CONFEDERATE FLAG FACTS

THE LOCHLAINN SEABROOK COLLECTION

Everything You Were Taught About the Civil War is Wrong, Ask a Southerner!
Everything You Were Taught About American Slavery is Wrong, Ask a Southerner!
Give This Book to a Yankee! A Southern Guide to the Civil War For Northerners
Honest Jeff and Dishonest Abe: A Southern Children's Guide to the Civil War
Confederacy 101: Amazing Facts You Never Knew About America's Oldest Political Tradition
Slavery 101: Amazing Facts You Never Knew About America's "Peculiar Institution"
The Great Yankee Coverup: What the North Doesn't Want You to Know About Lincoln's War!
Confederate Blood and Treasure: An Interview With Lochlainn Seabrook
Confederate Flag Facts: What Every American Should Know About Dixie's Southern Cross
A Rebel Born: A Defense of Nathan Bedford Forrest - Confederate General, American Legend (winner of the 2011 Jefferson Davis Historical Gold Medal)
A Rebel Born: The Screenplay
Nathan Bedford Forrest: Southern Hero, American Patriot - Honoring a Confederate Icon and the Old South
The Quotable Nathan Bedford Forrest: Selections From the Writings and Speeches of the Confederacy's Most Brilliant Cavalryman
Give 'Em Hell Boys! The Complete Military Correspondence of Nathan Bedford Forrest
Forrest! 99 Reasons to Love Nathan Bedford Forrest
Saddle, Sword, and Gun: A Biography of Nathan Bedford Forrest For Teens
Nathan Bedford Forrest and the Battle of Fort Pillow: Yankee Myth, Confederate Fact
Nathan Bedford Forrest and the Ku Klux Klan: Yankee Myth, Confederate Fact
The Quotable Jefferson Davis: Selections From the Writings and Speeches of the Confederacy's First President
The Quotable Alexander H. Stephens: Selections From the Writings and Speeches of the Confederacy's First Vice President
The Alexander H. Stephens Reader: Excerpts From the Works of a Confederate Founding Father
The Quotable Robert E. Lee: Selections From the Writings and Speeches of the South's Most Beloved Civil War General
The Old Rebel: Robert E. Lee As He Was Seen By His Contemporaries
The Articles of Confederation Explained: A Clause-by-Clause Study of America's First Constitution
The Constitution of the Confederate States of America Explained: A Clause-by-Clause Study of the South's Magna Carta
The Quotable Stonewall Jackson: Selections From the Writings and Speeches of the South's Most Famous General
Abraham Lincoln: The Southern View - Demythologizing America's Sixteenth President
The Unquotable Abraham Lincoln: The President's Quotes They Don't Want You To Know!
Lincolnology: The Real Abraham Lincoln Revealed in His Own Words - A Study of Lincoln's Suppressed, Misinterpreted, and Forgotten Writings and Speeches
The Great Impersonator! 99 Reasons to Dislike Abraham Lincoln
The Quotable Edward A. Pollard: Selections From the Writings of the Confederacy's Greatest Defender
Encyclopedia of the Battle of Franklin - A Comprehensive Guide to the Conflict that Changed the Civil War
Carnton Plantation Ghost Stories: True Tales of the Unexplained from Tennessee's Most Haunted Civil War House!
The McGavocks of Carnton Plantation: A Southern History - Celebrating One of Dixie's Most Noble Confederate Families and Their Tennessee Home
Jesus and the Law of Attraction: The Bible-Based Guide to Creating Perfect Health, Wealth, and Happiness Following Christ's Simple Formula
The Bible and the Law of Attraction: 99 Teachings of Jesus, the Apostles, and the Prophets
Christ Is All and In All: Rediscovering Your Divine Nature and the Kingdom Within
Jesus and the Gospel of Q: Christ's Pre-Christian Teachings As Recorded in the New Testament
Seabrook's Bible Dictionary of Traditional and Mystical Christian Doctrines
The Way of Holiness: The Story of Religion and Myth From the Cave Bear Cult to Christianity
Christmas Before Christianity: How the Birthday of the "Sun" Became the Birthday of the "Son"
Britannia Rules: Goddess-Worship in Ancient Anglo-Celtic Society - An Academic Look at the United Kingdom's Matricentric Spiritual Past
The Book of Kelle: An Introduction to Goddess-Worship and the Great Celtic Mother-Goddess Kelle, Original Blessed Lady of Ireland
The Goddess Dictionary of Words and Phrases: Introducing a New Core Vocabulary for the Women's Spirituality Movement
Princess Diana: Modern Day Moon-Goddess - A Psychoanalytical and Mythological Look at Diana Spencer's Life, Marriage, and Death (with Dr. Jane Goldberg)
Aphrodite's Trade: The Hidden History of Prostitution Unveiled
UFOs and Aliens: The Complete Guidebook
The Caudills: An Etymological, Ethnological, and Genealogical Study - Exploring the Name and National Origins of a European-American Family
The Blakeneys: An Etymological, Ethnological, and Genealogical Study - Uncovering the Mysterious Origins of the Blakeney Family and Name

CONFEDERATE FLAG FACTS

What Every American Should Know About Dixie's Southern Cross

LOCHLAINN SEABROOK

JEFFERSON DAVIS HISTORICAL GOLD MEDAL WINNER

LAVISHLY ILLUSTRATED
EXTENSIVELY RESEARCHED

Sea Raven Press, Nashville, Tennessee, USA

CONFEDERATE FLAG FACTS

Published by Sea Raven Press,
the literary wing of the pro-South movement
Cassidy Ravensdale, President
PO Box 1484, Spring Hill, Tennessee 37174-1484 USA
SeaRavenPress.com • searavenpress@gmail.com

1st paperback edition: November 2015
ISBN: 978-1-943737-09-3
LCCN: 2015952103

Confederate Flag Facts: What Every American Should Know About Dixie's Southern Cross, by Lochlainn Seabrook. Includes an index, endnotes, and bibliographical references.

Front and back cover design and art, book design, layout, and interior art by Lochlainn Seabrook
All images, graphic design, graphic art, and illustrations copyright © Lochlainn Seabrook
Cover art: "Taking Battery A," copyright © John Paul Strain
Portions of this book have been adapted from the author's other works

The views on the American "Civil War" documented in this book *are* those of the publisher.

The paper used in this book is acid-free and lignin-free. It has been certified by the Sustainable Forestry Initiative and the Forest Stewardship Council and meets all ANSI standards for archival quality paper.

PRINTED & MANUFACTURED IN OCCUPIED TENNESSEE, FORMER CONFEDERATE STATES OF AMERICA

DEDICATION

To Dixie's Starry Cross,
under which my intrepid Southern ancestors
fought and perished in the cause of freedom.

EPIGRAPH

For over sixty years the civilization of the South has been almost destroyed by the falsehoods written about it, and now when one has in hand the authenticated facts to prove these falsehoods to be false, many of our own Southern people as well as the press, largely responsible for them, are unfair and say, "It will do no good to bring these facts to light, for you will only stir up strife." Why not stir up strife, rather than allow these falsehoods to forever remain in history? Shall fear of attacks from those responsible for them silence us? Have we lost our courage? The truth is all we ask . . . Prejudice has no part in history.

Mildred Lewis Rutherford, 1923

CONTENTS

A wartime Confederate print entitled "Our Heroes and Our Flags." In the center stand three of the author's cousins (from left to right): General Thomas "Stonewall" Jackson, General Pierre G. T. Beauregard, and General Robert E. Lee. Surrounding them are the four principle Confederate flags: the Seven-Star First National (upper left), the Confederate Battle Flag (upper right), the Second National (lower left), and the Third National (lower right). Around the border are eighteen well-known Confederate officials and military officers with their signatures, familiar to all traditional Southerners.

NOTES TO THE READER

THE TWO MAIN POLITICAL PARTIES IN 1860

☛ In any study of America's antebellum, bellum, and postbellum periods, it is vitally important to understand that in 1860 the two major political parties—the Democrats and the newly formed Republicans—were the opposite of what they are today. In other words, the Democrats of the mid 19th Century were Conservatives, akin to the Republican Party of today, while the Republicans of the mid 19th Century were Liberals, akin to the Democratic Party of today.

Thus the Confederacy's Democratic president, Jefferson Davis, was a Conservative (with libertarian leanings); the Union's Republican president, Abraham Lincoln, was a Liberal (with socialistic leanings). This is why, in the mid 1800s, the conservative wing of the Democratic Party was known as "the States' Rights Party."[1]

Hence, the Democrats of the Civil War period referred to themselves as "conservatives," "confederates," "anti-centralists," or "constitutionalists" (the latter because they favored strict adherence to the original Constitution—which tacitly guaranteed states' rights—as created by the Founding Fathers), while the Republicans called themselves "liberals," "nationalists," "centralists," or "consolidationists" (the latter three because they wanted to nationalize the central government and consolidate political power in Washington, D.C.).[2]

The author's cousin, Confederate Vice President and Democrat Alexander H. Stephens: a Southern Conservative.

Since this idea is new to most of my readers, let us further demystify it by viewing it from the perspective of the American Revolutionary War. If Davis and his conservative Southern constituents (the Democrats of 1861) had been alive in 1775, they would have sided with George Washington and the American colonists, who sought to secede from the tyrannical government of Great Britain; if Lincoln and his Liberal Northern constituents (the Republicans of 1861) had been alive at that time, they would have sided with King George III and the English monarchy, who sought to maintain the American colonies as possessions of the British Empire. It is due to this very comparison that Southerners often refer to the "Civil War" as the Second American Revolutionary War.

THE TERM "CIVIL WAR"

☛ As I heartily dislike the phrase "Civil War," its use throughout this book (as well as in my other works) is worthy of an explanation.

Today America's entire literary system refers to the conflict of 1861 using the Northern term the "Civil War," whether we in the South like it or not. Thus, as all book searches by readers, libraries, and retail outlets are now performed online, and as all bookstores categorize works from this period under the heading "Civil War," book publishers and authors who deal with this particular topic have little choice but to use this term themselves. If I were to refuse to use it, as some of my Southern colleagues have suggested, few people would ever find or read my books.

Add to this the fact that scarcely any non-Southerners have ever heard of the names we in the South use for the conflict, such as the "War for Southern Independence"—or my personal preference, "Lincoln's War." It only makes sense then to use the term "Civil War" in most commercial situations.

We should also bear in mind that while today educated persons, particularly educated Southerners, all share an abhorrence for the phrase "Civil War," it was not always so. Confederates who lived through and even fought in the conflict regularly used the term throughout the 1860s, and even long after. Among them were Confederate officers such as Nathan Bedford Forrest, Richard Taylor, and Joseph E. Johnston, not to mention the Confederacy's vice president, Alexander H. Stephens.

In 1895 Confederate General James Longstreet wrote about his military experiences in a work subtitled, *Memoirs of the Civil War in America*. Even the Confederacy's highest leader, President Jefferson Davis, used the term "Civil War,"[3] and in one case at least, as late as 1881—the year he wrote his brilliant exposition, *The Rise and Fall of the Confederate Government*.[4]

THE CONCEPT OF RACE

☛ Contrary to popular opinion, and in particular the opinion of racists, there is no "race gene" that makes one white, black, red, yellow, or brown. There is no abrupt genetic line of demarcation between a Caucasian, a Negro, or an Asian. What actually exists is an infinite spectrum of human skin colors, from white on the far left to black on the far right, with every known color variation in between.

The reason for this is that we are all merely products of our ancestors and where and how they lived: *generally speaking*, the closer they dwelt to the heat and bright Sun at the equator the darker their skin and eyes, the curlier their hair, the taller their height; the further away they lived from the equator, the lighter their skin and eyes, the straighter their hair, the shorter their height.

What we call "race" then is simply the end result of the human body's biological adaptation to environment; in other words, it is a survival mechanism that has evolved over millions of years that has helped maintain and protect our species.

This makes the very concepts of "race" and "racism" delusions; nothing more than convenient but highly subjective, misleading, useless, and wholly unscientific methods of categorizing human beings by skin color. Thus I reject the ambiguous concept of "race"; not on liberal *moral* principles, but on conservative *scientific* ones.[5] My use of the words race, racist, and racism throughout this book therefore is a concession to currently accepted social tradition and opinion, and does not reflect my personal view.[6]

QUOTATIONS & ENDNOTES

☛ In an effort to preserve the authenticity of the early American writers and speakers I quote in this work, I have retained the exact wording and grammatical peculiarities (such as long-running paragraphs) inherent to that era. Bracketed words within quotes are my additions and clarifications, while italicized words within quotes are my emphasis.

As always, in quoted material I identify unnamed, obscure, and often even well-known historical figures, events, items, and places for those readers, particularly my foreign readers, who may not be familiar with American history. Finally, the sources for most or all of the information in an entry will (usually) be found in the endnote at the close of that entry.

TO LEARN MORE

☛ Lincoln's War on the American people and the Constitution can never be fully understood without a thorough knowledge of the South's perspective of the conflict. As *Confederate Flag Facts* is only meant to be a brief introductory guide, one cannot hope to learn the whole truth about the "Civil War" here. For those who are interested in a more in-depth study, please see my other more scholarly books, listed on page 2. Additionally, these works contain the original references (footnotes and bibliographical listings) for the notes in the present volume, material that could not be included here due to length restrictions.

THE SOUTHERN BATTLE FLAGS

NOTE: THIS POEM, WRITTEN BY CONFEDERATE VETERAN FRANKLIN H. MACKEY, IS A SOUTHERN REPLY TO THOSE UNION VETERANS "WHO OBJECTED TO THE CHEERING OF THESE FLAGS BY THE CONFEDERATE VETERANS AT THE RICHMOND REUNION IN JULY 1896."

Now, Southern men, take off your hats, and ho! ye all the world,
Stand up and with uncovered heads, salute those flags unfurled!
Though faded much and tattered more, they once were banners bright.
As once were young those men whose hairs old age has rendered white.
And who so bravely followed them, in battle line arrayed.
In those discordant days of death when roared the cannonade.

All harmlessly for many a year those battle flags have lain
Upon the closet shelves of those who fought for them in vain.
The sore at first was hard to heal, as ever is the case
When fiercely meet in civil strife one nation and one race.
Yet, praised be God! 'tis ended now, and foreign foes shall dread
But all the more the Stars and Stripes for all the blood we've shed.

Yet why should not we Southern men who once, as Southern boys,
'Mid shot and shell and canister and battle's dreadful noise.
Followed a flag o'er many a field where comrades, falling fast,
Gave for the cause they loved so well their best blood and their last,
Take off our hats at sight of it just one day in the year?
Think of the memories that well up and flow into that cheer!

In ragged clothes we marched with it the hot and dusty road,
And felt our haversacks grow light, our cartridge box a load.
And here and there, on wintry days, we saw the frozen sod
And trampled snow tinged with the blood of bleeding feet unshod;
Yet we were rich in high resolve, and though we oft lacked food,
We had what most a soldier needs—a flag and fortitude!
Oh! where is he, of North or South, who lives and bravely fought.
Who does not know how easily he finds himself o'erwrought
By all the memories of those days, so suddenly aroused
By his old flag, whichever be the cause that he espoused?

At Seven Pines we saw it borne amid the smoke and din.
While whistling bullets tore its folds and our full ranks grew thin;

At Gaines' Mill and at Frazier's Farm, and Malvern Hill it fell,
We saw it lifted up again and gave the "Rebel yell."
With Pickett's men at Gettysburg, it led the charge to death.
While bleeding heroes cheered it on with their last dying breath.

At Spottsylvania, Wilderness, and Chickamauga's field.
And twice a hundred more, its foes had learned to it to yield.
At last it fell no more to rise—God's wisdom willed it so—
And few are left who fought with it, and they, too, soon must go;
Yet of the years still left to us we love one day in each
To see and cheer the flag we bore into the deadly breach.

You are the victors. Brave you were, you boys who wore the blue.
And Valor never yet denied a fallen foe his due.
The fight is o'er. Our wounds are healed. We clasp your hand again;
But while we hold it fast and fair, remember we're but men
Who cannot quite forget the flag for which our brave ones fell,
And so whene'er we see its folds, we feel our bosoms swell.

Then grudge us not, brave boys in blue, that once or so a year
We meet our comrades of lang syne and give the flag a cheer.
We have no cause for quarrel now, and never more shall face
Each other in intestine war, but rather would embrace,
And teach our children to defend the old Red, White and Blue—
The flag our common fathers loved, the only one they knew;
But give us credit for good faith, and it will all be well.
And ask us not to scorn the flag for which our brothers fell.

Do it dishonor? That battle flag? Look on it with disdain?
No: never while our pulses beat our honor will we stain:
Yet we will touch our elbows close to yours, if comes the need
That we for our united land be called upon to bleed.
And North and South as friends again shall be to each so true
That both can march to "Dixie's Land" and "Yankee Doodle," too;
But never ask that we shall be so false unto our dead
That we can turn our backs upon the flag for which they bled.[7]

FRANKLIN H. MACKEY
U.C.V., Camp 171. Company A., 5th South Carolina infantry
Washington, D.C., July 20, 1896

Our president. God bless Jefferson Davis.

INTRODUCTION

AS A CIVIL WAR HISTORIAN and scholar who wishes to record authentic history, I must deal in cold, hard, sometimes uncomfortable facts. As such I go directly to the source for my material: the writings of 19th-Century eyewitnesses; that is, from individuals who lived during the War period or who were actually at the scene.

This approach is quite the opposite of typical anti-South writers, who, because they detest and ignore facts, instead base their work on personal feelings, beliefs, opinions, and biases, or just as bad, the defamatory error-filled anti-South work of uneducated amateurs who came before them.

Every year the anti-South movement publishes thousands of pro-North books filled with both misinformation and disinformation about Lincoln's War. One can never hope to learn the truth about the conflict through such revisionist, poorly researched, highly biased history, whose main goal is to propagandize rather than educate.

Though this vindictive group daily churns out countless thousands of books, articles, blogs, social media posts, TV programs, and films that slander the South, the Confederacy, our heroes, our monuments, our literature, our culture, and our heritage, they fail to back any of this up with genuine historical evidence. It is all opinion and speculation—and that based on gossip, hearsay, and erroneous propaganda.

Worse still are the anti-South movement's practices of wantonly rewriting history to fit its left-wing sociopolitical ideologies, while giving immunity to those who protect what I refer to as "The Great Yankee Coverup": the Big Lie about the Civil War.[8] Having taken over and monopolized the entire media industry (TV, film, radio, social media), the publishing industry, and both the educational and library systems, it is free to create, regulate, ban, suppress, encourage, promote, and market any ideas it likes. The innocent public is thus brainwashed unawares. As Albert Einstein noted many decades ago:

> The ruling class has the schools and press under its thumb. This enables it to sway the emotions of the masses.

Second only to the self-righteous, progressive, South-hating Hollywood elite, the worst offenders and most influential members of this group are the so-called "university presses." Masquerading as "educational publishers," this propaganda arm of the Liberal Establishment nefariously fills our bookstores and libraries with all manner of historically inaccurate, anti-South literature. Because these titles have the stamp of academia on them, they are annually hailed as "great, scholarly works," and their authors are showered with ceremonies, accolades, and awards—by other Liberals, of course.

While he was alive Abraham Lincoln—the man directly responsible for the deaths of untold thousands of Americans, the erosion of the Constitution, the destruction of the Founding Fathers' voluntary Union, and the first massive expansion of the central government—was understandably voted the worst president up until that time. Yet his deification by modern pro-North writers has transformed him into our country's "favorite" and "greatest" chief executive.

In the Left's process of redacting American history, they have, for example, transformed big government Liberal, racist, anti-Christian, anti-Constitution, war criminal, and political thug, Abraham Lincoln, into a gentle, kindly, fatherly god, one worthy of his own Paganesque temple in Washington, D.C., and his visage permanently enshrined on our money, license plates, and Mount Rushmore. Conversely, the noble, erudite Southern gentleman, scholar, strict constitutionalist, racially tolerant, and ingenious Christian Conservative, Jefferson Davis, has been recast as the worst villain of the entire War, his cabinet members and military officers depicted as treasonous cowards who deserved nothing less than execution without trial.

Tennessee's state capitol, Nashville, 1940. Like the South's other capitol buildings, the Confederacy's Stars and Bars once flew over this one as well. It was long ago replaced by the Stars and Stripes.

As I pen these words, paintings, memorials, and statues of our beloved chief executive are being quietly removed from various locations around Dixie at the request of uninformed, mean-spirited Leftists; sanctimonious dullards with no interest in facts, historical accuracy, or even intellectual growth. Just a sadistic thirst for vengeance and a cowardly impulse to further shame and punish the South for something she was not responsible for: slavery!

And yet it is from this very group of uneducated pro-North propagandists that the masses are being taught American history in our schools and universities, on TV, in film, on the radio, and on the Internet. Getting your information about the American Civil War from the works of pro-North Liberals, however, is not recommended. It is the equivalent of trying to learn about God from the writings of atheists.

Of course, the anti-South movement saves its most poisonous venom for its most detested Southern symbol of all: the Confederate Battle Flag, which it relentlessly delights in labeling a "controversial" and "racist" emblem. And though this particular banner has never had anything to do with politics (it was created strictly as a military flag), it could not escape the progressive's proclivity for politicizing everything, even the weather.[9] Now widely seen as a "political symbol," politicians, even Southern ones (who should know better), have turned their backs on the Confederate Battle Flag, removing it from state capitols and courthouses across Dixie to appease liberal America's flourishing victim culture.

This unwarranted nationwide attack on our beautiful "Southern Cross" has been so effective that for many traditional Southerners it is now too dangerous to display it, whether on a flag pole, a vehicle, a window, or clothing. For many uninformed Americans the mere reference to it, not to mention the actual sight of it, is like waving a red flag before a bull. I myself have been spit on, threatened, yelled at, and called a "Nazi," a "racist," and a number of expletives that are unprintable, for displaying the Confederate Battle Flag. All this mainly from members of the self-styled "party of tolerance and compassion," the Democratic Party.

The racial and cultural crimes committed by Yankees under the auspices of the U.S. Flag are beyond counting, beginning with the founding of the American slave trade in the early 1600s. My own third great-grandparents were killed by Union soldiers who were carrying the Star-Spangled Banner. Yet we do not see the Left crying out against it, stigmatizing it, labeling it "racist," tearing it from flagstaffs, or trying to prohibit its display—as it has done with the C.S. Flag.

This abysmal ignorance of history may be acceptable in the strange, upside-down world of Liberals, socialists, Marxists, communists, PC thought police, cultural terrorists, cultural cleansers, and South-loathers in general, where fact is fantasy and fantasy is fact. But not in highly literate, conservative Dixie. Here, we value facts, honor the past, and are passionate about genuine, unadulterated history. We are especially proud of our heritage and we will never let it be hijacked and rewritten, distorted, and perverted by enemies of the South ever again. Our history and our flag stay right where they are.

If we Southerners sometimes get angry about attempts to misrepresent, besmirch, and ban our flag—a reaction that will be better understood after reading this book—it is because it is part and parcel of our collective heritage, an integral aspect of our family histories; a flag under which thousands of our ancestors died defending a great cause.

My own third great-grandparents, Elias Jent Sr. and Rachel Cornett, were murdered in Perry County, Kentucky, in 1864 by a passing Union regiment; hanged from a tree in front of a relative's house at gunpoint for no other reason than that Elias was a Confederate soldier. He was on furlough at the time, and Rachel, of course, was a civilian non-combatant, making this war crime especially heinous and an unconstitutional act of supreme savagery.

Some 150 years later, this story of senseless Yankee violence against my kin continues to reverberate through my family. Please do not ask a Southerner with Confederate ancestors why he or she is so emotionally attached to the Confederate Battle Flag.

In closing let me quote the words of Confederate officer John A. Richardson, for they mirror my thoughts exactly. Captain Richardson wrote them in 1914 as part of the preface to one of his own books:

> The writer makes no apology for issuing this volume. Its *prime object* is to refute the atrocious accusations against the South *before, during* and *after* the war; and to *do this* within such a limited space as will be adapted to the wants of the general reader. . . . We challenge an investigation of the facts upon which our conclusions are based. *They are incontrovertible.*
>
> *Before the war*, we were most bitterly and world-widely denounced because of the institution of slavery, for which both sections were equally responsible.
>
> *During the war*, we were officially, and otherwise, denounced as traitors to our common country, and as rebels against the plan of the Constitution we had sworn to obey; and this, too, by those who had declared this same Constitution, *"A Compact with Death and a league with Hell."*
>
> *After the war*, we were still called rebels and traitors. As late as July 12, 1911, Senator [Weldon B.] Heyburn, of Idaho, in the United States Senate, denounced our cause as *"infamous."* . . . We propose to enlighten this benighted Westerner and others, and to prove that it was *a glorious cause.*
>
> If in this volume any expressions seem harsh and bitter let it not be attributed to any lingering animosity on the part of the author, but to the facts that falsely proclaimed him a traitor. . . . Nor let it be attributed to the failure of the Confederacy, but to the base misrepresentations and vituperations heaped on the people of the South. The home of secession was not in the South, but in the North, in the midst of the enemies of the Constitution, the anti-slavery agitators of the North. It was there [that] the abusers of the South and the Constitution lived, and there [that] they multiplied till they were sufficiently strong to disregard both the demands of the Constitution and the rights of the South.
>
> We, therefore, ask that all our words which are seemingly severe be regarded in the light of the facts.

> Just one other word here; every true Southern veteran is an American citizen of the truest type, as loyal as the loyalest, as willing to imperil his life in the interests or defense of the common country, as the most patriotic son of any section of this great American Republic. *But they will never confess that their cause was not that of the fathers—that of the common Constitution of the American States forming the American Union.*
>
> They believe that their unparalleled devotion to the American Constitution has a tendency to enshrine it in the American heart as never before; and to give it a place of security unknown before their great sacrifice for its principles. If constitutional government is to be preserved unimpaired for the coming generations, it *must be*, and it *will be* through the *conservative* spirit of the South.[10]

As part of my ongoing anti-propaganda campaign—my effort to preserve authentic Southern history while combating the lies of Northern mythology—I offer this informational book on the world's most beautiful ensign, the Confederate Battle Flag, a military banner belonging to the most remarkable government ever created by the mind of Man and the hand of God: the Confederate States of America.

May my words go to every corner of the world and enlighten the darkness.

Lochlainn Seabrook
Nashville, Tennessee, USA
October 2015

1

ORIGINS OF THE SOUTHERN CONFEDERACY

DIXIE OUR OWN

Dixie, when first waved thy flag in the sunshine,
Brave soldiers in gray gladly answered its call,
Marching so fearlessly into the firing line,
Knowing that some of them surely must fall.
Horrors of war! Ah, how dauntless they proved you!
Thin grew the ranks of the soldiers who loved you.
Countless souls carried to bright worlds above you—
Souls who had fought for you, Dixie, their own.

Dixie, on fields which once thrilled to the beating
Of drums and of fearless hearts thy people prize,
Golden-eyed daisies the mornings are greeting,
Lifting their faces to bright southern skies.
Peace they are speaking—aye, peace that is given
To men who have done their best, though they be driven
At last to surrender; souls surely are shriven
Who fought for thy honor, fair Dixie, our own.

Dixie, the flag that thy soldiers marched under
Long since is furled and forever laid low.
Hushed is the cannon whose deep voice of thunder
Brought on thy people such ruin and woe.
Dixie, thy glory passed not with surrender;
Deep in our hearts, that are loving and tender,
Ever we'll praise thee and sweet homage render
To men who once fought for thee. Dixie, our own.[11]

LURA W. LOVE, 1916

CHAPTER 1

WHAT YOU WERE TAUGHT: The Southern Confederacy, that is, the Confederate States of America (C.S.A.), had no connection to the United States of America, and was in fact nothing more than a treasonous attempt by the South to take over the Union, the U.S. government, destroy the Constitution, and preserve slavery.
THE FACTS: Like all of the other Northern myths created to hide the truth about Lincoln's War, this one too has been fabricated by the anti-South movement for self-serving purposes. And like all of the others, authentic history proves this one wrong as well, and we will expose it now by taking a brief look at the origins of both the U.S.A. and the C.S.A.

To begin with, the Southern states seceded for one reason and one reason only: the election of Abraham Lincoln on November 6, 1860. This is why, despite the fact that they had been discussing secession for decades, the Southern states did not begin leaving the Union until *after* November 6. Indeed, South Carolina, which had been considering secession for many years, only seceded on December 20, 1860, a mere five weeks after Lincoln's election.

Yes, as we will see, ultimately the South went to War in defense of the Constitution. But this was only because they knew that Constitution-loathing, anti-Christian, big government Liberal Lincoln—who believed that there was a "higher law" than the Constitution—planned on altering it once he got in office; actions that would move the country away from being a confederate republic to a government-centered empire, the dream of every Leftist. Let us allow Lincoln to speak for himself on this topic.

In February 1861, while meeting with a Southern peace

commission at Willard's Hotel in Washington, D.C., the president-elect was asked by New York businessman William E. Dodge what he was going to do to prevent war with the South. Lincoln's response is chilling. When I get to the Oval Office, he said,

> I shall take an oath to the best of my ability to preserve, protect, and defend the Constitution. This is a great and solemn duty. With the support of the people and the assistance of the Almighty I shall undertake to perform it. I have full faith that I shall perform it. *It is not the Constitution as I would like to have it*, but as it is that is to be defended.[12]

Liberals, like big government progressive Lincoln, have disliked the U.S. Constitution and its limits on governmental power since its inception, and have never tried to hide either their disdain for it or their desire to modify it to fit their own leftist agenda.

(As we will discuss later, socialist Liberal and Lincoln-worshiper, U.S. President Barack Hussein Obama, once made a similar statement, calling the U.S. Constitution "an imperfect document.")

Reading between the lines, it is obvious that even prior to becoming president, Lincoln was plotting to alter, and even destroy, the Constitution of George Washington, Thomas Jefferson, James Madison, Benjamin Franklin, George Mason, Charles Pinckney, and the other Founders. Under such circumstances the Constitution-loving Southern states then had every reason, and right, to secede.

Let us read the sentiments of the North's Left-wing leaders (at that time, the Republicans) for ourselves. Though they lived 150 years ago, their open criminality and smug contempt for Federal law and the Constitution still appalls us to this day:

> "*There is a higher law than the Constitution which regulates our authority over the domain*. Slavery must be abolished, and we must do it." — William H. Seward

"The time is fast approaching when the cry will become too overpowering to resist. Rather than tolerate national slavery as it now exists, *let the Union be dissolved at once*, and then the sin of slavery will rest where it belongs." — New York *Tribune*

"The Union is a lie. The American Union is an imposture—a covenant with death and an agreement with hell. *We are for its overthrow!* Up with the flag of disunion, that we may have a free and glorious republic of our own." — William Lloyd Garrison

"*I look forward to the day when there shall be a servile insurrection in the South*; when the black man, armed with British bayonets, and led on by British officers, shall assert his freedom and *wage a war of extermination against his master*. And, though we may not mock at their calamity nor laugh when their fear cometh, yet *we will hail it as the dawn of a political millennium*." — Joshua Giddings

"In the alternative being presented of the continuance of slavery or a dissolution of the Union, *we are for a dissolution, and we care not how quick it comes*." — Rufus P. Spaulding

"The fugitive-slave act [a Federal law at the time] is filled with horror; *we are bound to disobey this act*." — Charles Sumner

"The *Advertiser* has no hesitation in saying that *it does not hold to the faithful observance of the fugitive slave law* of 1850." — *The Portland Advertiser*

"I have no doubt but the free and slave States ought to be separated. . . . *The Union is not worth supporting in connection with the South*." — Horace Greeley

"The times demand and *we must have an anti-slavery Constitution*, an anti-slavery Bible, and an anti-slavery God." — Anson P. Burlingame

"There is merit in the [Liberal] Republican party. It is this: *It is the first sectional party ever organized in this country. . . . It is not national; it is sectional. It is the North arrayed against the South*. . . . The first crack in the iceberg is visible; you will yet hear it go with a crack through the center." — Wendell Phillips

"[The only infallible remedy for slavery is this:] . . . *men must foment insurrection among the slaves in order to cure the evils*. It can never be done by concessions and compromises. *It is a great evil, and must be*

> *extinguished by still greater ones*. It is positive and imperious in its approaches, and must be overcome with equally positive forces. You must commit an assault to arrest a burglar, and *slavery is not arrested without a violation of law* and the cry of fire." — The *Independent Democrat*, leading Republican [Liberal] paper in New Hampshire[13]

With menacing comments such as these flowing from the North, is it any wonder that the South, *the region of strict law and order*, wished to break away from the Liberal-led Union, *the region of negligent lawlessness and disorder*? In short:

> In 1860 it was plain to the world that the people of the North were determined to spurn the compact of union with the Southern States and to deny to those States all right to control their own affairs.[14]

In November 1860, only days after Dishonest Abe was voted president, even many Liberal Yankees understood why the South was now planning to secede. Wrote Greeley of New York at the time:

> The telegraph informs us that most of the cotton States are meditating a withdrawal from the Union, *because of Lincoln's election*.[15]

Just five years later, in 1865, "the Confederate Joan of Arc," famed Rebel spy Belle Boyd, commented on the same subject:

> *The secession of the Southern States, individually or in the aggregate, was the certain consequence of Mr. Lincoln's election*. His accession to a power supreme and almost unparalleled was an unequivocal declaration, by the merchants of New England, that they had resolved to exclude the landed proprietors of the South from all participation in the legislation of their common country.[16]

It is clear from these few facts alone that the Southern states did not separate from the Union in order to "take over the U.S. government, destroy the Constitution, and preserve slavery." As we are about to see, it was for the opposite reasons: they wished to start their own Union, create their own Constitution, and abolish slavery in their own time and manner.

Now let us examine the charge that "the Confederate States of America, the C.S.A., *had no connection* to the United States of America, the U.S.A."

With the issuance of the Declaration of Independence and the start of the American Revolutionary War in 1776 (inaugurating America's secession from England), the original 13 colonies set about forming a government of their own. After much debate the form of government chosen was a confederacy, or a "confederate republic," as Alexander Hamilton called it, which is defined as "a confederation of independent sovereignties, delegating a small portion of their power to a central government."[17]

Baron de Montesquieu was a brilliant 18th-Century French political scholar whose conservative ideas about confederation and dividing the government into three branches (the "separation of powers") were adopted by the Founders of both the U.S. Confederacy (1781-1789) and the Southern Confederacy (1861-1865).

In essence the first U.S. Confederacy was a purely unique, European-American form of government, one comprised of ideas that the Founding Fathers borrowed from not only the views of earlier political scholars, like Baron de Montesquieu, but also real Old World confederations, such as the famed Greek confederacies that dated back to the 4th Century B.C.

The personal papers of American Founder James Madison, for example, reveal that he studied and was very familiar with the "Achaean Confederacy," the "Belgic Confederacy," the "Amphictyonic Confederacy," the "Lycian Confederacy," the "German Confederacy," the "Dutch Confederacy," and the "Swiss Confederacy," founded in 1291. Similarly, the writings of American Founding Father Thomas Jefferson show that he was a keen student of the many early Native-American confederacies.

Like many of both early Indian and European confederacies, the original U.S. Confederacy was defined, not as a body of "united states," but as a body of "states united," its purpose being to form a loose

Founding Father Alexander Hamilton recognized the importance of states' rights, calling them "essentially necessary" to our form of government.

"association" in which the states retained all sovereign power, while the central government was given limited powers and was legally dependent on the will of the states. It was this first "friendly compact" between the colonies that *permanently established* the U.S.A. as a confederacy rather than a nation, the latter which is defined as "a community of people ruled by a strong national government." Thus, technically the U.S. is *not* a nation, despite the assertion of Liberals to the contrary, and despite the fact that this false notion, that we are "*one nation* under God," is promoted in "The Pledge of Allegiance"—which was written, quite naturally, by a *socialist*: big government progressive Francis Bellamy.

We are, in actuality, not a nation made up of states, but rather a union made up of nation-states. This fact is so little known or understood by most Americans that it bears examining more closely. Confederate Captain John Levi Underwood noted that

> *from the very nature of the formation of our [U.S.] government there can be no organized Nation*. . . . It is a Union of States and can be made nothing else.

Alexander Hamilton wrote:

> *The State governments are essentially necessary to the form and spirit of the general system*. . . . They can never lose their powers till the whole of America are robbed of their liberties.

George Bancroft, the lionized Victorian historian, said:

> *But for states' rights the Union would perish from the paralysis of its limbs*. The States, as they gave life to the Union, are necessary to the

continuance of that life.

James Madison likewise declared:

> *The assent and ratification of the people, not as individuals composing the entire nation, but as composing the distinct and independent States to which they belong, are the sources of the Constitution. It is therefore not a National but a Federal [that is, a Confederal or Confederate] compact.*[18]

In other words, though we have been steadily creeping toward nationhood since the late 1700s, the U.S. was originally designed to be a confederacy not a nation.

Continuing with our history, it was the representatives of the first thirteen colonies (later states) that made up the U.S. Confederacy who, in turn, were made responsible for creating a constitution, a collection of rules and regulations governing the Confederacy and its citizens. And it is this document that makes the U.S.A. *a republic, a country ruled by law*, rather than *a democracy, a country ruled by the majority*. (Let us note here that not only did the Founders never intend America to be a nation, they also never meant it to be a democracy, and to this day it is still neither—despite the claims of Liberals.)[19]

Being members of a confederacy it was only natural that in 1781, the year the U.S.A. ratified its first constitution, the Founding Fathers called it the "Articles of Confederation." Though the Articles referred to the new republic as "the United States of America," few at the time actually called it by that name. To most it was, as Jefferson fondly referred to it, "our Confederacy," "our Confederation," "the Confederation," or more commonly "the Confederacy."

Article 1 of the Articles themselves refers to the United States of America as "the Confederacy." This was the name given to the original U.S. at its founding, during the Confederate period (1781 to 1789), and even long after the Articles of Confederation were replaced in 1789 with our second constitution, the Constitution of the United States of America.

This shows, as nothing else does, that after 1789, even though the country began to move away from confederation (strong states and a weak central government) and forward toward federation (weak states and a strong central government), the U.S. was still considered a confederacy, with all that which was implied by confederation.

With the ratification of our first Constitution, the Articles of Confederation, on March 1, 1781, the Continental Congress became the "Confederate Congress" and Continental Congressmen became "Confederate Congressmen." The union of the first "Confederate States of America" was born.

The U.S. Capitol, Washington, D.C. The Founding Generation never intended our Federal government to have the power it has assumed today, as an objective study of the history of the Articles of Confederation and the U.S. Constitution reveal.

Countries that were not members of the U.S. Confederacy began to be invited to join it under the designation "this confederation." Article Eleven of the Articles of Confederation in its entirety, in fact, was written as an invitation to Canada to join

> *this confederation*, and joining in the measures of the United States, shall be admitted into, and entitled to all the advantages of this Union.[20]

Patterned on ancient and Medieval European confederacies, and quite probably Native-American confederacies as well, under their new confederate government all Americans were now literally confederates, living in a confederacy under a one-of-a-kind confederated political organization known to the Founders as a "confederate republic."

Most importantly, under confederation the colonists were able to avoid their greatest fear: the formation of a single monolithic *nation*, with all of its autocratic, dictatorial overtones, enslavement under monarchical rule, political corruption, and dearth of personal freedom. In place of one large nation, as we have seen, the colonies or nation-states very purposefully chose to form a loose compact—that is, a "firm league of friendship"—with one another, while retaining their individual powers, rights, and freedoms, the very definition of a confederacy.

The first Confederate president of the U.S. during the period of confederation, Samuel Huntington of Connecticut.

The U.S. Confederacy in turn operated under the auspices of a republican form of government, a political body based on laws (rather than majority rule, as in a democracy) in which the supreme power lay with the people rather than with their political leaders. This was, in essence, the "Confederate Republic" intended by the Founders, one that served a very specific purpose, as Hamilton noted:

> It appears that the very structure of the confederacy affords the surest preventatives from error, and the most powerful checks to misconduct.

The U.S. Confederacy of 1781 was a legitimate republic, with all of the rights, powers, functions, and leaders of a confederacy, including a chief executive. Thus in all, there were ten U.S. confederate presidents who held that office prior to George Washington—our first president under the later emerging U.S. Constitution.

The first president of the U.S. under the Articles of Confederation was Samuel Huntington of Connecticut, who served from September 28, 1779 to July 6, 1781. Though it was officially known as "President of the United States in Congress Assembled," the position was that of a true *confederate* chief executive.

Black Confederate soldiers like this one, who adored the Confederate Battle Flag as much as any white Confederate soldier, were a common sight on the battlefield. Indeed, five times as many African-Americans served with the Confederacy in one capacity or another as served with the Union, a fact you will never read in any mainstream history book.

What follows is a complete list of our first ten presidents and the dates they served. Note that under the Articles of Confederation there was no executive branch, making the office of "President of the Confederate Congress" far less onerous and rigorous than that of a modern U.S. president. As specified in Article Nine of the Articles of Confederation, each presidential term was limited to one year.[21] Several men served partial terms, otherwise there would have only been eight U.S. confederate presidents:

1. America's First Confederate President: Samuel Huntington of Connecticut (1731-1796): served from September 28, 1779, to July 6, 1781.
2. America's Second Confederate President: Thomas McKean of Delaware (1734-1817): served from July 10, 1781, to November 4, 1781.
3. America's Third Confederate President: John Hanson of Maryland (1715-1783): served from November 5, 1781, to November 4, 1782.
4. America's Fourth Confederate President: Elias Boudinot of New Jersey (1740-1821): served from November 4, 1782, to November 3, 1783.
5. America's Fifth Confederate President: Thomas Mifflin of Pennsylvania (1744-1800): served from November 3, 1783, to June 3, 1784.
6. America's Sixth Confederate President: Richard Henry Lee IV of Virginia (1732-1794): served from November 30, 1784, to November 23, 1785. (Robert E. Lee's first cousin.)
7. America's Seventh Confederate President: John Hancock of Massachusetts (1737-1793): served from November 23, 1785, to June 6, 1786.
8. America's Eighth Confederate President: Nathaniel Gorham of Massachusetts (1738-1796): served from June 6, 1786, to November 13, 1786.
9. America's Ninth Confederate President: Arthur St. Clair of Pennsylvania (1737-1818): served from February 2, 1787, to October 29, 1787.
10. America's Tenth Confederate President: Cyrus Griffin of Virginia

(1748-1810): served from January 22, 1788, to March 4, 1789.[22]

On April 30, 1789, just two months after President Griffin's term ended, George Washington was sworn in on the balcony of Federal Hall on Wall Street in New York City as the first president of the United States of America under the newly effective U.S. Constitution.

In 1787, when Congress began discussing the idea of discarding the Articles of Confederation and strengthening the central government, an alarmed Patrick Henry came forward in defense of the original U.S. Confederacy. "I am extremely uneasy at the proposed change of government," he declared. "Who authorized [my Liberal colleagues] . . . to speak the language of, 'We, the people,' instead of 'We, the states?' States are the characteristics and the soul of a confederation."

In order to fully understand how the Southern Confederacy and the Confederate Flag (1861-1865) are integrally connected to the U.S. Confederacy, our first Confederate States of America, and her constitution, the Articles of Confederation (1781-1789), let us now find out what became of the latter.

Though Jefferson and the rest of the Founding Fathers expected the U.S. Confederacy to be a "lasting confederacy," soon the Liberals of the day began moving to expand the powers of the national government and weaken the powers of the states, which, at the time, were considered "thirteen *nations* who have agreed to act and speak together," as Jefferson phrased it.[23] Conservatives pushed back, trying to retain the original confederacy as laid out under the Articles of Confederation.

The crisis culminated at the Philadelphia Convention in the Spring of 1787. Here, with conservative voices like Thomas Jefferson and Patrick Henry missing from the meeting,[24] the Liberals were able to have the Articles tossed out and replaced with our second constitution, the "Constitution of the United States of America." It was here that the U.S. first began its long and gradual transformation from confederation (powerful states) toward federation (powerful government).

Adopted on September 17, 1787, ratified on June 21, 1788, and made effective on March 4, 1789, the establishment of the new federal government and the U.S. Constitution marked the formal end of the American Confederation period. It had lasted only eight short years, from 1781 to 1789.[25]

Yet, despite the fact that the new Constitution more clearly defined and strengthened the powers of the national government, two important amendments, Nine and Ten, were added that severely restricted these powers, while insuring that the sovereign rights of the states and the people were maintained. In other words, technically the U.S. was still a confederate republic, and it remains so to this day.

After the Articles of Confederation were replaced by the U.S. Constitution in 1789, George Washington, our first post-Articles president, referred to the country as "the new Confederacy," proving that the United States was still regarded as a confederacy by our leaders.

Proof that the U.S.A. got its start as a confederacy, and that it retained this governmental form right up to Lincoln's War, is the fact that every single American president and statesman from 1781 to 1861 publicly and privately referred to the U.S. as "the Confederacy." This included even Lincoln, who used the phrase just prior to becoming president, as well as during the brief period he was president-elect. Even the U.S. Constitution itself refers to the country as "the confederacy" (see Article Six).

Liberals will tell you that after the Articles of Confederation were replaced with the U.S. Constitution in 1789, America was no longer thought of as a confederacy. However, the words of none other than George Washington refute this. With the signing of the U.S. Constitution, our country's first post-Articles chief executive referred to the newly refurbished government as "the new Confederacy." This definitively establishes that he viewed the new governmental system under the U.S. Constitution as being identical to the old one under the Articles of Confederation.[26]

Furthermore, from this it is clear that the Founding Generation continued to see the U.S. as a confederacy, as *the* Confederacy, even after the adoption of the U.S. Constitution that year.

Most revealing is the fact that the United States of America—which Madison called "the present Confederation of the American States"—was, from the very beginning, known to both American citizens and foreigners as not only "the confederate states," but more importantly as "the Confederate States of America."

In 1779, for example, in the midst of the American Revolutionary War, and two years before the original 13 colonies were first confederated under the Articles of Confederation in 1781, Reverend David S. Rowland, Minister of the Presbyterian Church at Providence, Rhode Island, published a small book with the unwieldy title: *Historical Remarks, with Moral Reflections: A Sermon Preached at Providence, June 6, 1779, Wherein are Represented, the Remarkable Dispensations of Divine Providence to the People of these States, Particularly in the Rise and Progress of the Present War, Between the Confederate States of America, and Great-Britain*.

Three years later, in 1782, an anonymous English author using the pseudonym "a Man of No Party," referred to the U.S.A. as "the confederate states of America." That same year minister Robert Smith of Pequea, Pennsylvania, penned a book entitled: *The Obligations of the Confederate States of North America to Praise God*. This was 79 years before the official formation of the Southern Confederacy in 1861.

A half century later, writing in the early 1830s, French aristocrat and tourist Alexis de Tocqueville made the following statements after visiting the U.S., all some 30 years prior to the formation of the Southern Confederacy:

> . . . the *confederate states of America* [that is, the United States of America] had been long accustomed to form a portion of one empire before they had won their independence: they had not contracted the habit of governing themselves, and their national prejudices had not taken deep root in their minds. Superior to the rest of the world in political knowledge, and sharing that knowledge equally among themselves, they were little agitated by the passions which generally oppose the extension of federal authority in a nation, and those passions were checked by the wisdom of the chief citizens.

The plain fact is that *all* of America's early presidents, statesmen, politicians, judicial scholars, and citizens viewed the United States as a confederate republic. This even included 18th- and 19th-Century

Liberals, each who unfailingly maintained that the country was a "confederation of sovereign states." This is indeed why nearly everyone endearingly referred to the U.S.A. variously as "the Confederate States," "our Confederacy," "our Confederation," the "American Confederacy," or most accurately, "the Confederate States of America."[27]

From such facts the conclusion is self-evident: the United States of America began as a voluntary confederation of 13 individual nations with a weak central government, a confederated Union that was subordinate to those states.

Thomas Jefferson called the U.S. "the Confederacy," and in 1801 he referred to states' rights as an "essential principle" and the best and strongest barrier against Liberal "tendencies."

As noted, after the Constitutional Convention of 1787 at Philadelphia, the Articles of Confederation were replaced by the U.S. Constitution. But our government remained a confederate republic, and each of the states retained all of the rights originally accorded to them as individual nation-states by the Declaration of Independence, the Articles of Confederation, the U.S. Constitution, and finally the Bill of Rights.[28]

Moving forward in time, by the end of 1861, the Southern Confederacy, the C.S.A., possessed 13 seceded states in all, which were symbolized by a 13 star circle on its First National Flag. This, of course, was the identical number of colonies that had seceded from England to form the first Confederate States of America in 1781, and which were astrally symbolized on the U.S. Confederate Flag of that period, still known as the "Betsy Ross Flag." Clearly, as we will see, the C.S.A. adopted this same "stars and stripes" pattern for it own first official flag. (Incidentally, the 13 colonies represented on the Betsy Ross, the first official flag of the U.S., were Delaware, Pennsylvania, New Jersey, Georgia, Connecticut, Massachusetts, Maryland, South Carolina, New Hampshire, Virginia, New York, North Carolina, and Rhode Island.)

Furthermore, despite a few significant alterations, the Southern Confederacy very precisely patterned its Constitution on the

Constitution of the United States, a document that was, in turn, built around our country's first Constitution, the Articles of Confederation, formulated during the period of American Confederation (1781-1789).

Lastly, like the U.S.A., the C.S.A. was intentionally formed to be a "lasting confederacy": a perpetual union of powerful autonomous states existing under a small limited central government. In other words, just as the former was built on states' rights, the latter was to be as well.

Speaking for the U.S., President Thomas Jefferson uttered the following words in his Inaugural Address on March 4, 1801. The "essential principles" of the newly formed U.S. Confederacy, he asserted, include

> the support of the state governments in all their rights [i.e., states' rights], as the most competent administrations for our domestic concerns and the surest bulwarks against anti-republican [i.e., Liberal] tendencies. . . .[29]

Eighty years later, in 1881, former Southern Confederate President Jefferson Davis, agreed, writing:

> If the State government is instituted with certain powers which become "just powers" by the formal consent of the governed, for the purpose of enforcing security to the unalienable rights of man, it must be evident that any interference with those rights by which their enjoyment is diminished, endangered, or destroyed, is not only an obstruction to the operation of the "just powers" of the State government, but is subversive of the purpose which it was instituted to effect.[30]

It is obvious then why the Southern Confederate Founding Fathers gave their new republic the name "the Confederate States of America" in 1861. This was the name given to the original U.S.A. by both American citizens and foreigners, and more loosely by the American Founding Fathers and countless subsequent statesmen and politicians, from George Washington and Thomas Jefferson to Jefferson Davis and Abraham Lincoln.

This was far more than just mere name-borrowing, however: *the second Confederate States of America (1861) was meant to be a literal continuation of the first or original Confederate States of America (1781)*, not a rebellion intent on "destroying the United States," as anti-South critics continue to misleadingly assert.[31] Thus, at the outset of Lincoln's War in early 1861, Southern Confederate President Davis exclaimed: "Let us stand by the government established by the wisdom of our fathers."[32] In 1912 Confederate writer Robert M. Howard concurred:

> The men of the South [the Democrats, the Conservatives at the time] were absolutely loyal to the Government as it was organized and had been administered from the beginning. *They were upholding the fundamental law of the land* against the advocates [the Republicans, the Liberal Party at the time] of a new nationalism, *who proposed to substitute their ideas of justice and right for that law.*[33]

Betsy Ross creating the first official flag of the U.S. Confederacy in 1776, later used by the Southern Confederacy as a template for the "Stars and Bars," or First National Flag. Though her story is considered a legend by some, the "Betsy Ross Flag" itself certainly was not: a number of paintings from the time period include the familiar banner with 13 red and white stripes and 13 stars encircled on a blue background.

This developmental connection, in which the C.S.A. evolved from out of the original U.S.A.—and even shared the same name and similar flags and constitutions—is one that no card-carrying Leftist wants you to know about. Why? Because the innumerable lies and myths they have created about the American "Civil War" would be exposed for all to see. Yet, for Liberal South-haters, this is the very point, for their goal is to erase, edit, suppress, and rewrite European-American history to such an extent that the factual truth can never be known. Fortunately for both posterity and truth-seekers, their plot has failed. All is being dug back up, resuscitated, and revealed!

Now let us address the charge of "treason" against the Southern Confederacy, long one of the North's favorite pieces of anti-South propaganda.

It has been proven time and time again over the past 150 years that secession was legal in 1860 and 1861, and it is still legal to this day. If it had not been, the law-abiding Southern states would not have seceded. As it was legal, secession was not treasonous. If it had been, the Southern people would not have fought. And as their fight was legal, they were not traitors. It is that simple.

In 1904 former Confederate officer Charles T. O'Ferrall, a cavalry colonel under Robert E. Lee, explained why the South took up arms:

> At this late day it is unnecessary for me to declare that the Confederate soldier believed his cause was just. No body of men would ever have enlisted under a flag and for four years exposed their lives and scattered their wounded and dead from the Pennsylvania hills to the plains of Texas, fought until they were shoeless and almost naked, suffered the pangs of hunger almost to starvation, left mothers, wives, daughters and sisters to struggle unaided to keep body and soul together—unless they believed in the righteousness of *their cause* and the sacredness of *the principles* they were maintaining and defending.[34]

"Their cause" was freedom from tyranny, and "the principles" Confederate soldiers fought to "maintain and defend" were the rights of the states as laid out in the Constitution, one of which was secession. In 1912 Confederate defender Mildred Lewis Rutherford wrote:

> Was Secession Rebellion? The very fact that President [Jefferson] Davis and the leaders of the South could not be brought to trial disproves this. [Yankee] Chief Justice [Salmon P.] Chase said, "If you bring these [Confederate] leaders to trial it will

condemn the North, for *by the Constitution secession is not rebellion.*" Wendell Phillips said, and he was no friend of the South, "Looking back upon the principles of '76 *the South had a perfect right to secede.*" Horace Greeley said so, [before becoming president] Lincoln himself said so, and Daniel Webster had said so.

[In fact,] there have been eight distinct secessions in the United States and very many threatened ones.

1. The thirteen colonies seceded from England and formed a Perpetual Union under the Articles of Confederation in 1776.

2. The thirteen States seceded from the Perpetual Union and formed a Republic of Sovereign States in 1787.

3. Texas seceded from Mexico and became a Republic in 1836.

4. The Abolitionists, led by William Lloyd Garrison, seceded from the Constitution at Framingham, Mass., and publicly burned it, calling it a "league with hell and covenant with death," the assembled multitude loudly applauding.

5. Eleven States seceded from the Union in 1861 and formed a Southern Confederacy.

6. The North seceded from the Constitution in 1861 when she attempted to coerce the eleven States back into the Union.

7. Under President [William] McKinley in 1898 the United States forced Cuba to secede from Spain.

8. Under [Theodore] Roosevelt in 1905 the United States forced Panama to secede from Colombia.

Why should all of these secessions be justifiable save the one by the South in 1861?[35]

William Rawle, arguably the most important constitutional scholar of the 19th-Century, and whose famous 1829 work, *A View of the Constitution of the United States of America*, was once used as a textbook in universities and military schools across the country, made these remarks about secession:

The Union is an association of the people of republics; its preservation is calculated to depend on the preservation of those republics. . . . The principle of representation, although certainly the wisest and best, is not essential to the being of a republic, but to continue a member of the Union, it must be preserved, and therefore the guarantee must be so construed. *It depends on the state itself to retain or abolish the principle of representation, because it depends on itself whether it will continue a member of the Union. To deny this right would be inconsistent with the principle on which all our political systems are founded, which is, that the people have in all cases, a right to determine how they will be governed.*

This right must be considered as an ingredient in the original composition of the general government, which, though not expressed, was mutually understood, and the doctrine heretofore presented to the reader in regard to the indefeasible nature of personal allegiance, is so far qualified in respect to allegiance to the United States. It was observed, that it was competent for a state to make a compact with its citizens, that the reciprocal obligations of protection and allegiance might cease on certain events; and it was further observed, that allegiance would necessarily cease on the dissolution of the society to which it was due.

The states, then, may wholly withdraw from the Union, but while they continue, they must retain the character of representative republics. Governments of dissimilar forms and principles cannot long maintain a binding coalition. "Greece," says Montesquieu, "was undone as soon as the king of Macedon obtained a seat in the amphyctionic council." It is probable, however, that the disproportionate force as well as the monarchical form of the new confederate had its share of influence in the event. But whether the historical fact supports the theory or not, *the principle in respect to ourselves is unquestionable.*[36]

Leading 19th-Century American constitutional scholar William Rawle declared that the U.S. right of secession is indispensable and its legality "unquestionable."

Ten years later, in 1839, former U.S. President John Quincy Adams gave a speech before the New York Historical Society which included these sagacious words:

> But the indissoluble link of Union between the people of the several States of this confederated nation is, after all, not in the right, but in the heart. *If the day should ever come (may Heaven avert it!) when the affections of the people of these States shall be alienated from each other*, when the fraternal spirit shall give way to cold indifference or collisions of interest shall fester into hatred, the bands of political association will not long hold together parties no longer attracted by the magnetism of conciliated interests and kindly sympathies; and *far better will it be for the people of the disunited States to part in friendship from each other, than to be held together by constraint*. Then will be the time for reverting to the precedents which occurred at the formation and adoption of the Constitution, to form again a more perfect Union by deploring that which could no longer bind, and to leave the separated parts to be re-united by the law of political gravitation to the centre.[37]

On November 9, 1860, just before South Carolina seceded, the editor of the New York *Tribune*, Liberal Northerner Horace Greeley, published the following public commentary:

> If the cotton States consider the value of the Union debatable, we maintain their perfect right to discuss it. Nay: *we hold, with Jefferson, to the inalienable right of communities to alter or abolish forms of government that have become oppressive or injurious; and, if the cotton States shall decide that they can do better out of the Union than in it, we insist on letting them go in peace. The right to secede may be a revolutionary one, but it exists nevertheless: and we do not see how one party can have a right to do what another party has a right to prevent.*[38]

All three of the men just cited were Yankees: Rawle, a lawyer, was from Pennsylvania; Adams, a politician, was from Massachusetts; and Greeley, a newspaperman, was from New Hampshire. Clearly, Northerners from across a wide spectrum of the population understood and recognized the legality of secession right up to 1861.

Lincoln himself had once accepted this fact, even calling secession a "most sacred right." On January 12, 1848, in a speech before the U.S. House of Representatives, he declared:

> *Any people anywhere, being inclined and having the power, have the right to rise up, and shake off the existing government, and form a new one that suits them better.* This is a most valuable, a most sacred right—a right which, we hope and believe, is to liberate the world. Nor is this right confined to cases in which the whole people of an existing government may choose to exercise it. *Any portion of such people that can may revolutionize, and make their own of so much of the territory as they inhabit.*[39]

Why did Lincoln change his mind on the subject 13 years later upon becoming U.S. president? Because it was politically expedient. He was a Liberal, after all, a political species known for its contempt for, and even hatred of, the Constitution.

Thus, on July 4, 1861, in his "Message to Congress in Special Session," the newly elected chief executive called the Southern Confederacy an "illegal organization," and the constitutional right of secession an "ingenious sophism," an "insidious debauching of the public mind," and, ridiculously, a "sugar-coated invention" of the South. Those who challenged these views were labeled "traitors" and "rebels." All of this despite the fact that the U.S. itself was a country founded on secession; in this case, by breaking away from the tyrannical English monarchy.[40]

The question we Southerners are often asked is, why, if secession is legal, is this right not clearly articulated in the U.S. Constitution?

To begin with, let us note here that there is nothing in the Constitution that prohibits secession. As for the answer to this question, it was stated, as we have just seen, by Rawle nearly 200 years ago: "though not expressed, it was mutually understood." In other words, the concept was so well-known and accepted at the time the U.S. Constitution was written that the Founders felt no need to mention it. Jefferson Davis answered the question this way:

> It was not necessary in the Constitution to affirm the right of secession, because *it was an attribute of sovereignty*, and the states had reserved all which they had not delegated [to the central government].

Thus, as it was understood by Victorian Southerners—and even many

Northerners—under the unwritten but assumed right of secession, a state could leave the Union anytime it wished, *legally and independently*. This is quite in contrast to the more complicated right of *accession* (entrance into the Union), which requires the consent of Congress before a new state can be admitted (see Article Four, Section Three, Clause One of the U.S. Constitution).

The fact is that *up until 1865 secession was the most frequently discussed political issue in both the United States and the Confederate States*. Thus to the Framers and the general populace it was merely another common law that was universally recognized and automatically accepted by every American citizen.[41]

What all of this amounts to is simple: secession was legal in 1860 and 1861, therefore the Southern states broke no laws when they left the Union. And because their exit was legal, not only was there no treason involved, this also means that the Confederate States of America was a separate, legal, and constitutionally created political body, one intentionally formed around, and even named after, the original U.S.A.—a country also founded on secession. In short, on March 4, 1861, the day the C.S.A. was officially born, America possessed two individual countries, with two individual nationalities and two individual flags.

This, in turn, makes *all* Confederate Flags, whatever their state and origins, legitimate American emblems. Not of racism, treason, or slavery. But of *Southern independence*. For not only was secession legal, there was never such a thing as a "Pro-Slavery Party," not in the South, or anywhere else in America. The preservation of slavery was *never* the sole focus of anyone; not of any organization, nor of any political group, period.[42] Thus *all* 19th-Century wartime Southern flags, whether governmental, military, state, or unofficial, were and remain *historical* banners: flags of Southern history, heritage, and honor.

Writing in 1912, Confederate soldier Robert M. Howard looked back and captured the mood of the South during the beginning stages of secession in 1860:

> I lived in LaFayette, Ala., in 1860 where I had charge of grading a railroad from there to Opelika. I contributed to a fund with which to erect a [John] Bell and [Edward] Everett liberty pole 125 feet high from which to float a Bell and Everett campaign flag. I was a

> secessionist *per se* believing that *each state had the inalienable right to secede from the Union at its own discretion and will.* When Lincoln was declared elected president I had a large secession flag made; some one cut the rope to prevent me from hoisting it. I went up to the arm eighty-five feet above the ground, nailed it to the pole, stood up, spoke about fifteen minutes, and descended to the ground. When I left there in January 1861 it was still proudly floating to the propitious breezes of Heaven.[43]

In 1914 former Confederate Captain John Anderson Richardson of Georgia declared what every Southerner, then as now, knows to be true: "The South was right."

Howard makes it clear that he was not "rebelling" against the Union to "preserve slavery." He raised the Secession Flag in the cause of the Constitutional guarantee of states' rights, for it is the Bill of Rights which makes America exceptional, and which makes our Confederate Republic the best country in the world. The Bill of Rights, so detested by Liberals then as now, is why Conservative Jefferson Davis referred to the Southern Confederate States of America as "the last best hope of liberty." For these all-important ten rights were later incorporated directly into the C.S. Constitution, with the hope of preserving them after what they believed would be the overthrow of the U.S. Constitution by Lincoln and his Liberal constituents. As it turns out, "the South was right," just as Confederate champion John A. Richardson asserted in 1914.[44]

Despite the legality of the South's separation from the Union, the overwhelming military might of Lincoln and his Northern armies decided the future course the U.S.A. would take. And that course was meant to gradually remake our confederate republic (a country based on state sovereignty and law) into a socialist democracy (a country based on governmental domination and majority rule), something that was both feared and fiercely resisted by the Founding Generation. Unfortunately, as Howard writes:

> When the Confederacy fell [at Appomattox on April 9, 1865], the Republic formed by the Fathers and composed of sovereign States in Federation, perished. The States were robbed of their independence. In fact, if not in name, they ceased to be sovereign, and became subject provinces, whose people owe their highest political allegiance, not to them, but to a centralized national authority. They tell us that it is best; that the Government established by the Fathers, under which the States retained their sovereignty and were united by compact, served well enough in the beginning, but could not meet the demands of new conditions resulting from the country's growth; and that it was necessary to lose the sovereignty of the States in the sovereignty of the nation, in order that we might become a great world-power and successfully compete with the kingdoms of the earth for political and commercial supremacy. It may be so; but I beseech you to pardon an old Confederate soldier, who is perhaps blinded by memories that sometimes fill his eyes with tears, if he can not see it so; and believing, as history teaches, that *patriotism is most ardent and freedom most secure in small communities*, would to-day rather have his own State as his crowned queen, and owe to her his highest political allegiance, than be a subject of the mightiest, richest and most glorious Empire that ever was or can be reared by the wisdom and power of man.[45]

Christopher Gadsden of South Carolina, the designer of the Gadsden Flag (after whom it was named), was just one of many early American statesmen who longed for a government built on individual freedom.

These are words that all traditional Southerners can relate to.

Enemies of the South like to call our fight "The Lost Cause." But the cause of freedom was not lost at Appomattox, and, in fact, it can never be lost; not through intolerance, coercion, prohibitions, or even war. As our birthright it is inborn; it is one of what English philosopher John Locke called our "natural rights: life, liberty, and property"; bestowed upon us, not by government, but by God. And what is ordained by Spirit cannot be undone by Man.

Thus today's Confederates have not given up on the Confederate Republic of the Founding Fathers. And they never will. They will continue to resist the empire-making tendencies of America's Left-wing while pressing forward in the constitutional cause of self-government, self-reliance, capitalism, private enterprise, and individual freedom. And the flags they march under are primarily Southern in origin. For it was the South—under such great Southerners as George Washington, Thomas Jefferson, James Madison, George Mason, Christopher Gadsden, Thomas Burke, John C. Calhoun, Christopher G. Memminger, Alexander H. Stephens, and Jefferson Davis—which first dreamed of a land based on personal liberty, and inspired, and in many cases actually first drew up, the documents that would create it: the Declaration of Independence, the Articles of Confederation, the U.S. Constitution, the Bill of Rights, and finally the C.S. Constitution.

In 1899 Lieutenant Governor of Virginia, James Taylor Ellyson, uttered these words before the United Confederate Veterans at New Orleans:

> There is no danger that we who fought under the Stars and Bars [the Confederate First National Flag], shall ever forget the memories of four stormy years or prove false to the generous motives that then animated our lives; but *there is danger, and real danger, that our children may be taught that the cause for which we fought was treason and we but traitors.* From such a fate may a kind Providence spare us! *Then let us see that histories are written which shall contain the true story of Southern patriotism and valor, and which teach our children that the soldiers of the Southern Confederacy were not rebels, but were Americans who loved Constitutional liberty as something dearer than life itself. Let us be certain that our children know that the War between the States was not a contest for the preservation of slavery, as some would have them believe, but that it was a great struggle for the maintenance of Constitutional rights*, and that the men who fought—
>
> Were warriors tried and true,
> Who bore the Flag of a nation's trust;
> And fell in a cause though lost, still just,
> And died for me and you.[46]

Writing from the same period, Jacob Owen McGehee, who

served in George Pickett's Division under Confederate General James Longstreet, continues this line of thought:

> Nor was the cause for which we fought entirely "lost," [for] "truth crushed to earth will rise again."
>
> Though we failed to establish permanently an independent government, yet, *the eternal truth and right and justice of our cause still lives*; and that it is steadily gaining ground in the minds and convictions of calm, dispassionate thinkers everywhere is shown by the fact, among many other instances, that one of the most distinguished and forceful writers of Massachusetts said in a recent publication, treating of the Confederacy and its people:
>
> > "Such character and achievement were not all in vain; though the Confederacy fell as an actual, physical Power, *it lives eternally in its just cause—the cause of Constitutional liberty*."[47]

In the early 1900s, conservative Virginian and former Confederate officer George Llewellyn Christian, made the following comments at a memorial for Robert E. Lee:

> I am just as firm a believer today in the justice of the Confederate cause as I was when I enlisted to defend that cause in 1861, and I am never going to stultify myself by saying, I am sorry that cause did not succeed.
>
> [A] . . . Northern writer of two hundred years of New England ancestry, has written that after studying the questions at issue in the late war honestly and thoroughly, he had reached the conclusion that *the Northern cause was the "lost cause," and not that of the South*. And even Mrs. Harriet Beecher Stowe's youngest son [Charles Edward Stowe] has recently said, that whilst there was a rebellion in this country in 1861, *the Northern people were the rebels, and that the Southern people were the patriots, fighting for the maintenance of the constitution as it was delivered to them by their fathers*. And a more recent Northern writer thus refers to the Army of Northern Virginia and our cause in these words:
>
> > "Army of Northern Virginia, sleep on; the Confederacy's star will hang in your country's sky, and the day is coming when your children will rejoice in the fact that to whatsoever height of glory the reunited country rises,

> prouder will it and they be of you and your valor, and above all in those trying times to come of that display of willingness to lay your lives down for a political principle that is the very foundation on which your whole governmental system is based."

Is there wonder, then, that we old veterans are proud both of our cause and of our matchless leaders?[48]

14th-Century "rebel" Sir William Wallace gave his life for the cause of Scottish independence, a burning passion for personal freedom that was transmitted down through the centuries all the way into the Victorian South. Here it found a home in the heart of every Confederate soldier, each one a "William Wallace" in his own right.

To prove that the "Southern" Cause is both immortal and universal, we need look no further than the words spoken by Scottish "rebel" leader Sir William Wallace—the Nathan Bedford Forrest of Scotland—at his trial for "treason" in 1305. Here the famed the Liberator of Caledonia vigorously defended himself against his oppressor English King Edward "Longshanks" I. Tellingly, if we replace the word "English" with Yankee, "King" with president, and "Edward" with Lincoln, this could be Forrest or any other a Confederate officer speaking 556 years later. Said Wallace:

> I can not be a traitor, for I owe Edward of England no allegiance. He is not my Sovereign; he never received my homage; and whilst life is in this persecuted body, he never shall receive it. To the other points whereof I am accused, I freely confess them all. As

> Governor of my country I have been an enemy to its enemies; I have slain the English; I have mortally opposed the English King; I have stormed and taken the towns and castles which he unjustly claimed as his own. If I or my soldiers have plundered or done injury to the houses or ministers of religion, I repent me of my sin; but it is not of Edward of England I shall ask pardon.[49]

You cannot kill an idea. What Wallace fought and died for carried on into the American South nearly six centuries later through the bloodlines of her Scottish-American sons and daughters, with Saint Andrew's Cross emblazoned on our Confederate Battle Flag. The concept of confederation, symbolized by the lively colorful banners of the South, will indeed flourish until the end of time, for *it is the very definition of freedom.* Not just for the European-American community, the African-American community, the Hispanic-American community, the Native-American community, or the Asian-American community; and certainly not even specifically for the South. It is a symbol of liberation for all humanity, whatever their skin color, religion, or nationality.

The inauguration of Jefferson Davis on February 18, 1861, at Montgomery, Alabama. The Yankee propagandists who created this print in 1888 entitled it: "The Starting Point of the Great War Between the States," certainly one of the most inaccurate and deceitful statements ever made about Lincoln's War! In truth it was on this day that the Southern Confederacy—the second "Confederate States of America"—installed its first official leader, *relaunching* what Thomas Jefferson said he had hoped would be a "lasting confederacy." Lincoln himself would initiate the War two months later after devilishly tricking the Confederacy into firing the first shot at Fort Sumter.

This is precisely why the Confederate Battle Flag can be seen on display in oppressed countries all over the world, from Europe to South America. It is the exact opposite of what South-loathers have long claimed: a "flag of slavery." In truth, it is the universal standard of personal liberty, humankind's most valued spiritual and political inheritance!

Belle Boyd, one the Confederacy's most fascinating, patriotic, romantic, indomitable, and enduring figures. Born Maria Isabella Boyd in 1844 in what is now Martinsburg, West Virginia, Belle lived a life of adventure and intrigue that few could imagine. Raised in a cultured home, she received a thorough education, lived as a debutante in Washington, D.C., murdered a Yankee soldier who insulted her mother, spent her twenties working as a Confederate spy for Generals Stonewall Jackson and Pierre G. T. Beauregard, married three times, had several children, served numerous (brief) sentences in Yankee prisons, traveled by ship to Europe to deliver secret Confederate documents, wrote an autobiography, gave lectures, and finally became an actress, passing away during a performance in Wisconsin at the age of 56. Her delightful habit of singing "Dixie" in her jail cell while waving Confederate flags from her prison windows, earned her a number of Yankee epithets, including: "the Rebel Joan of Arc," "the Siren of the Shenandoah," and "La Belle Rebelle." The nickname she gave herself was the "Cleopatra of Secession."

2

ORIGINS OF THE FOUR CONFEDERATE FLAGS

THAT GLORIOUS FLAG WHICH SLUMBERS

Gallant nation, foiled by numbers,
Say not that your hopes are fled;
Keep that glorious flag which slumbers,
One day to avenge your dead.
Keep it, widowed, sonless mothers,
Keep it, sisters, mourning brothers,
Furl it with an iron will;
Furl it now, but keep it still,
Think not that its work is done.
Keep it till your children take it,
Once again to hail and make it
All their sires have bled and fought for,
Bled and fought for all alone.

All alone! aye, shame the story,
Millions here deplore the stain;
Shame, alas! for England's glory,
Freedom called, and called in vain.
Furl that banner, sadly, slowly,
Treat it gently, for 'tis holy,
Till that day—yes furl it sadly,
Then once more unfurl it gladly,
Conquered banner, keep it still.[50]

SIR HENRY HOUGHTON OF ENGLAND, 1865

CHAPTER 2

WHAT YOU WERE TAUGHT: There is only one Confederate Flag: the infamous red banner with the blue cross and 13 white stars, the same one seen on the TV series *The Dukes of Hazzard*. This is the national flag of the Southern Confederacy, and it flew over the Confederate capitol at Richmond. Therefore it is a vile symbol of slavery and white racism, and of the murder, torture, and death of thousands of African-Americans.

THE FACTS: Contrary to Yankee mythology, what is commonly called the "Confederate Flag" is not and never was the official flag of the Confederates States of America. This particular flag was specifically created for the Confederate military, which is why it is called the "Confederate Battle Flag"—its bright colors and impactful cross design were meant to make it more easily recognizable on the battlefield.

What then was the official flag of the Confederacy?

The C.S.A. had three national flags during its brief four-year history. The true story of how they, as well as the Battle Flag, came about forms the very foundation of this book, and explains the undying adoration the Southern people have for them.

As Abraham Lincoln's inauguration loomed on March 4, 1861, Confederate authorities scrambled to select a flag for their new republic, which was to be presented that same day at a flag-raising ceremony at the Confederate capitol, then located in Montgomery, Alabama. To this end the Provisional Confederate Congress set up the "Committee on Flag and Seal," installing William Porcher Miles of South Carolina as chairman.

While hundreds of ideas were submitted, some even from Confederate supporters in the Northern states (known derogatorily by South-hating Northerners as "Copperheads"), only four were taken seriously enough to be put forward to the committee.

The first of these proposed designs, submitted by Miles, was what would later become the Confederate Battle Flag. The second possessed seven white stars and seven red and blue stripes symbolizing the original seven Southern states that had seceded. The third design was a simple red flag with a large blue ring in the middle. All three of these were rejected by the Confederate Congress.[51]

It was the fourth design, however, created by the flag committee itself,[52] that was adopted, and this was primarily because it resembled the first U.S. Flag, one known as the "Betsy Ross Flag": Southern sentiment toward the U.S. Union was still so strong at the time that the Confederate public demanded that their new flag be similar.[53] According to early accounts, the general public favored a flag that should "differ from the Stars and Stripes only enough to make it easily distinguishable." One prominent Southern newspaper noted that "there was a general desire to depart as little as possible from the old [U.S.] flag."[54]

The U.S. "Betsy Ross Flag," according to the author the probable model for the Southern Confederacy's First National Flag, the "Stars and Bars."

On March 4, 1861, the newly selected C.S. flag design was described by Miles in the following words:

> Your committee, therefore, recommend that the flag of the Confederate States of America shall consist of a red field with a

> white space extending horizontally through the center, and equal in width to one-third the width of the flag. The red spaces above and below to be of the same width as the white. The union blue extending down through the white space and stopping at the lower red space. In the center of the union a circle of white stars corresponding in number with the States in the Confederacy. If adopted, long may it wave over a brave, a free, and a virtuous people. May the career of the Confederacy, whose duty it will then be to support and defend it, be such as to endear it to our children's children, as the flag of a loved, because a just and benign, government, and the cherished symbol of its valor, purity, and truth.[55]

This seven-star flag, representing the current number of seceded Southern states (South Carolina, Georgia, Florida, Alabama, Mississippi, Texas, and Louisiana), was nicknamed the "Stars and Bars," and also the "tri-barred flag,"[56] but its official moniker was the "First National Confederate Flag."[57]

During the Winter and Spring of 1861, the beautiful Stars and Bars could be seen popping up all over the South, hanging in windows, from porches, on flagstaffs, and floating jauntily above Southern homes and buildings. The lapels and hats of thousands of proud Confederates were decorated with cockades and pins featuring the First National in miniature.[58] Kentuckian Eliza Ripley, who wrote about her life in Louisiana during Lincoln's War, described the festive flag-embracing mood of the Confederacy, at which time her family raised the first Confederate flag in the Pelican State:

> It was during the temporary absence of my husband [James Alexander McHatton], and Arlington [Plantation, just south of Baton Rouge] full of gay young guests, when our city paper described the device for "the flag," as decided upon at Montgomery, the cradle of the new-born Confederacy. Up to and even far beyond that period we did not, in fact could not, realize the mightiness of the impending future. Full of wild enthusiasm, the family at Arlington voted at once that the banner should unfold its brave States-rights constellation from a staff on our river-front. This emblem of nationality (which, on account of its confusing resemblance to the brilliant "Stars and Stripes," was subsequently discarded) consisted of a red field with a horizontal bar of white across its center; in one corner was a square of blue with white

stars. There were red flannel and white cotton cloth in the house, but nothing blue could we find; so a messenger was hastily dispatched to town with orders for goods of that color, no matter what the quality or shade.

On a square of blue denim the white stars were grouped, one to represent each seceded State. We toiled all that Saturday, and had no little difficulty in getting our work to lie smooth and straight, as the red flannel was pieced, the cotton flimsy, and the denim stiff. From the negroes who had been spending their half-holiday catching drift-wood, which in the early spring floats from every tributary down on the rapidly swelling bosom of the broad Mississippi, we procured a long, straight, slender pole, to which the flag was secured by cords, nails, and other devices. When the staff was firmly planted into the ground, on the most prominent point on the river-front, and its gay banner loosened to the breeze, the enthusiastic little party danced round and round, singing and shouting in exuberance of spirit. At that critical moment a small stern-wheel Pittsburg boat came puffing up the stream; its shrill whistle and bell joined in the celebration, while passengers and crew cheered and hallooed, waving newspapers, hats, and handkerchiefs, until the little Yankee craft wheezed out of sight in a bend of the river. Of all the joyous party that danced and sung round that first Confederate flag raised on Louisiana soil, I am, with the exception of my son, then a very small boy, the only one living to-day.

It made such a brave show, and we were so exhilarated, that we passed all that bright Sunday in early spring under its waving folds, or on the piazza in full view of it.

When my husband, after a two weeks' absence, boarded the steamer *Quitman* to return home, the first news that greeted him was, "There is a Confederate flag floating over your levee!" He was thunderstruck! That far-seeing, cautious man was by no means an "original secessionist," and did not, in his discretion, and the hope that lingered long in his breast of an amicable adjustment of the difficulties, countenance the zealous ardor of his hasty and impetuous household. Our flag was already beginning to look frayed and ragged-edged. We had no means of lowering it, and its folds had flapped through fog and sunshine until the sleazy cotton split and the stars shriveled on the stiff blue ground. The coming of the "general commanding," as we now playfully called him, signalized the removal of our tattered banner; but we had the satisfaction of knowing that advantage of his absence had been taken to float it a whole week, and that it was no hostile hand that furled it at the last.[59]

The Confederacy's first First National Flag, the "Stars and Bars," seven-star version.

For the next four years raising the "Secession Flag," as it was called, would remain the most popular political act in the South. And though, as mentioned, it was already unofficially flying over private Southern homes, public buildings, churches, and courthouses,[60] it did not appear over the Confederate Capitol at Montgomery, Alabama, for the first time until March 4, 1861, when it was hoisted aloft by Letitia Tyler, the granddaughter of former U.S. President John Tyler. Miss Tyler, born at the White House in Washington, D.C., had been invited by President Jefferson Davis to "raise the first flag of the Confederacy."[61] Fifty-five years later the famous Southern belle recalled not only that glorious occasion, but also the Yankee hatred directed toward her father, who happened to be living in the North at the time:

> It has been so long ago that many of the details of the event have faded from my memory. I know that great crowds of people were constantly about the Statehouse and Capitol grounds, as companies of [Confederate] soldiers were being mustered into service, and interested people were on hand to watch the doings of the Provisional Congress of the Confederacy. I cannot now recall, even if I ever had heard, who designed the flag. I clearly remember ascending the stairs that led to the dome of the building and that I was escorted by Hon. Alex B. Clitherall, one of the Confederate officials. Dr. and Mrs. Thomas Taylor and several other persons accompanied us to the top of the Capitol. Below us were vast

throngs of people, who were watching and waiting for the signal to unfurl the flag of the new nation. On reaching the base of the dome I found the flag all ready, and the cord was handed me. Then I began to pull it, and up climbed the flag to the top of the pole and floated out boldly on the stiff March wind. The hundreds of people below us sent up a mighty shout. Cannon roared out a salute, and my heart beat with wild joy and excitement. May I recall further that *my father, although residing in the North, never lost one whit of his love for the South; but he never taught us sectional things. Because he was so much a Southerner, his position was one of suspicion and hate on the part of the people there; and when it became known that his daughter had actually raised a Confederate flag, feeling against him became very intense. It was not long before he removed South with his family.*[62]

The Capitol Building at Montgomery, Alabama, where Jefferson Davis took his oath of office on February 18, 1861, and where the initial raising of the Confederate First National Flag took place on March 4, 1861. Today the U.S. Flag flies over its dome. Below it, however, can still be seen floating the Alabama state flag, with a Saint Patrick's Cross (or a "crimson" Saint Andrew's Cross) on a white field, the Yellowhammer State's tribute to both its Celtic heritage and the second Confederate States of America, the C.S.A.

The memorable flag-raising at Capitol Hill in Montgomery was accompanied by an unexplained supernatural phenomenon, as described by an editor at the *Montgomery Weekly Advertiser*, March 6, 1861:

> Ere [that is, before] there was time to take one hasty glance at the national ensign, the eyes of all were upturned to gaze at what would perhaps at any time have attracted unusual attention, but on this occasion seemed really a providential omen. Scarcely had the first report from the [cannon] salute died away when *a large and beautifully defined circle of blue vapor* rose slowly over the assemblage of Southern spirits there assembled to vow allegiance to the Southern banner, rested for many seconds on a level with the flag of the Confederate States, then gradually ascended until lost to the gaze of the multitude. *It was a most beautiful and auspicious omen*, and those who look with an eye of faith to the glorious future of our Confederacy could but believe that the same God that vouchsafed to the Christian emperor [Constantine I] the cross in the heavens as a promise of victory had this day given to a young nation striving for liberty a divine augury of hope and national durability.[63]

Not surprisingly, just as Letitia Tyler's father had been attacked by Yankees shortly after the Stars and Bars was made official, the flag itself began to be assailed by ill-willed Northerners almost immediately. The following story is worth recording here at length, not only for its historical interest, but also to show how, from the very beginning, the North has used disinformation to slander our beloved Southern flags and turn the naive against them. This article, entitled *First Confederate Flag on the Atlantic*, was written by C. H. Beale of Montgomery, Alabama, in 1907. Note the mention of the crew of Southern "free negroes," all who were ready to defend the ship's Confederate flag with their lives:

> When the wave of secession began to roll over the South, I was living in Newbern, N. C., which was a considerable seaport town. My honored father was one of the first to espouse the cause, and I, his oldest son, followed him.
>
> Too young to aid our cause, however, but full of love and adventure, my school companion, John Hall, and I persuaded our parents to let us take a voyage in one of the many merchant vessels that plied between Newbern and Northern ports and the West India Islands. Owners of these merchant vessels in the South, fearing trouble because of the agitation of war, refused to allow them to take cargoes to Northern points. We finally enlisted with Capt. Bob Robbins, commander of the schooner *Pearl*, bound for the island of Demarara, in the West Indies. This schooner was owned by Theodore Hughes.
>
> On the 5th of March, 1861, the schooner *Pearl*, two

hundred and forty-seven tons burden, sailed from Newbern loaded under hatches with white oak staves and a deck load of lumber. She was a flat-bottomed schooner, centerboard, with two masts. Her sails consisted of a mainsail, foresail, standing jib, flying jib, two gaff topsails, and a staysail. Her crew consisted of one mate (white), *four sailors and one cook (who were all free negroes)*, John Hall, and myself.

At our main topmast we had unfurled the first Confederate flag [the First National] that ever kissed the breeze of the Atlantic, so we claim and believe. The design of this flag was adopted in Montgomery [on March 4, 1861] and telegraphed throughout the country.

On the 9th of March, 1861, we crossed the bar at Hatteras Inlet, headed for Demarara. On the 12th we were struck by a gale that lasted four days and nights, during which time we were compelled to reef all sails except the standing jib (that was double-reefed), and we scudded under bare poles with the standing jib holding her to the wind. When the gale subsided, we had been blown entirely out of our course. After repairing damages, we found that our gallant little vessel was taking in considerable water by reason of leaks caused by the severe strain she had undergone. The discovery compelled us to keep up some extra pumping, which was done by hand, and right here our love of adventure had vanished, and we did some tall praying for boys of our age.

The leaks were stopped, the sails were unfurled, and everything went along lovely. The first land we sighted in three weeks was the Island of Antigua, which belonged to the English, and which of course we hailed with delight. We set our colors for a pilot to take us in to the harbor of St. John's, a nice little city. When entering the harbor, which was commanded by a fort, boom! came a shot across the bow of the vessel, which meant for us to lay to,. and we did.

The commandant of the fort came out to us in a small boat, and when aboard asked where we were from and what flag we were flying. We informed him that *we hailed from North Carolina, and the flag was that of the anticipated Confederacy*. He remarked that he had sighted the flag as we were coming in, and had consulted the map of all nations and flags and found nothing like it, and for that reason had caused us to lay to. *After complimenting the flag*, he gave his permission for us to enter the harbor, and we got in about midday. Here we lay in the stream at anchor and took samples of our stores ashore to sell the cargo. We consigned our vessel to Johnson & Son, an English commission firm.

As may be imagined, our flag created considerable excitement.

In the harbor all about us were small schooners commanded by New England captains in the fish trade, and they commenced to talk about it, calling it the "slavery" flag. Mr. Johnson, Jr., asked permission to take the flag ashore and show it to the Governor of the island. The request was granted, and *the Governor complimented it.*

All of these commission merchants had flag poles, and Mr. Johnson raised this flag upon his pole. *Threats were made by these New England captains to tear it down; bribes were offered to cut the flag's halyards*; but Hall and I, aided by young Johnson, kept the natives [blacks] and all others from attempting to do so, swearing we would shoot the first man who put his hand upon the halyards. The next morning the feeling against the flag seemed to have subsided, and on that evening we accepted a very kind invitation from Mr. Johnson to dine with him between the hours of five and six. *While at dinner we were informed that our flag had been cut down*, and we lost no time in running to its protection, even though it was on a foreign shore. *To our horror, we found that the mob of [native] negroes, incited by the [Yankee] crews of the fishing vessels, had torn the flag down, tied the stars and stripes [the U.S. Flag] to the halyards above it and raised it on the pole, fired pistol balls through our flag, then tore it down and tore it into strips and tied it around their ankles and trampled it in the dirt to disgrace it.* We were maddened to desperation, and would have rushed headlong into certain death, but older heads kept us down.

The design of this flag [the Confederate First National] was a blue field with seven stars in the field and the red and white bars, and was made of oil calico.

We failed to sell our cargo in St. John's, and decided to sail for another port next morning. *We were constantly eyed by the mob, who said that if we raised another such flag they would scuttle our vessel.* Our captain, though a "down-Easter" [Yankee] by birth, married in the South, and was as true a man to the Southern cause as ever lived. He said the *Pearl* should fly the stars and bars, and if necessary he would sink with his vessel in attempting it.

Leaving the vessel under the watch of a guard, the mate and three seamen, we determined on having a new flag made. Some English ladies volunteered their services, and by rapid work of fair hands it was not long before we had another flag made of bunting. Before daylight next morning the stars and bars was again unfurled from the main topmast of the *Pearl*, and as daylight appeared we sailed out of the harbor in full view of all the citizens and headed for the Island of Guadeloupe. *Our crew of negroes had caught our spirit, and were as ready to fight for the flag as any of us, and for this reason we felt somewhat secure against anything like a hand-to-hand encounter.*

At the port of Bastarre, where we took dinner, the flag was

> *highly complimented by the French officers and consuls on the island, this island belonging to France.* Nothing of interest transpired here, and we soon sailed for the Island of Nevis, which is owned by the English and has fine sugar estates. Filling our casks with fresh water, we sailed for St. Kitts, just opposite Nevis. We had to land there in our small boats, as our schooner got in a dead calm five miles out. Not selling the cargo here, we sailed for the Island of Dominique, which belonged to the English. Here we made the port of Roseo, and there sold our cargo for a good price. We were compelled to lay at anchor and unload in small boats, as there were no wharves. *Our flag was much admired here and considerably talked about.*[64]

On April 12, 1861, just a few weeks after Beale's March excursion, the First National flew over Fort Sumter. It was on this day that Lincoln tricked the South into firing the first shot of the War.[65]

As the War progressed and more and more Southern states left the Union, the First National went through a change in the number of stars it possessed. In May two more stars were appended when two states seceded (Virginia and Arkansas), making nine stars; in July two more states separated (Tennessee and North Carolina), adding two stars, now eleven in total. In November and December portions of the final two Southern states seceded (Kentucky and Missouri), and the First National attained its final form with 13 stars.

The Confederate First National Flag, the "Stars and Bars," final 13-star version.

Despite the fact that it appears that the C.S.A. never established a Flag Act of 1861,[66] the First National was displayed and flown as the country's official flag from March 4, 1861, to May 1, 1863.[67]

As the conflict continued, the savage realities of Lincoln's War began to negatively affect every facet of Southern society. The brutal impact of the Yankee invaders and their war crimes forced a change of attitude in the Confederate people toward their flag, the First National, and its resemblance to the U.S. Flag. In 1862 Kate Cumming, a nurse who tended the wounded of the Confederate Army of Tennessee throughout the conflict, expressed the feelings of many Southerners. One day she happened to spot a U.S. flag printed on the back of a Bible belonging to a Yankee prisoner in her care:

> Some of us were looking at it; one of the ladies remarked that it was still sacred in her eyes. This astonished me, after the suffering which we had seen it the . . . cause of. I said that it was the most hateful thing which I could look at; as every stripe in it recalled to my mind the gashes I had witnessed upon our men.[68]

With such feelings growing across Dixie, by early 1862 the Confederate Congress, having moved to the new Confederate Capitol at Richmond, Virginia, sought to change the flag design to one more properly representing a free and venerable people; one not associated with the detested remorseless trespassers to the North.

The First National was also disliked by the Confederate military since, through the smoke and haze of the battlefield, it was often mistaken for the U.S. Flag.[69] As historian Edward S. Ellis put it: "This flag bore considerable resemblance to the old one—so much so, indeed, that fatal mistakes sometimes took place in battle."[70] On the battlefield Confederate General Gilbert M. Sorrel likewise found the Southern Stars and Bars to be "dangerously similar to the Northern Stars and Stripes."[71]

To this end the Confederate Joint Committee on Flag and Seal was formed, with instructions to come up with a new design for the national flag. After one proposal that received little support, the more pressing demands of the War caused the idea to be shelved until the following year.

April 22, 1863, brought another flag submission before the Confederate Congress, an attempt to create a design as dissimilar to the

U.S. flag as possible. Senate Bill No. 132 read:

> The Congress of the Confederate Stales of America do enact, That the flag of the Confederate States shall be as follows: A white field with the battle flag [of the Army of Northern Virginia] for a union: which shall be square and occupy two-thirds of the width of the flag, and a blue bar, one-third of the flag in its width, dividing the field lengthwise.[72]

After much discussion the bill was amended with the following words:

> The field to be white, the length double the width of the flag, with the union (now used as the battle flag) to be a square of two-thirds the width of the flag, having the ground red, thereon a saltier [saltire] of blue, bordered with white and emblazoned with mullets or five-pointed stars, corresponding in number to that of the Confederate States.[73]

The bill was passed and signed by President Jefferson Davis that same day. The Confederacy's new emblem, the Second National Flag, nicknamed the "Stainless Banner," was now official. It would fly above the Confederate Capitol from May 1, 1863, to March 4, 1865.

The Confederate Second National Flag, the "Stainless Banner," was eventually replaced due to its similarity, on windless days, to a white flag of truce.

This flag was not to be the last and final design change to the national flag of the C.S.A., however. The white field of the Stainless Banner, which took up the majority of the space, could sometimes make it appear as a flag of truce, especially in calm weather. This was an issue particularly irksome to the Confederate navy, for without wind the flag hung limp, showing all white.[74]

After many more months of debate and consideration, the final national flag bill, No. 137, was introduced with these words:

> The Congress of the Confederate States of America do enact, That the Flag of the Confederate States shall be as follows: The width, two-thirds of its length, with the union (now used as the Battle Flag) to be in width three-fifths of the width of the flag, and so proportioned as to leave the length of the field on the side of the union twice the width of the field below it; to have the ground red and a broad, blue saltier [saltire] thereon, bordered with white and emblazoned with mullets or five pointed stars, corresponding in number to that of the Confederate States; the field to be white except the outer half from the union to be a red bar extending the width of the flag.[75]

The Confederate Third National, the "Blood-Stained Banner," still the authorized flag of the Confederate States of America, which was never officially closed down—not by the C.S. Congress or the U.S. Congress. Legally speaking, with her Constitution still alive, all that is needed to reactivate the C.S.A. are political candidates and elections.

In 1916 Judge Walter A. Montgomery of Raleigh, North Carolina, commented on the Third National:

> The flag was, in fact, a duplicate of the second Confederate flag, with the addition of a broad transverse strip of red at the end of the whole width of the flag.[76]

The flag was unofficially adopted on February 4, 1865. One month later, on March 4, 1865, the bill easily passed the Confederate House and Senate, and that same day the Flag Act of 1865 was established, President Davis signed the bill into law, and the Confederacy's final flag, the Third National, was authorized.[77]

From that date to this day, the Third National, nicknamed "The Blood-Stained Banner," remains the official flag of the Confederate States of America.[78]

An interesting account of the C.S. government's transition from the First National to the Second National was recorded by Confederate Midshipman James Morris Morgan in May 1863:

> There was little sleep on the *Georgia* the night of our arrival [at All Saints' Bay, off the Brazilian city of Bahia]. Day broke and we found ourselves very near . . . two men-of-war. What was their nationality? It seemed an age before the hour for colors [the flag] arrived, but when it did, to our great delight, the most rakish-looking of the two warships broke out the Stars and Bars [First National]! "It is the *Alabama*!" we gasped, and commenced to dance with delight. The officers hugged one another, each embracing a man of his own rank, except the captain and myself. Like the commander, I was the only one of my rank aboard, so I hugged myself.
>
> *The Confederate Government had changed its flag since we had left home, and the Stars and Bars had given way to the white field with a St. Andrew's cross [the Second National] which we fondly believed represented the Southern Cross.* The *Alabama* had not yet heard of the change [from the Stars and Bars to the Stainless Banner], and we furnished the anomalous and embarrassing spectacle of two warships belonging to the same Government and flying flags which bore no resemblance to each other! Fortunately the new [Second National] flag was not a difficult one to make, and the *Alabama's* sailors soon had the new colors proudly fluttering from her peak.[79]

One evening in the Summer of 1861, after one of his many sea battles with the Union, Confederate Rear Admiral Raphael Semmes stood aboard his ship, the *Sumter*, and described the mixed emotions he felt due to switching his allegiance from the U.S. Flag to the C.S. Flag:

> As I leaned on the carriage of a howitzer on the poop of my ship, and cast a glance toward the quarter of the horizon whence the land had disappeared, memory was busy with the events of the last few months. How hurried, and confused they had been! It seemed as though I had dreamed a dream, and found it difficult, upon waking, to unite the discordant parts. A great government [the U.S.] had been broken up, family ties had been severed, and war—grim, ghastly war—was arraying a household against itself. A little while back, and I had served under the very [U.S.] flag which I had that day defied. Strange revolution of feeling, how I now hated that flag! It had been to me as a mistress to a lover; I had looked upon it with admiring eyes, had dallied with it in hours of ease, and had had recourse to it, in hours of trouble, and now I found it false! What wonder that I felt a lover's resentment?[80]

Having explored the origins of the three official flags of the Confederate government, the First, Second, and Third Nationals, let us return now to the South's military standard, the Confederate Battle Flag, and record its true history for posterity.

The designer of the Confederate Battle Flag, South Carolina Representative William Porcher Miles.

As mentioned, the very first Confederate flag design ever proposed was what is now known as the Confederate Battle Flag, created by William Porcher Miles and submitted to the Provisional Confederate Congress on March 4, 1861. Miles seems to have patterned his flag design on the banner of the South Carolina Secession Convention, the "Sovereignty Flag," which was red with a blue Saint

George's Cross, fifteen white stars (representing the 15 slavery-optional states in the South), and the state's symbols: the palmetto tree and crescent Moon.[81]

The primary difference between South Carolina's Secession Flag and Miles' design was that he replaced the *horizontal* Saint George's (Latin) Cross with the *diagonal* Saint Andrew's (Greek) Cross. (Both crosses can still be seen overlaid in the Union Flag, the national flag of the United Kingdom, a country with which the C.S.A. and U.S.A. share much history.)

South Carolina's Secession Flag, with England's Saint George's Cross, the crescent Moon, palmetto tree, and 15 stars.

Though originally rejected by the Confederate Congress for use as the national flag, Miles' eye-popping banner eventually caught the attention of Confederate Generals Joseph E. Johnston and Pierre G. T. Beauregard: the C.S. Stars and Bars was so similar to the U.S. Stars and Stripes that at the Battle of First Manassas, July 21, 1861, their soldiers had had difficulty differentiating Rebels from Yankees. Later, Confederate General James Longstreet wrote of the incident in his memoirs:

> The mistake of supposing [Confederate General Edmund] Kirby Smith's and [Confederate General Arnold] Elzey's approaching

> troops to be Union reinforcements for [Yankee General Irvin] McDowell's right was caused by the resemblance, at a distance, of the original Confederate flag [the First National] to the colors of Federal regiments [the U.S. Flag]. This mishap caused the Confederates to cast about for a new ensign, brought out our battle-flag, led to its adoption by General Beauregard, and afterwards by higher authority as the union shield of the Confederate national flag [Second and Third Nationals].[82]

The issue of confusion on the field, compounded with the fact that at this time, early in the conflict, the two sides were wearing both blue and gray uniforms, made it essential to come up with a new Confederate battlefield flag, one that had no resemblance to any state or federal flag.[83]

The Confederate Battle Flag, the 13-star rectangle version, with Saint Andrew's Cross.

All of the submissions were rectangular, but General Johnston insisted on a square flag, probably because it would be easier to handle on the field of action. With the final design approved, the first three square Confederate Battle Flags ever made were sewn by Hettie and Constance Carey, and given to Generals Johnston, Beauregard, and Earl Van Dorn.[84] Of the selection General Beauregard wrote:

> We finally adopted in September, 1861, the well-known battle flag of the Army of the Potomac [as it was first called] to which our soldiers became so devoted. Its field was red or crimson; its bars were blue and, running diagonally across from one corner to the other, formed the Greek cross; the stars on the bars were white or gold, their number being equal to the number of States in the Confederacy; the blue bars were separated from the red field by a small white fillet. The size of the flag for infantry was fixed at 4 x 4 feet, for artillery at 3 x 3 feet, and for cavalry 2.5 x 2.5 feet.[85]

The details of how the Confederate Battle Flag came into existence are best told by someone who was there to experience it firsthand. One of these individuals was Confederate Private Carlton McCarthy, a member of (Wilfred E.) Cutshaw's Battalion Artillery, Second Corps, Army of Northern Virginia:

> This banner, the witness and inspiration of many victories, which was proudly borne on every field from Manassas to Appomattox, *was conceived on the field of battle, lived on the field of battle*. . . . But the men who followed it, and the world which watched its proud advance or defiant stand, see in it still the unstained banner of a brave and generous people, whose deeds have outlived their country, and whose final defeat but added lustre to their grandest victories.
>
> *It was not the flag of the Confederacy, but simply the banner, the battle-flag, of the Confederate soldier. As such it should not share in the condemnation which our cause received, or suffer from its downfall. The whole world can unite in a chorus of praise to the gallantry of the men who followed where this banner led.*
>
> It was at the [first] battle of Manassas, about four o'clock of the afternoon of the 21st of July, 1861, when the fate of the Confederacy seemed trembling in the balance, that [Confederate] General Beauregard, looking across the Warrenton turnpike, which passed through the valley between the position of the Confederates and the elevations beyond occupied by the Federal line, saw a body of troops moving towards his left and the Federal right. He was greatly concerned to know, but could not decide, what troops they were, whether Federal or Confederate. The similarity of uniform and of the colors carried by the opposing armies, and the clouds of dust, made it almost impossible to decide.
>
> Shortly before this time General Beauregard had received from the signal officer, Captain Alexander, a dispatch, saying that from the signal station in the rear he had sighted the colors of this

column, drooping and covered with the dust of journeyings, but could not tell whether they were the Stars and Stripes or the Stars and Bars. He thought, however, that they were probably [Union General Robert] Patterson's troops arriving on the field and reenforcing the enemy.

General Beauregard was momentarily expecting help from the right, and the uncertainty and anxiety of this hour amounted to anguish. Still the column pressed on. Calling a staff officer, General Beauregard instructed him to go at once to General [Joseph E.] Johnston, at the Lewis House, and say that the enemy were receiving heavy reinforcements, that the troops on the plateau were very much scattered, and that he would be compelled to retire to the Lewis House, and there re-form, hoping that the troops ordered up from the right would arrive in time to enable him to establish and hold the new line.

Confederate General Pierre G. T. Beauregard experienced the battlefield problems connected with the Stars and Bars firsthand, and was instrumental in getting it replaced with the Battle Flag.

Meanwhile, the unknown troops were pressing on. The day was sultry, and only at long intervals was there the slightest breeze. *The colors of the mysterious column hung drooping on the staff. General Beauregard tried again and again to decide what colors they carried.* He used his glass repeatedly, and handing it to others begged them to look, hoping that their eyes might be keener than his.

General Beauregard was in a state of great anxiety, but finally determined to hold his ground, relying on the promised help from the right; knowing that if it arrived in time victory might be secured, but feeling also that if the mysterious column should be Federal troops the day was lost.

Suddenly a puff of wind spread the colors to the breeze. It was the Confederate flag,—the Stars and Bars! It was [General Jubal A.] Early with the Twenty-Fourth Virginia, the Seventh Louisiana, and the Thirteenth Mississippi. The column had by this time reached the extreme right of the Federal lines. The moment the flag was recognized, Beauregard turned to his staff, right and left, saying, "See that the day is ours!" and ordered an immediate advance. In the mean time Early's brigade deployed into line and charged the enemy's right; [General Arnold] Elzey, also, dashed upon the field, and in one hour not an enemy was to be seen south of Bull Run.

While on this field and suffering this terrible anxiety, General Beauregard determined that the Confederate soldier must have a flag so distinct from that of the enemy that no doubt should ever again endanger his cause on the field of battle.

Soon after the battle he entered into correspondence with Colonel William Porcher Miles, who had served on his staff during the day, with a view to securing his aid in the matter, and *proposing a blue field, red bars crossed, and gold stars.*

They discussed the matter at length. Colonel Miles thought it was contrary to the law of heraldry that the ground should be blue, the bars red, and the stars gold. *He proposed that the ground should be red, the bars blue, and the stars white. General Beauregard approved the change*, and discussed the matter freely with General Johnston. Meanwhile it became known that designs for a flag were under discussion, and many were sent in. One came from Mississippi; one from J. B. Walton and E. C. Hancock, which coincided with the design of Colonel Miles. The matter was freely discussed at headquarters, till, finally, when he arrived at Fairfax Court House, General Beauregard caused his draughtsman (a German) to make drawings of all the various designs which had been submitted. With these designs before them *the officers at headquarters agreed on the famous old banner,—the red field, the blue cross, and the white stars. The flag was then submitted to the War Department, and was approved.*

The first flags sent to the army were presented to the troops by General Beauregard in person, he then *expressing the hope and confidence that they would become the emblem of honor and of victory.*

> The first three flags received were made from "ladies' dresses" by the Misses [Hettie and Constance] Carey, of Baltimore and Alexandria, at their residences and the residences of friends, as soon as they could get a description of the design adopted. One of the Misses Carey sent the flag she made to General Beauregard. Her sister presented hers to General [Earl] Van Dorn, who was then at Fairfax Court House. Miss Constance Carey, of Alexandria, sent hers to General Joseph E. Johnston.
>
> General Beauregard sent the flag he received at once to New Orleans for safe keeping. After the fall of New Orleans, [his wife] Mrs. [Marguerite Caroline Deslonde] Beauregard sent the flag by a Spanish man-of-war, then lying in the river opposite New Orleans, to Cuba, where it remained till the close of the war, when it was returned to General Beauregard, who presented it for safe keeping to the Washington Artillery, of New Orleans.
>
> This much about the battle-flag, to accomplish, if possible, two things: first, preserve the little history connected with the origin of the flag; and, second, place the battle flag in a place of security, as it were, *separated from all the political significance which attaches to the Confederate flag, and depending for its future place solely upon the deeds of the armies which bore it, amid hardships untold, to many victories.*[86]

It was beneath the beautiful folds of the *final* battle flag design, issued in 1863, that General Robert E. Lee fought at such battles as Gettysburg, the Wilderness, Cold Harbor, and Petersburg, among others.[87] And it was under this same flag's blood red field that thousands of Southern soldiers, along with countless non-combatants (Southern men, women, and children of all races), died, casualties of the needless, illegal, and avoidable war instigated by Lincoln and his meddling Yankee cohorts.

Three of General Lee's color-bearers, just prior to the Battle of Cold Harbor.

It is for these reasons (and others that we will examine shortly) that to this day traditional Southerners embrace, honor, and display the Confederate Battle Flag; not as a tribute to "racism and slavery," as the pro-North movement disingenuously teaches. But in memory of those

Southern ancestors who fell fighting in defense of the Constitution, their land, and their families—mine among them.

The great irony, of course, is that Northerners have always permitted themselves the right to honor their flag with obsessive devotion, but still will not accord Southerners the right to honor theirs. This is harsh, churlish, selfish, and arrogant in the extreme, and yet this practice has been going on since the War itself.

William B. Mumford, across Dixie regarded as a Southern martyr, hero, and patriot to this day.

One of many examples that could be provided involves William Bruce Mumford, a Confederate soldier with Company B, First Regiment, New Orleans. His story reveals not only the love the South has always had for her flag, but also the heartless and unreasonable demands the North has so often placed on Southerners regarding it.

In the Spring of 1862, after Union forces landed at the Crescent City, they immediately went to the top of the town's mint, tore down the Confederate Flag, and hoisted up a U.S. Flag in its place. As these were the first Yankee soldiers to arrive, the town was not yet occupied by the Federal army and so legally was still under Confederate dominion. "What right had anyone to issue such a command," asked Southern belle Marion Southwood, "when the city had *not* yet surrendered? It was the supposed right of *brutal might* alone."[88]

Mumford, watching from the street as the U.S. Flag went up, was incensed, as he had every right to be. Running to the top of the mint, he quickly tore it down (with the help of a young man named Harper) to the sounds of cheering onlookers. He intended to carry the captured banner to the mayor, John T. Monroe, but as he tried to escape he was shelled by the Federal fleet anchored in the river and injured. Furthermore, as he limped through the streets toward city hall, excited pro-South crowds pulled the U.S. Flag from his hands and ripped it to pieces.

A few days later Union General Benjamin F. Butler had Mumford arrested on charge of "treason," after which he was tried, convicted, and sentenced to death. Since New Orleans was still a Confederate city at the time Mumford seized the U.S. Flag, history proves that the entire trial was nothing but a political farce meant to humiliate, intimidate, and provoke the Southern populace.

On June 7 Mumford was taken to a scaffold set up in the courtyard of the scene of the crime, the mint, where he gave a speech on Confederate patriotism. Union officers at the scene offered to spare the Rebel's life if he would renounce his country and swear allegiance to the U.S. Refusing the offer, the noose was placed around his neck and he was hanged, leaving behind a grieving wife (who had unsuccessfully begged the Yanks for clemency) and three children.

Union General Benjamin F. Butler of New Hampshire was nicknamed "the Beast" by the South, and for good reason.

Naturally Mumford's illegal and unjust execution caused a furor across the South. Confederate President Davis issued a proclamation stating that Butler was a "felon deserving capital punishment," General Lee wrote to Union Generals George Brinton McClellan and Henry Wager Halleck demanding to know why a Confederate soldier had been executed for a crime against the U.S. when New Orleans was still under C.S. control, and Louisiana governor Thomas O. Moore pronounced Mumford a Southern role model. Said Moore:

> The patriotism of the hero Mumford has placed his name high on the list of our martyred sons. . . . He met his fate courageously and

> transmitted to his countrymen a fresh example of what men will do and dare when under the inspiration of fervid patriotism.

After Mumford's burial, his widow, Mary (Baumlin) Mumford, placed a tablet at his grave which read:

> William Bruce Mumford, executed by Benj. F. Butler June 7, 1862, for taking down the United States flag from the mint.

Yankee soldiers snuck into the cemetery at night, however, and removed the tablet. When an outraged Mrs. Mumford complained to Federal authorities, she was told she was not allowed to use such language on the stone, and would only be allowed a simple grave message.[89]

Though at first Mumford was buried in the family vault at Cypress Grove Cemetery (New Orleans), in 1950 his remains were reinterred in the Confederate section of Greenwood Cemetery (New Orleans) by the Ladies Confederate Memorial Association. His grave marker today reads: "William B. Mumford: Martyr to the Cause of the Confederacy, June 7, 1862, aged 42 years."

In the Spring of 1861 Union officer Ephraim E. Ellsworth lost his life in Virginia tampering with a Confederate Flag.

Mumford was not the first Southerner nor would he be the last to be *unlawfully* killed by Yanks for defending the Confederate Flag.

A little over a year earlier, on May 24, 1861, Virginia lost its first victim to Lincoln's War, when Yankee Colonel Ephraim Elmer Ellsworth stormed into the Marshall House Inn in Alexandria, and illegally removed a First National Flag from atop the hotel. As he came down the stairs with the prize in his hand, Ellsworth yelled out, "This is my trophy!" The owner, passionate Southern secessionist James W. Jackson, who was waiting at the bottom of the staircase, cried, "And you are mine!" and angrily shot Ellsworth dead with a double-barrel shotgun. The colonel's infantrymen then promptly stepped forward and killed Jackson, pinning him to the wooden floor with their bayonets. The story of the tragic dual murder quickly spread around both the South and the North.[90]

A Yankee propaganda postcard from 1861, celebrating the gruesome murder of Southerner James W. Jackson at the hands of Union Corporal Francis "Frank" Brownell—one of the infantrymen who was with Ellsworth at the Marshall House Inn that day. On the left Ellsworth lies on the floor bleeding; on the right Jackson falls backward from Brownell's bayonet thrust. The caption reads: "Father, Col. Ellsworth was shot dead this morning. I killed his murderer. Frank."

Catherine Copper Hopley, a Confederate-supporting Briton living in Virginia at the time, later commented on Jackson's death:

> This was the first blood shed upon Virginian soil, and for some days nothing else could be thought of. Jackson, the victim, was called "the first martyr;" and his heroic bravery was the theme of many a song. The story of the double deaths created no less of sorrow in both sections, the young Colonel Elsworth having been so great a favourite that Mr. Lincoln was said to have shed tears over his remains; and his death was described in the Northern papers as having been thus avenged: "Our brave men hacked the miscreants in pieces with their bayonets." But poor Jackson was not so mutilated as this horrible statement would lead one to suppose. Afterwards, during the summer, I became acquainted with many persons who had been in Alexandria at the time, the result of whose various accounts of the tragedy being, that the Northern troops had sent word that the town was to be vacated in a given

> number of hours, but whether owing to a delay of the messenger, or some other mistake, the mandate and the Union soldiers all arrived together, while yet one-half of the inhabitants were wrapped in sleep. That [Confederate First National] flag from the cupola of Jackson's hotel had been visible from the [U.S.] Capitol [across the river]. He had received several orders from the Union government to take it down, and, in refusing, had sworn to defend it with his life's blood. Elsworth had promised President Lincoln to bring it to him as a trophy, and perhaps hoped by a sudden *coup de main* to effect his purpose. He walked into the hotel, accompanied by a few of his men, while Jackson was yet in his bed, and hastily ascending to the top of the house, succeeded in bringing down the offending flag to the lower flight of stairs, where he was met by the landlord, who put a bullet through his heart. Then the infuriated soldiers rushed upon Jackson and stabbed him to death in the presence of his wife and family. Thus were two reckless men hurled into eternity, and each extolled as a hero.[91]

The Marshall House Hotel, Alexandria, Virginia, site of James W. Jackson's murder.

Confederate women, *both white and black*, were equally as courageous in the face of Yankee terrorism. Indeed, they repeatedly risked their own lives standing up for the Confederate Flag and against the tyranny of the "Federal Flag." Rebel spy, Belle Boyd, for instance, gave the following account of one of her wartime experiences with the ill-mannered, mean-spirited Union soldier:

> About ten o'clock General [Stonewall] Jackson's army, in admirable array, marched through Martinsburg [Virginia, now West Virginia]. They were in full retreat, their object being to effect a junction with the main body, under [Confederate] General J. E. Johnston, who had evacuated Harper's Ferry, and was falling back, by way of Charlestown, upon Winchester.
>
> Jackson's retreat was covered by a few horsemen under the gallant [Confederate] Colonel [Turner] Ashby; and scarcely were these latter disengaged from the streets of the town, when the shrill notes of the fife and the roll of the drum announced the approach of a Federal army, which proved to be 25,000 strong.
>
> It was to us a sad, but an imposing sight. On they came (their colours streaming to the breeze, their bayonets glittering in the sunlight), with all the "pomp and circumstance of glorious war." We could see from afar the dancing plumes of the cavalry . . . we could before long hear the rumbling of the gun-carriages, *and, worse than this, the hellish shouts with which the infuriated and undisciplined soldiers poured into the town.*
>
> At the time of their entry I was in the hospital, with my negro maid and some ladies of my acquaintance, in attendance upon two of our Southern soldiers, who had been stricken down with fever and were lying side by side. These were the sole tenants of the hospital: all the others had been borne off by the retreating army.
>
> I was standing close by the side of one of these poor men, who was just then raving in a violent fit of delirium, when I was startled by the sound of heavy footsteps behind me; and, turning round, I confronted a captain of Federal infantry, accompanied by two private soldiers. He held in his hand a Federal [U.S.] flag, which he proceeded to wave over the bed of the sick men, at the same time calling them "[goddam] rebels."
>
> I immediately said, with all the scorn I could convey into my looks, "Sir, these men are as helpless as babies, and have, as you may see, no power to reply to your insults."
>
> "And pray," said he, "who may you be, miss?"
>
> I did not deign to reply; but my negro maid answered him, "A rebel lady."
>
> Hereupon he turned upon his heel and retired, with the courteous remark that "I was a [goddam] independent one, at all events."
>
> I hope my readers will pardon my quoting his exact

words: without such strict accuracy I should fail to do justice to his gallantry.

Notwithstanding this interruption to our "woman's mission," the ladies to whom I have before alluded and myself were not discouraged; and before long we contrived to get our patients moved to more comfortable quarters. *They were taken away on litters; and, while they were in this defenceless condition, a condition which would have awakened the sympathy and secured the protection of a brave enemy, the Federal soldiers crowded round and threatened to bayonet them.*

Their gesticulations and language grew so violent, their countenances, inflamed by drink and hatred, were so frightful, that I nerved myself to seek out an officer and appeal to his sense of military honour, even if the voice of mercy were silent in his breast. Let me do him the justice to say, he restrained his turbulent men from further molestation, and I had the unspeakable satisfaction of conveying my sick men to a place of safety. The satisfaction was immeasurable; for I never for one moment forgot that insults such as I had just seen offered to defenceless men might at any moment be heaped upon my own father [Benjamin Reed Boyd Sr.].[92]

The ever captivating and dauntless Belle Boyd.

This Victorian Southern illustration features the Confederate Second National Flag, surrounded by scenes of war, including the Battles of the Wilderness (upper left) and the Crater (upper right). Above the battle flag shield at the bottom center are the words: "The Warrior's Banner Takes Its Flight to Greet the Warrior's Soul."

Boyd recalled another episode from the same period, again risking her life for the Confederate Flag, her family, friends, and black servants:

> Shall I be ashamed to confess that I recall without one shadow of remorse the act by which I saved my mother from insult, perhaps from death—that the blood I then shed has left no stain on my soul, imposed no burden upon my conscience?
>
> The encounter to which I refer was brought about as follows:—A party of [Yankee] soldiers, conspicuous, even on that day, for violence, broke into our house and commenced their depredations; this occupation, however, they presently discontinued, for the purpose of hunting for "rebel flags," with which they had been informed my room was decorated. Fortunately for us, although without my orders, my negro maid promptly rushed up-stairs, tore down the obnoxious emblem, and, before our enemies could get possession of it, burned it.
>
> They had brought with them a large Federal [U.S.] flag, which they were now preparing to hoist over our roof in token of our submission to their authority; but to this my mother would not consent. Stepping forward with a firm step, she said, very quietly, but resolutely, "*Men, every member of my household will die before that flag shall be raised over us*."
>
> Upon this, one of the soldiers, thrusting himself forward, addressed my mother and myself in language as offensive as it is possible to conceive. I could stand it no longer; my indignation was roused beyond control; my blood was literally boiling in my veins; I drew out my pistol and shot him. He was carried away mortally wounded, and soon after expired. (All our male relatives being with the army, we ladies were obliged to go armed in order to protect ourselves as best we might from insult and outrage.)
>
> Our persecutors now left the house, and we were in hopes we had got rid of them, when one of the servants, rushing in, cried out—
>
> "Oh, missus, missus, dere gwine to burn de house down; dere pilin' de stuff ag'in it! Oh, if massa were back!"
>
> The prospect of being burned alive naturally terrified us, and, as a last resource, I contrived to get a message conveyed to the Federal officer in command. He exerted himself with effect, and had the incendiaries arrested before they could execute their horrible purpose.[93]

The actions displayed here, as well as the sentiments expressed, are things that many will never comprehend. In fact, only the words of a Confederate veteran could ever do them justice and make the Southern love of the Confederate Battle Flag, and the cause it represented, understandable to non-Southerners. In 1894 Confederate Captain C. H. Andrews of Company D, and historian of the 3rd Georgia Regiment, wrote:

> The Third Georgia Regiment (Infantry) rendezvoused in Augusta April 26, 1861, and at Portsmouth, Va., May 8, organized by the election of field officers.
>
> Mrs. Wright, the wife of Ambrose R. Wright, first colonel of the regiment, later brigadier general and then major general, presented the command with a handsome stand of colors, painted from an original design submitted by a celebrated artist in Norfolk.
>
> The Third Georgia Regiment was actively engaged in outpost and on detached service during the first year of the war, and this handsome regimental flag was much used.
>
> When Norfolk was abandoned to the enemy, and the Third Georgia moved to the vicinity of Richmond, it became necessary to have the uniform flag then just adopted [i.e., the Confederate Battle Flag]. Col. Wright secured from the proper department this now tattered banner, and it was the only battle flag this regiment ever had. It waved over every battlefield upon which the regiment appeared, from May, 1862, to the surrender, in April, 1865. The hand of an enemy never touched it.
>
> It was a bright and beautiful morning, May 18, 1862, when this glorious flag was flung to the breeze on the heights at Petersburg. Its colors were then bright, fresh, and pure. Some two years passed, and this flag floated again on these heights; but its folds were torn with shot and rent by shell, and these "tricolors of liberty" were made dim by the smoke of battles and stained with the blood of the brave. In its worn and tattered condition, it was the more glorious in the love of its defenders for the victories at Richmond, Manassas, and Chancellorsville; and no less sacred for the struggle at Sharpsburg, the slaughter at Gettysburg, and the defense at Cold Harbor.[94]

An anonymous sonnet from the postwar period (read at a dedication ceremony honoring the unknown Confederate dead buried in Kentucky's Bardstown Cemetery) encapsulates Captain Andrews' words in poetry:

THEY WORE THE GRAY

This sculptured shaft guards but a grave
In soil that's hallowed loam;
For quick in memory be the brave,
And hearts give them a home.
This graven stone 'neath which they rest,
The myrtle at their head,
The sigh that stirs a loyal breast—
Love's tribute to its dead.
For 'neath this turf in slumber lay
A Spartan band that wore the gray.

A nameless grave, a sacred mound,
Enshrined in Southern heart,
For braver men hath ne'er been found,
Nor bore more noble part.
In haste they came to Southland's call
With Morgan and with Bragg;
They gave to it their life, their all,
And died beneath its flag.
But whence they came, tongue may not say;
But 'tis enough—they wore the gray.

These fallen ones, their splendid deeds
Demand the world's applause;
And grandest epitaph which reads:
"They fell in freedom's cause."
They to the Southland gave a fame
That all mankind can see,
And on eternity ascribed the name
Of their immortal Lee.
The names they bore we may not say;
Sufficient this—they wore the gray.

A thin gray line of trenchant swords,
Whose duty 'twas to check
The vast, plethoric Northern hordes
Or perish in the wreck.
Mars, God of war, by it was taught
Stern lessons in his craft,
When gray-clad men for homeland fought
'Gainst whelming Northern draft
But kith and kin their God can say;
But this we know—they wore the gray.

Against advancing spoilers blue
Their banners floated fair;
They did what mortal arm could do
To keep them flying there.
True to the end, this gallant troop
The crisis nobly met.
'Twas numbers caused their flag to droop,
But it's unconquered yet;
And sleeping here, attrition's prey,
Are matchless men who wore the gray.

When triple lines this gray line crushed,
New strength it seemed to grow;
Then, Phoenixlike, it rose and rushed
To battle with the foe.
Large is the heritage they gave
In valor, truth, and love.
They bartered life their cause to save;
They pleaded for it above.
'Twas thus they fell in duty's way,
These nameless men who wore the gray.

They followed well where honor led,
Their daring deeds were rife;
They gave to duty heart's blood red
When it demanded life.
They strove with might, both true and well,
On many a hard-fought field
And, facing the invaders, fell;
They knew not how to yield.
No cravens here, not faint hearts they,
But vanguard men who wore the gray.

In hearts aglow with love and pride
These gray-clad martyrs dwell;
And of their might in battle tide
Posterity shall tell.
Sons they were of that sun-kissed land
That gave to freedom birth,
That gave to it the guiding hand
Who taught a world its worth.
By rank or gold ne'er turned astray,
The sires of these who wore the gray.

As long as time our love shall last

And hearts for Southland thrill,
But though its deeds be of the past,
Its glory's living still.
A hero band lie waiting here
Beneath this slumb'rous green.
They went to death devoid of fear
And left escutcheons clean.
But when and how, no man can say;
But 'tis enough—they wore the gray.

The Southland grand, of it I sing,
To courage firm as oak;
'Twas first to brave the British king,
First to spurn his yoke.
A meed of praise to her let's give,
Her precepts value high;
'Twas she that taught for what to live
And showed for what to die.
And to protect her gracious sway
Fell these, her sons, who wore the gray.

The mothers of this peerless race
Gave husbands and sons,
Then met the foe with queenly grace,
Undaunted by his guns.
The women now, as women then,
The paths of duty show;
They gave their love to Southern men,
But eased the stricken foe,
And on these mounds their offerings lay,
Still true to those who wore the gray.

But Time has poured a soothing balm
And healed all hearts anew,
For now the gray-clad soldier's palm
In friendship clasps the blue.
But Southern men are sleeping here,
Though name and rank unknown.
We give to them a rose, a tear;
These soldiers were our own.
Of rank or file, we may not say;
But 'tis enough—they wore the gray.[95]

The Confederate Battle Flag was truly a banner that Southerners, both military and civilian, would "follow anywhere."[96] So devoted was the Confederate populace to our Starry Cross, that when every last one had been shredded by bullets or captured by the Yanks, Southern women cut up U.S. Flags and "converted" them into C.S. Flags.[97]

A Confederate regiment "baptizing the flag."

This was a banner, after all, that not only represented the grand constitutional cause of the South, but which also had powerful personal associations. In many cases it was taken into battle as a gift from sisters, daughters, mothers, sweethearts, and wives, who had sewn it using material from their own dresses.[98] And sadly at war's end it was often returned to these same women covered in the blood of their brothers, fathers, sons, lovers, and husbands. In 1901 several Confederate officers with the Fifth Regiment North Carolina remembered the valor of their men at the Battle of Yorktown in the Spring of 1862:

> Instances of individual heroism would fill a volume. The members of the color-guard [flag-bearers] were shot down one by one, and as each man fell the battle flag was passed to the successor. When the last sergeant fell, Captain Benjamin Robinson, of Company A, took it and bore it at the head of his company until the staff was shot to pieces. The officers and men were falling rapidly under the withering fire of grape and canister and musketry.[99]

This was called "baptizing the flag." But the liquid used was not water. It was blood; the blood of Confederate soldiers, which, for every man on the field, imbued the military emblem with spiritual overtones. Of the Spotsylvania Campaign in the Spring of 1864, Confederate Colonel Hamilton A. Brown made the following notes:

> On the night of the 7th [of May] the movement was commenced by the right flank and the march was continued throughout the next day, the 8th, through the dust, heat and smoke (the woods being on fire), the regiment arriving in the evening near Spottsylvania Court House. The enemy was marching on a road nearly parallel with ours, and where the roads came together, at sundown, a brisk engagement took place. While going into this action, on the right by file into line, color-bearer W. H. Lee was decapitated by a shell. Captain Thompson picked up the colors [that is, the Confederate Battle Flag], and bore them until the regiment had finished the movement and taken its place in line. Just before advancing a volunteer was called for to bear the colors in the battle. A stripling, with gosling voice, tattered jacket, ragged trousers and powder-burnt face, in the immediate presence of the murderous legions of [Union General Winfield Scott] Hancock, and bearing the thenceforth honored name of Reams, stepped to the front and said: "I'll take the flag, Colonel," and the flag, its folds still dripping with the warm blood of noble Willie Lee, was delivered into his hands. Lieutenant-General [Richard Stoddert] Ewell, who had witnessed the tragic death of gallant Lee, inquired: "What youth is that who has left his father's fold and come here and assumed the duties of a veteran?" On being told that it was John Reams, of Company F, he said that he would gladly approve any recommendation that might be made for his promotion, but the 12th came before the promotion, and on that day the regiment was captured by the enemy. Color-bearer Reams, determined not to surrender the flag, tore it from the staff and carried it in his bosom to a Northern prison.[100]

The South's love for her Confederate soldiers began with the commission of the very first officer and the enrollment of the very first private in the Spring of 1861. This adulation has not only never diminished or even wavered, it has grown with each passing year, despite constant attempts by the anti-South movement to crush the Southern spirit and rid her of every last vestige of what I call "the Confederate Religion": Southern history, Southern heritage, and Southern honor.

At the Battle of Cedar Mountain, August 9, 1862, Confederate troops (left) proudly carried the First National Flag to victory under the command of General Stonewall Jackson. The author's cousin Rebel General William Winder perished in the conflict.

In 1900 former C.S. colonel of cavalry, Robert C. Wood, further clarified the reasons for the undying idolization we have for our Confederate heroes—as well as for our staunch resistance to the ongoing attempts to undermine it by Northern and New South partisans. Wood wrote the following under the title, "Confederate Memorial Work":

> When the Confederate soldiers returned to their homes at the close of the war they were confronted by conditions more trying than any perils they had encountered on the field of battle. Disappointed in their hopes; enfeebled by four years of hardship and privation; without money, credit or the implements of labor; unaccustomed to manual labor, and in many instances, without a roof to shelter their heads, they commenced a struggle to earn a support for themselves and those dependent upon them. Enduring want and suffering without a murmur; submitting to the oppressions of carpet-bag rule because of a determination to comply with the obligations of their paroles; moved by a stern purpose to succeed and cheered by the sympathy and example of their wives and mothers, they toiled as men had never toiled before. They showed all the high qualities that had marked them as *the most magnificent soldiers of the age*. Step by step, slowly but surely, they moved forward in the path of love and duty. Never discouraged, but always hopeful, they attacked and overthrew

every obstacle to their progress.

During the long and weary years of their toil they ever kept loved and lost comrades in tender remembrance. When dawning prosperity enabled them to divert something from their daily needs they turned to *memorial work.* At first modest headboards, here and there throughout the South, marked the resting places of fallen comrades. Later, when improved conditions justified larger expenditures, cemeteries were established in which were gathered the remains of the dead, and monuments commenced to replace the simple headboards. To-day, lofty and beautiful shafts in every part of the South stand in mute but eloquent evidence of the loving devotion of the Confederate soldiers to the memory of their dead. The appended partial list of monuments will convey an idea of the large amount of memorial work that has been done up to the present.

Attention has not been directed solely to local work. The grand memorial structure to Jefferson Davis at Richmond will be a tribute from the people of every section of the South. The erection of a national mausoleum has been the subject of consideration for a number of years, and efforts are being made in that direction. The matter was first presented in a tangible form by Miss Nannie Nutt, a bright and accomplished daughter of the "Land of Sun and Flowers." In July, 1898, she wrote of a Confederate Westminster as follows:

> "As time advances, removing the actors of the tragedy of the Confederacy from the world's stage, and their memory becomes less and less a matter of personal knowledge and more of tradition, literature and art should be invoked as custodians of their fame.
>
> "War is terrible, but *never were soldiers endowed with military genius, so unpolluted by its demoralizing breath, as Davis, Lee, Jackson, Johnston, and many others who have identified their names with the Confederacy. Their deeds and lives we can place without fear of comparison by the brightest episodes in history. Defeat can not vitiate such virtue and genius as theirs*, and for them, and the principles which inspired their valor before all the world, let us ordain fitting sepulture for ashes, fitting monument for a just, though lost, cause, for genius and virtue an apotheosis. Can these ends be achieved more co-ordinately than by the erection of a

> *Confederate Westminster*—so to speak, *a national mausoleum?*"

In 1895 a Confederate veteran of large means proposed a plan embodying the idea of Miss Nutt. He proffered a subscription of $100,000, conditioned upon a like amount being contributed by the Confederate veterans. Up to the present this condition has not been complied with. At the Confederate Veteran reunion in 1896 a plan was submitted for the establishment of a grand memorial and educational institution at Washington, D. C, at a cost of $1,000,000. As in the previous instance, one-half of the amount was proffered conditionally. This plan found no favor and was abandoned.

Westminster Abbey, London, England. The idea of a "Confederate Westminster," which would hold the remains and honor the names of America's most notable Confederate dead, was being discussed over a century ago. Once the truth about both Lincoln's War and the Confederacy become more widely known and accepted, the author believes that it will become a reality.

The results of these two efforts do not indicate any lack of interest by the Confederate veterans in memorial work. Notwithstanding their disinclination to part with valued relics and records, which would be the most precious heirlooms to their children, they are contributing liberally to the collections in the Confederate Museum at Richmond and to the Confederate Memorial Hall at New Orleans. These two institutions have attained national proportions and importance. They contain a wealth of materials of inestimable value to the future historian of the great Civil War. They are rich in object lessons that inspired the youth of the South with a more reverent love for the memory of the brave men and noble women who suffered and sacrificed so much to preserve the rights that would be the richest inheritance of their descendants.

Union General Phillip H. Sheridan, who banned Confederate organizations and prohibited the erection of Confederate monuments in New Orleans after the War, is an archetypal example of the intolerance and cruelty which many Yankees levied against Confederate soldiers and their families.

From the commencement of Confederate memorial work, every obstacle to its prosecution was thrown in the way by the Federal [Yankee] authorities. The following order is a fair reflex of *the antagonistic sentiment that prevailed.* Lesser military lights followed in the wake of [Union General Philip H.] Sheridan:

"Headquarters Military District Of
The Gulf, New Orleans, July 18, 1866.

"1. Notification is hereby given for the information of all concerned that *no monument intended to commemorate the late rebellion [that is, the Confederacy] will be permitted to be erected within the limits of the military division of the Gulf.*

"2. *All organizations of Confederate companies, batteries, regiments, brigades or divisions for whatever purpose are hereby dissolved, and the maintenance of such organizations either in a public or private manner is prohibited.*

"3. Department commanders will be held strictly responsible for the faithful execution of this order.

"By command of Major General P. H. Sheridan. George Lee, Asst. Adjt. Genl."

The Confederate burial grounds at Rose Hill Cemetery, Columbia, Tennessee, photographed by the author. At the base of the monument are the words: "Our Fallen Heroes, 1861-1865." Honoring the Confederate dead has been a deeply cherished tradition in the patriotic South since the death of the very first Rebel soldier.

This attempt to destroy a custom that always had honored observance among civilized nations, failed of effect. While the Confederate veterans abstained scrupulously from any acts that could be construed into a violation of the obligations of their paroles, they never ceased to formulate plans and collect funds to honor the memory of their worthy dead.

An examination of the following list of completed monuments will convey some idea of the amount of memorial work that has been accomplished.

Confederate Monuments and Cemeteries: From the remotest days of antiquity to the present time, the custom of honoring the dead has been observed throughout the world. Savage and barbaric people as well as civilized nations, although they differ widely in their methods of manifestations, are moved by the same reverence for the dead. The Egyptians, who bestowed great care upon the homes of the living, gave greater attention to the homes of the dead. In the "Valley of the tombs of the Kings" are twenty-five sepulchres which display the highest order of the painter's and sculptor's art. The Pyramids, those wondrous structures which have puzzled modern architects and engineers, are known universally as the "Tombs of the Pharos."

More than 350 years B.C. the widow of Mausolus, King of Carria, in accordance with an existing custom, erected to the memory of her husband a sepulchre so magnificent in design, so grand in proportions and of such indestructible materials as to make it one of the seven wonders of the world. Time has not destroyed its massive beauty.

What student of history has not been interested in the accounts of the grand funeral rites and honors accorded by the Greeks and Romans to their distinguished dead? What reader of modern annals has not wondered at the Escurial, with its twelve thousand doors and windows; at Westminster Abbey, with its long array of entombed and illustrious dead; at the Indian mounds, wherein rest the remains of mighty chiefs and warriors. In the centres of population, in hamlets, on the hillsides and in the valleys of civilized countries and in the forests and caverns of savage lands can be found evidences of the universal reverence of the living for the dead.

Countries that have waged successful wars are most lavish of monuments to the memory of great military leaders. *Very rarely have those who suffered defeat been accorded memorial honors. The South has made no such unjust discrimination. She has woven wreaths of immortelles for all who died under her banners, although they were lowered in the gloom of defeat. She has erected statues and monuments to her great leaders, and has built as lofty shafts to the memory of her "private soldiers" and her "unknown dead." All those who served her faithfully have been embraced in the circle of her mournful love.*

Immediately after the fall of the Confederacy, the women of the South took upon themselves the duty of collecting and reinterring the remains of the scattered Confederate dead. With only such aid as the impoverished Southern veterans could give them; with the scantiest means at their disposal and under the most discouraging conditions, they entered upon this labor of love. Their constancy and perseverance stands revealed to-day in beautiful monuments and cemeteries throughout the broad expanse of our Southland. All that generosity could supply, all that taste could suggest and all that labor could accomplish has been expended in the erection of memorial shafts and in the care of the "homes of the Confederate dead." *All the millions expended by the Federal [Yankee] Government upon statues to military leaders and in the care of national cemeteries have not wrought such marvelous results as have been accomplished by the women of the South.*

Another Confederate monument, this one at Fayetteville, Tennessee, photographed by the author. Untold thousands of such memorials dot the South. Despite their importance to the Southern people, bigoted cultural cleansers have been desecrating them and demanding their removal since the time of the War, a hateful movement that is only increasing in intensity due to the spreading of anti-South propaganda by the ignorant and the heartless. Only widespread education can save such monuments from the fiendish designs of enemies of the South. The author calls on all those who read these words to help assist him and the pro-South movement in this noble mission.

At Winchester, Va., as in other places, a Federal and a Confederate cemetery may be seen side by side. In one, the mourning of a nation is evidenced by rows of expensive headstones; in the other are more beautiful but less pretentious proofs of the love of a sorrowing people. In one, salaried officials stand "watch and ward;" in the other, gentle women keep loving and voluntary vigil. In one, the annual ceremonies of "Decoration Day" momentarily dispel funereal gloom; in the other perennial tributes of flowers gladden the eye.

Confederate Monuments: It has been impossible to secure a full record of the memorial structures that have been erected throughout the South, but the partial list of monuments which follows shows how general the work has been of honoring and perpetuating the memory of the Confederate dead. Opposite the names of the different States is noted the location of monuments within their respective borders:

Alabama: Montgomery, Mobile, Gainesville.

Arkansas: Helena, Fayetteville, Fort Smith, Little Rock, Van Buren, Camden.

Florida: Pensacola, Tallahassee, Olustee, Jacksonville, Quincy, St. Augustine.

Georgia: Augusta, Atlanta, Thomson, Elberton, Washington, Sparta, Milledgeville, Athens, Oxford, Marietta, Rome, Resaca, Dalton, Macon, Barnesville, Griffin, Forsyth, Columbus, Americus, Albany, Cuthbert, Savannah, Newman, La Grange, Sandersville, Crawfordsville, Decatur, Oalaoun, Greensboro, Chickamauga.

Illinois: Chicago.

Kentucky: Hopkinsville, Louisville, Nicholasville, Frankfort, Georgetown, Paris, Lexington, Lawrenceburg, Owensboro, Munfordville.

Louisiana: Baton Rouge, New Orleans.

Maryland: Point Lookout, Hagerstown, Frederick, Woodside.

Mississippi: Jackson, Holly Springs, Vicksburg, Baldwyn, Corinth, Union Church, Canton, Crystal Springs, Boonville, Liberty, Woodville, Natchez, Columbus.

Missouri: St. Louis, Springfield, Lexington.

New York: New York City.

North Carolina: Raleigh, Windsor, Bentonville, Goldsboro, Washington, Greensboro, Hugh's Point, Wilmington, Charlotte.

South Carolina: Charleston, Florence, Darlington, Cheraw, Sumter, Lexington, Camden, Columbia, Orangeburg, Newberry, Greenville, Georgetown, Beaufort, Fort

Mill, Edgefield, Saluda, Rivers' Bridge, Summerville.
Tennessee: Knoxville, Columbus [Columbia], Nashville, Clarksville, Jackson, Memphis, Franklin, Chattanooga.
Texas: Dallas, Sherman, Austin.
Virginia: Richmond, Alexandria, Lexington, Chancellorsville, Luray, Petersburg, Portsmouth, Suffolk, Winchester, Powhattan, Clarkville, Fredericksburg, Norfolk, Front Royal, Staunton, Manassas, Warrenton, Harrisonburg, Charlottesville.
West Virginia: Shepherdstown, Romney, Charlestown, Huntington.

Dead Confederate artillerymen near Dunker Church after the Battle of Sharpsburg, September 1862. These brave soldiers perished for a "glorious cause," and we, their descendants, will never let them be forgotten.

The above list does not embrace all the monuments that have been erected, nor does it indicate the number of structures located at the different places named. Charleston, S. C., has six monuments and a number of memorial tablets; Richmond, Va., has eleven monuments and several tablets; New Orleans, La., has five monuments and a number of tablets; Winchester, Va., has eight monuments and several tablets. A number of other places have more than one memorial structure each. *Among the monuments erected are two at Fort Mill, S. C.; one to the women of the Confederacy and one to the faithful slaves.*

A number of monuments are in process of erection throughout the South, and others are in contemplation for which funds are being raised. Each Confederate State that had troops in the battle of Chickamauga will have its participation marked by a shaft in the Chickamauga National Park. In the near future, like action will be taken on the battlefields of Gettysburg and Antietam. *There will be no cessation in memorial work. When the men and women of the Civil War have passed to "eternal rest," their sons and daughters will take up the task of perpetuating the memories that are dearest to the Southern heart. Generation after generation will succeed to this sacred duty.*

Confederate Cemeteries: Wherever battles were fought or hospitals were located within the limits of the Confederacy, the women of the South devoted themselves actively to the care of the Confederate dead. Cemeteries were established, in which were gathered the remains of those who perished on the field of battle or fell the victims of disease. In some instances, churches set aside a portion of their consecrated ground for the interment of the Confederate dead; in others, donations of land were made for burial purposes; in some few cases, ground was bought by the Southern women, organized into memorial associations. In every instance, these Confederate burial plots have been kept entirely separate and distinct from all others.

There are hundreds of Confederate cemeteries located within the limits of the South, but only those are named that contain the largest number of Confederate dead in each State:

Alabama: Mobile, Gainesville.
Arkansas: Camden, Fort Smith.
Florida: Olustee, Lake City, Pensacola.
Georgia: Atlanta, Chickamauga.
Kentucky: Louisville, Lexington,
Louisiana: New Orleans, Baton Rouge, Mansfield.
Maryland: Point Lookout, Sharpsburg.
Mississippi: Vicksburg, Jackson, University.
Missouri: Springfield, Higginsville.
North Carolina: Goldsboro, Raleigh; Wilmington.
South Carolina: Charleston, Columbia, Cheraw.
Tennessee: Nashville, Memphis, Knoxville, Chattanooga, Franklin.
Texas: Dallas, Sulphur Springs.
Virginia: Winchester, Richmond, Staunton, Charlottesville.

West Virginia: Charles Town, Shepherdstown.[101]

The McGavock Confederate Cemetery, Franklin, Tennessee, photographed by the author. Here lie the bodies of nearly1,500 Rebel soldiers who perished at the Battle of Franklin II, November 30, 1864, one of the most devastating Confederate defeats of the War. Many of the author's cousins fought here, among them Generals John Bell Hood, Nathan Bedford Forrest, Stephen Dill Lee, Edmund W. Rucker, and States Rights Gist. One of them, John Byars Womack, now rests peacefully in the McGavock Confederate Cemetery, whose grounds are said to still be haunted by ghosts in gray.

In 1912 one of Stonewall Jackson's men, John H. Worsham, gave the world a glimpse of the searing emotional attachment that Confederate soldiers had for their battle flags:

> You would like to know what became of the colors of the 21st Va. Regt. After it was known positively that Gen. Lee was going to surrender, the gallant John H. Cumbia, who had carried the colors [regimental flag] for such a long time, tore them from the staff—which was a short one, as it had been shot off by a cannon ball some months before—broke the staff and threw it away! *Then he tore the flag into small pieces, giving to each man a piece. That was a great flag!* It had inscribed upon it the names of all the battles from Kernstown on, in which Jackson's old division had been. Three cannon balls had been shot through it, and when I left it, in

September, 1864, over one hundred musket shots through it could be counted![102]

Confederate surgeon Dr. John Henry King, who spent nearly a year in a Yankee prison at Camp Chase, Ohio, wrote of a prisoner exchange in February 1865. A member of the first division of Rebels to be freed, he wrote of his reaction to once again seeing the Confederate Flag and his native soil:

> By railway we were moved to Baltimore via Wheeling, Va., and from Baltimore to Aikens Landing on the James River and from that place marched through the picket lines of our enemies, on our way to Richmond, the capital of our beloved land of Dixie.
>
> *Can I ever forget the emotions I experienced when I looked upon the grand battle flag and the national colors of the Confederacy*, when I was again with my own people and breathing once more the soft air of the land of the pessamine and the gay woodbine? As soon as my comrades realized that they were freed from the presence of the hated Yankee, and were again under the aegis of *the flag that symbolized the chivalry of Dixie*, a mighty cheering yell of gratitude was given that might have been heard for miles.
>
> I felt a thrill of emotion passing from my heart to the extremities of my body as if some elixir had been given to me from the hand of a gracious God. Yes, I was indeed free from the curses and insults of a brutal guard. It was true, that I saw around me a deserted country, but, oh! it was my homeland, and I was now on the way to my own sweet home, where every love of my soul centered itself.
>
> Yes, again, through the mercy of a kind providence, I was again in the sunshine of my native land of flowers, the breeding place of noblest women and bravest men.[103]

The Confederate Flag was a living inspiration to the Confederate soldiery, one that served as a beacon of light in the darkest moments of Lincoln's War. One of these occurred between 1864 and 1865, in what has become known as the story of the "Immortal Six Hundred." Under order of U.S. Secretary of War Edwin McMasters Stanton, nearly 600 Rebel soldiers were confined in a stockade on Morris Island, South Carolina, where they were intentionally starved and used as human shields against the firing of their own guns. Most survived, in great part due to their love of the Confederate Flag and what it represented.

Confederate Major John Ogden Murray, one of the Confederates who lived through the experience, later made these comments:

> These six hundred Confederate officers—prisoners of war—who went through the fearful ordeal of fire and starvation were a noble body of men. . . . it is a proud record to present to the world, that, notwithstanding the ordeal of fire, starvation, and disease, there were but eighteen of the six hundred who faltered and took the oath of allegiance to the United States government, disgracing themselves, dishonoring their uniforms, leaving their comrades to suffer. What nation of the world can present a better record than this? And does it not prove the oft repeated claim that *the Confederate army was an army of heroes*, whose hearts were as true and brave as ever beat in the breast of an Alexander [the Great], or a [Marshal Michel] Ney? What could be said that would be flattery of the five hundred and eighty-three men who kept the faith throughout the terrible ordeal? No torture could wring from these men one whimper of pain, nor one regret that *they had linked their fortunes with the cause of the South and followed her flag whither it led. These men were heroes by nature's gift; they were Southern men by birth, noblemen whose right to nobility came from God.*[104]

Edwin McMasters Stanton, U.S. secretary of war under Lincoln, intentionally tortured some 600 Confederate soldiers over a period of several months, but we do not hear Liberals calling for the removal of his statues or the U.S. Flag from government buildings.

When Union Admiral David G. Farragut threatened to destroy New Orleans unless the inhabitants surrendered, they refused to leave or even lower the Confederate Flag. In the face of Yankee tyranny, all bravely "maintained their allegiance to the Confederate States."

Confederate soldiers were not the only ones fiercely devoted to their flag. Southern civilians of all kinds, young and old, male and female, were ready to risk even death to defend it. Southern nurse Kate Cumming wrote the following in April 1862:

> Every one is still down-hearted about New Orleans, as its fall has divided the Confederacy by opening the Upper Mississippi River to the enemy. All praise the spirited answer given by the mayor [John T. Monroe] when ordered to surrender the city. He said that the citizens of New Orleans yielded to physical force alone, and that they still maintained their allegiance to the Confederate States; and upon refusal to pull down the [Confederate] state flag from the city hall, [Yankee] Commodore [David G.] Farragut threatened to bombard the city. The mayor replied, *the people of New Orleans would not degrade themselves by the humiliating act of lowering their own flag*, and that there was no possible way for the women and children to leave; so he would have to do his worst. We can not but admire such spirited behavior; but it is nothing but what I expected from the proud Louisianians.[105]

Yankee Captain H. B. Doolittle pompously holds the U.S. Flag while disrespectfully standing on the Confederate First National Flag. Here we have more proof that many Northerners—besides being presumptuous, uncivilized, ill-bred, meddlesome, domineering, and culturally insensitive—have never grasped the true meaning of our Southern banners. Is it any wonder the two regions went to war?

In 1903, thirty-eight years after the War, John B. Gordon wrote about the Southern Flag and the soldiers who loved it as only a former Confederate officer could. This highly celebrated Rebel chieftain, who was instrumental in organizing the United Confederate Veterans (the forerunner of today's Sons of Confederate Veterans), later served as both a U.S. senator (three times) and a Georgia governor:

> When the proud and sensitive sons of Dixie came to a full realization of the truth that the Confederacy was overthrown and their leader [Robert E. Lee] had been compelled to surrender his once invincible army, they could no longer control their emotions, and tears ran like water down their shrunken faces. *The flags which they still carried were objects of undisguised affection. These Southern banners had gone down before overwhelming numbers; and torn by shells, riddled by bullets, and laden with the powder and smoke of battle, they aroused intense emotion in the men who had so often followed them to victory. Yielding to overpowering sentiment, these high-mettled men began to tear the flags from the staffs and hide them in their bosoms, as they wet them with burning tears.*
>
> The Confederate officers faithfully endeavored to check this exhibition of loyalty and love for the old flags. A great majority of them were duly surrendered; but *many were secretly carried by devoted veterans to their homes, and will be cherished forever as honored heirlooms.*
>
> There was nothing unnatural or censurable in all this. *The Confederates who clung to those pieces of battered bunting knew they would never again wave as martial ensigns above embattled hosts; but they wanted to keep them*, just as they wanted to keep the old canteen with a bullet-hole through it, or the rusty gray jacket that had been torn by canister. *They loved those flags, and will love them forever, as mementoes of the unparalleled struggle. They cherish them because they represent the consecration and courage not only of Lee's army but of all the Southern armies, because they symbolize the bloodshed and the glory of nearly a thousand battles.*[106]

Only the most stone-hearted individual could disregard such human sentiment, a passion that has been handed down from generation to generation into the present day, where it continues to manifest as an obsessive appreciation of the Starry Cross. It is this same love that causes soldiers from the American South to fly the Confederate Battle Flag in wars and conflicts all over the world: it is the ultimate symbol of freedom against political tyranny.[107]

Confederate General John Brown Gordon, later governor of Georgia, understood the importance of the various Rebel flags to his men. "They will love them forever," he wrote, for "they symbolize the bloodshed and the glory of nearly a thousand battles."

This plain fact, so simple that a third-grader could grasp it, seems to be far beyond the intellectual capacity of the average South-loather. We can only hope through education, using books like this one, that the history-illiterate enemies of the South will one day see the error of their ways, and that they too will come to recognize and value the patriotic fervor which thrives in the heart of every traditional Southerner for their flag, their cause, and their Confederate forebears.

These sentiments are identical to what today's descendants of Union soldiers feel toward their flag, their cause, and their Yankee ancestors. And that is something that *anyone* can understand.

WHAT YOU WERE TAUGHT: The Bonnie Blue Flag began as one of the official flags of the Confederacy, and is therefore also a symbol of racism and slavery.

THE FACTS: Another piece of Yankee propaganda. The Bonnie Blue Flag, a solid blue banner with a single white star in the center, has English and Spanish roots which predate the C.S.A. by six decades.

In the early 1800s disputes arose between Spain, France, and the U.S. over the territory that contained what are now the states of Louisiana, Mississippi, and Alabama. By 1810, with tyrannical Spain in control of the entire province, the English speaking, freedom-loving inhabitants of the area, by then known as "West Florida," rebelled.

On September 11 of that year a small West Florida militia set out for the Spanish capitol at Baton Rouge. Several "rebel" forces combined to overcome the Spaniards. The governor was arrested, a Declaration of Independence was issued, and the new republic of West Florida was born. Her official flag was blue with a single white five-pointed star in the center, the first known use of a lone star flag.[108]

The cover of the sheet music of *The Bonnie Blue Flag*, composed by Harry McCarthy.

Though the Republic of West Florida was dissolved only a month later when the U.S. placed it under the jurisdiction of the Louisiana Territory on October 27, 1810, her banner, now called the "Bonnie Blue Flag," was soon adopted as one of the emblems of the liberty-loving Southern states. Between 1836 and 1839 it became the flag of the Republic of Texas, and, for a brief time in 1861, the flag of the Republic of Mississippi when, on January 9, it was first flown over the Capitol Building in Jackson.[109]

In the Mississippi crowd that day was an Irish actor and Confederate soldier named Harry McCarthy, who went home and wrote a song about the thrilling flag raising at Jackson. His tune, "The Bonnie

Blue Flag," was first performed at the Varieties Theater in New Orleans in 1861, quickly becoming the second most popular song in the South after "Dixie."

McCarthy's jaunty composition so infuriated the U.S. government, Yankees, carpetbaggers, and scallywags that Union General Benjamin F. "The Beast" Butler took revenge by arresting the publisher of the song (A. E. Blackmar), destroying his copies of the sheet music, and penalizing him $500. Butler also fined anyone, man or woman, adult or child, $25 for singing it, playing it on any instrument, or even whistling it.[110] The lyrics of this immortal Southern song are as follows:

THE BONNIE BLUE FLAG
We are a band of brothers, and native to the soil,
Fighting for the property we gained by honest toil;
And when our rights were threatened the cry rose near and far:
Hurrah for the Bonnie Blue Flag that bears a single star!

Hurrah! hurrah! for Southern rights, hurrah!
Hurrah for the Bonnie Blue Flag that bears a single star.

As long as the Union was faithful to her trust,
Like friends and like brothers both kind were we and just;
But now when Northern treachery attempts our rights to mar,
We hoist on high the Bonnie Blue Flag that bears a single star.

Hurrah! hurrah! for Southern rights, hurrah!
Hurrah for the Bonnie Blue Flag that bears a single star.

First gallant South Carolina nobly made the stand;
Then came Alabama, who took her by the hand;
Next, quickly, Mississippi, Georgia and Florida—
All raised the flag, the Bonnie Blue Flag that bears a single star.

Hurrah! hurrah! for Southern rights, hurrah!
Hurrah for the Bonnie Blue Flag that bears a single star.

Ye men of valor, gather round the banner of the right;
Texas and fair Louisiana join us in the fight.
Davis, our loved president, and Stephens statesman are;
Now rally round the Bonnie Blue Flag that bears a single star.

Hurrah! hurrah! for Southern rights, hurrah!

Hurrah for the Bonnie Blue Flag that bears a single star.

And here's to old Virginia. The Old Dominion State
With the young Confederacy at length has linked her fate.
Impelled by her example, now other states prepare
To hoist on high the Bonnie Blue Flag that bears a single star.

Hurrah! hurrah! for Southern rights, hurrah!
Hurrah for the Bonnie Blue Flag that bears a single star.

Then cheer, boys, cheer! Raise the joyous shout!
For Arkansas and North Carolina now have both gone out,
And let another rousing cheer for Tennessee be given!
The single star of the Bonnie Blue Flag has grown to be eleven.

Hurrah! hurrah! for Southern rights, hurrah!
Hurrah for the Bonnie Blue Flag that bears a single star.[111]

The Bonnie Blue Flag, with its solitary white star on a blue field, is one of the oldest American symbols of "rebellion" against despotism, making it a perfect emblem for the Confederate States of America, the people of Dixie, and Southern pride.

As is clear from McCarthy's 1861 lyrics, the Bonnie Blue Flag, like the Confederate Battle Flag, has nothing to do with slavery, racism, hatred, blacks, or even whites. It represents the original pre-Lincoln Union and, more importantly, "our rights," as the song calls them; Southern-speak for the rights of the individual states, self-government, secession, free enterprise, and personal freedom as tacitly guaranteed in the Constitution's Bill of Rights.

Although the "Lone Star" flag design was not a specifically Southern creation,[112] and although it was never officially used by the Confederate government, it has become a permanent fixture of the history and heritage of Dixie, lovingly adopted and embraced by the Southern people themselves.[113] It was incorporated, for example, into the state flag of Texas, the "lone star" symbolizing her readiness to "go it alone" by officially seceding from the U.S. on March 2, 1861.[114]

EVOLUTION OF THE CONFEDERATE BATTLE FLAG

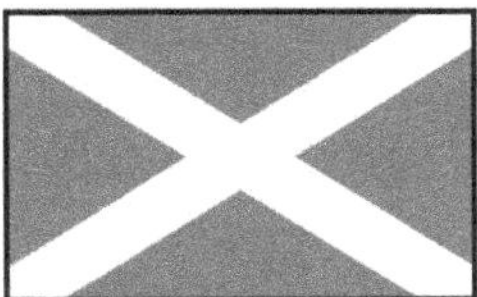

Saint Andrew's Cross, 832, the national flag of Scotland; a prototype for the Confederate Battle Flag. White Greek cross on a blue field.

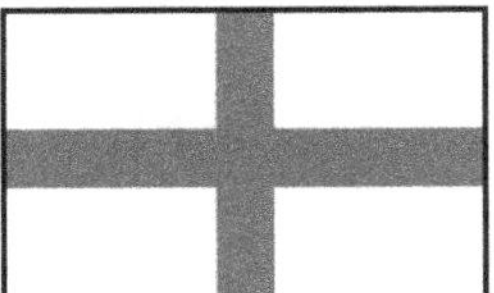

Saint George's Cross, 1270s, the national flag of England; a prototype for the South Carolina Sovereignty Flag. Red Latin cross on a white field.

Saint Patrick's Cross, 1783, a flag of Northern Ireland (unofficial); a prototype for the Confederate Battle Flag. Red Greek cross on a white field.

The Union Flag of 1801, which combines St. Andrew's Cross, St. George's Cross, and St. Patrick's Cross, is the national flag of the United Kingdom, and was a prototype for the Confederate Battle Flag. Red and white Greek and Latin crosses on a blue field.

South Carolina's Sovereignty Flag, December 1860; a prototype for the Confederate Battle Flag. Blue Latin cross with white stars on a red field.

The rectangle version of the Confederate Battle Flag, 1861, the "Starry Cross." Also the official flag of the Army of Tennessee as well as the C.S. Navy Jack. Blue Greek cross with white stars on a red field.

The square version of the Confederate Battle Flag, 1861, the "Southern Cross." Also the flag of the Army of Northern Virginia.

EVOLUTION OF THE CONFEDERATE NATIONAL FLAGS

The Family Coat of Arms of George Washington, 1346; a probable prototype for the U.S. Flag. Red stars and stripes on a white field.

The Grand Union Flag of the American Colonies, 1775-1777; a probable prototype for the U.S. Flag as well as the Confederate First, Second, and Third National Flags. Red and white stripes with a British Union Flag canton.

The "Betsy Ross" with 13 stars, 1777; the first official national flag of the U.S.A., and the prototype for the First National Flag of the C.S.A. Red and white stripes with a canton of encircled white stars on a blue background.

The Confederate First National Flag, 13-star version, 1861, the "Stars and Bars." Red and white stripes with a canton of encircled white stars on a blue background.

The Confederate Second National Flag, 1863, the "Stainless Banner." Also the C.S. Naval Ensign. White field with a Confederate Battle Flag canton.

The Confederate Third National Flag, 1865, the "Blood-Stained Banner"; to this day the official flag of the C.S.A. White field with a Confederate Battle Flag canton and a red bar extending the outer half of the width.

3

THE CONFEDERATE FLAG AND SLAVERY

RESURGAM

("I shall rise again")

Lost Cause! What grief upon the Southland dear,
And leaden burden, helpless sorrow lay
When Lee's brave, dauntless remnant of the Gray
Resigned the Cause for which their Chief, austere,
Renounced command and power and high career
In service of that Bond [the Constitution] whose lawful sway
Was trampled by the might of War's array
That left the stricken South bereft and sear!

But grieve no more, O faithful Southern heart!
Fraternal sov'reignty hath need of thee;
They Cause shall rise in light again, reborn.
This peerless Union never may depart
The noble visions [states' rights] of the Fathers free!
Not "Lost," but Herald of the Patriot Dawn![115]

A. W. LITTLEFIELD, 1916

CHAPTER 3

WHAT YOU WERE TAUGHT: American slavery is an institution that was born in and thus found only in the South, and is therefore properly called "the South's peculiar institution," and the Confederate Flag is its symbol.

THE FACTS: Since slavery and the Confederate Battle Flag are intimately connected in the minds of the uneducated, it is vitally important that we discuss, dissect, and debunk this anti-South myth once and for all.

The birth of American black slavery had nothing to do with the South. Rather it was the end product of thousands of years of worldwide slavery, as well as the direct actions of Africa herself. To hide this fact, anti-South historians have long referred to American slavery, and more specifically Southern slavery, as the "peculiar institution." Actually, there was nothing "peculiar" about it, and neither was it Southern, for it was once a common worldwide practice.

Indeed, slavery has been embraced by every known civilization, people, race, society, culture, and religion around the globe, from earliest recorded history right into present-day America. Some of the more notable slaving peoples have been the Egyptians, Assyrians, Babylonians, Sumerians, Akkadians, Mesopotamians, Phoenicians, Mycenaeans, Arameans, East Indians, Chaldeans, Hittites, Scythians, Persians, Arabians, Hebrews, Europeans, and Native-Americans, all who have a long history of enslaving their own citizens and neighbors.

An institution that has been found among nearly every people and on every continent since prehistoric times can hardly be considered "peculiar." In fact, as this chapter shows, it would be more appropriately and accurately called the universal, standard, or everyday institution.[116]

Slavery has literally nothing to do with the American South. Not only did Dixie never practice authentic slavery, but the institution has been an integral aspect of human society since before written records, and was once found on every continent, in every culture, society, and religion, and among every people. Thus, we are all descendants of both slaves and slave owners, no matter what our skin color, ethnic group, race, or nationality.

WHAT YOU WERE TAUGHT: Africa never practiced slavery within its own borders, which is why it was such a shock to Africans when American Southerners flying the Confederate Flag first came and kidnaped them from their homes.

THE FACTS: Everything in this statement is false. No region on earth has been more dependent on slavery over a longer period of time, practiced slavery more aggressively and widely on its own populace, or allowed slavery to become more entrenched, than Africa. Africa has been so intimately involved with slavery over such an immense duration—with slave majorities thought to be as high as 90 percent of the population in some regions—that its name is today synonymous with the institution. "The great womb of slavery," Yankee abolitionist Charles Sumner correctly called it.

Slavery was so intrinsic to the early African way of life that at one time slaves, known by their own people as "black ivory," could be found in nearly every African society, where—as in every other country where slavery is found—the minority population dominated and enslaved the majority population. These were not merely "insignificant traces of slavery," as African apologists maintain, but rather true African slave societies, built on and around the bondage of their own people, employing some of the most brutal and sadistic forms of slavery ever recorded.

Slavery's pivotal role in African society certainly explains why not a single organized slave revolt, or even an abolition movement for that matter, ever arose among the African populace during the entire pre-colonial period, and it is why African slavery was finally only outlawed by the efforts of non-Africans (mainly Europeans).

It also explains why there has long been a belief among the native population that due to domestic African slavery, "the whole land has been laid under a curse which will never be removed."[117]

The anti-South movement does not want you to know that Africa has been practicing slavery on her own people for thousands of years right into the present day, and that she employs forms of bondage so inhumane and cruel that they defy the English language. Indeed, no people on earth has engaged in the "peculiar institution" more aggressively, more enthusiastically, and over a longer period of time. Even 19th-Century Yankee abolitionists referred to Africa as "the great womb of slavery."

WHAT YOU WERE TAUGHT: African slavery got its start in America, under the Confederate Flag.

THE FACTS: Africans were practicing slavery on themselves for thousands of years before the arrival of Americans and Europeans. In point of fact, "African slavery was coeval with the existence of the African race . . . . [and thus] has existed in Africa since its first settlement," predating even the founding of ancient Egypt over 5,000 years ago.

It cannot be stressed enough that, it being a "characteristic part of African tradition" and a truly "universal" aspect of African society, *African slavery was of African origin.* Thus indigenous African slavery is nearly as old as Africa itself. Indeed, not only were slaves an integral part of the commerce of prehistoric and ancient Africa, but just as in early Sudan, as only one example, slave ownership was an accepted sign of wealth, and so was considered no different than owning precious metals or gems. Even the practice of Africans exporting African slaves out of the country can be definitively dated back to at least the 5th Century B.C. It can be truly said then that *early Africa literally revolved around the enslavement of its own people by its own rulers upon its own soil.*

The native victims of the pre-conquest African slave trade were captured inland or in East Africa by their African brethren, then exported to Persia, Arabia, India, and China. This means that the first European slavers to venture to Africa (Portuguese ship captain Antonio Gonzales arrived in 1434 and purchased several native African boys who he sold in Spain, while Portugal's trade in slaves with the continent began in 1441) only interrupted the booming, "well-developed" slave trade inaugurated by West Africans and various coastal tribes—one that had already been going on there for untold centuries with peoples like the Arabs. It was only much later that Europeans, and even later, Americans, helped stimulate the existing domestic business.

As we will see, however, these Americans were not Southerners flying the Confederate Flag. They were Northerners flying the U.S. Flag.[118]

WHAT YOU WERE TAUGHT: Africa never participated in any way in the slave trade with America, or any other country. White Confederates from America violently took them from their peaceful villages, back to their Southern plantations, where they brutally enslaved them.

THE FACTS: What Yankee historians, New South professors, and the Liberal media will not tell you is that Africans were never actually hunted down and captured directly by the white crews of any foreign slave ships. They were captives who had already been taken during yearly intertribal raids and then enslaved by enterprising African kings, kinglets, chiefs, and subchiefs, who quite eagerly traded them to non-African slavers for rum, guns, gunpowder, textiles, beads, iron, and cloth.

Sometimes these intra-African militaristic style raids and battles were carried on by slave armies led by slave officers. Though the attrition rate was extremely high (over the millennia millions upon millions of Africans died during these marauding attacks), greedy African kings would often purposefully start such wars, known as "slave hunts," in order to obtain slaves, a practice that eventually became "endemic" across large swaths of the African continent.

European and American white slave traders did not venture into the wilds of Africa to capture slaves, as our mainstream history books teach. African slavers kidnaped them from neighboring villages and marched them to the coast, where they sold them to waiting slave ship captains. The coffle on the lower left of this old illustration is made up of black African slaves, who have just been captured by fellow Africans, and are now on their way to a nearby slave market to be sold to African slave owners.

In other words, it was African chiefs who first enslaved other Africans, and it was African slave merchants—slave drivers known as *Slattees*—who then forcibly marched them to the coast in chains and sold them to Arabs, Europeans, and eventually Yankees. This means that when it came to African slaves, *all* of the slave hunting, slave capturing, slave abusing, slave torturing, slave marching, slave marketing, slave dealing, and slave selling went on *inside* Africa, perpetuated by Africans on other Africans on African land.

This is why before 1820 no free blacks ever came to the U.S. from Africa. All were imported *as slaves*—that is, they were already in bondage in their native country.

To put it another way, during the transatlantic slave trade, every one of the Africans brought to America on Yankee slave ships had already been enslaved in their home country by fellow Africans, after which they were marched to the Slave Coast (a 240-mile maritime strip roughly extending between the Volta River and the Akinga River), temporarily held in a *barracoon* (a small slave stockade or prison), then sold to white slavers by local African governments.

In short, whites only "bought [African] slaves after they had been captured" by their fellow Africans. Thus white people played no role in the actual enslaving process that took place in the interior, and had no idea what went on beyond the coastal areas. As one Yankee slave ship owner put it in the late 1700s:

> It is true, I have brought these slaves from Africa; but I have only transported them from one master to another.

Yes, *African slavery was purely an African-on-African business*.

And here is further proof: until the first part of the 19th Century, no white man had ever set foot in the interior of tropical Africa. Even the Europeans who first came to Africa's shores in the 1400s had no knowledge of anything "south of the desert." These were the African hinterlands, after all: utterly unnavigable and therefore unexplorable, due in great part to the ferocity of the native animals, and to the fact that it swarmed with cannibalistic tribes who practiced human sacrifice and other primitive customs.

At one time even radical abolitionists admitted as much. In 1835 Reverend George Bourne—the Briton who inspired fanatical New England abolitionist William Lloyd Garrison—noted that "no ancient and accessible part of the inhabited globe is so completely unknown as the interior of Africa." Thus whites could not have had any knowledge of what went on in the central regions of the continent during most of the Atlantic slave trade.

Truly, without Africa's encouragement, commitment, participation, and collusion there would have been no black slavery in

America. It is obvious then that Africa herself must be held accountable for taking part in the enslavement and forced deportation of some 10 to 50 million of her own people during the four hundred years between the 15th and the 19th Centuries.[119]

Without the help and encouragement of Africa, the transatlantic slave trade could not have arisen, nor could it have endured for as long as it did.

WHAT YOU WERE TAUGHT: The only race that has ever been enslaved is the black African race, and this is due to white racism in the American South.

THE FACTS: Our leftist schools focus only on black slavery, completely ignoring the reality of white slavery—and for good reason: America's liberalistic teachers do not want the truth to be known, for it would expose and demolish their false teachings about racism and capitalism. Let us correct this imbalance.

Not only did American slavery exist among native peoples—for example, the Aztecs, Incas, and Mayans—long before the arrival of Christopher Columbus (the man responsible for starting the European-American slave trade), but Western slavery itself began as a purely white man's occupation, one that had nothing to do with Indians, Africans, or any other people of color, or even racism.

Indeed, historically speaking, *both the earliest known slave traders and the earliest known slaves were Caucasians*: the Babylonians, Assyrians,

Sumerians, Akkadians, Mesopotamians, Phoenicians, Egyptians, Mycenaeans, Arameans, East Indians, Chaldeans, Hittites, Scythians, Persians, Arabians, and Hebrews—at some point in their history—all either enslaved other whites or were themselves enslaved by other whites. In India, for example, historic records show that Caucasian slavery was being practiced by 1750 B.C., nearly 4,000 years ago, though doubtlessly it arose there thousands of years earlier. Some maintain that white thralldom may have even once been an integral part of Hinduism, one of the world's oldest religions.

The earliest recorded slaves were white. This damaged ancient bas relief depicts a gang of Caucasian slaves at work in Mesopotamia. Such scenes were common in the area of the Tigris and Euphrates Rivers over 5,000 years ago.

The Vikings, Celts, Greeks, Italians, British, French, and, in fact, all European peoples, once enslaved other whites, a practice that has endured into the present day: in the 1940s Adolf Hitler enslaved nearly 8 million Caucasians, while in the 1930s Joseph Stalin enslaved as many as 18 million whites. The word slave itself derives from a European people, the Slavs, who were repeatedly enslaved by other whites throughout their history, such as the Celts.[120]

WHAT YOU WERE TAUGHT: There has never been such a thing as a "white slave," because non-whites are not racist and therefore would never enslave a white person.

THE FACTS: At one time Africans had enslaved so many whites in Africa that a series of wars, known as the Barbary Wars, were fought and an abolition society, known as the "Knights Liberators of the White Slaves in Africa," was formed to rescue and emancipate them.

The primary period of the enslavement of whites by African peoples lasted some 300 years, roughly from the 16th Century to the 19th Century. It has been conservatively estimated that between the years 1500 and 1800, 1 million to 1.5 million whites—from both Europe and America—were enslaved by the Barbary States, with an average of 5,000 white slaves entering the region each year. At about 14 new whites being imported a day, it was a commonplace occurrence. The city of

Algiers, the capital of the African nation of Algeria, alone possessed some 25,000 to 50,000 European bondsmen and women. Over the centuries countless tens of thousands of additional whites were killed during the process of African enslavement.

The Barbary Wars were comprised of several full scale U.S. military campaigns, launched in an effort to put a stop to the merciless enslavement of white Christians in Africa: the Tripolitan War (or First Barbary War, 1801-1805) under President Thomas Jefferson, and the Algerian War (or Second Barbary War, 1815) under President James Madison. Shortly thereafter, in 1816, the British, led by Lord Exmouth (Edward Pellew), conducted their own assault on African white slavery in the famed conflict known as the "Battle of Algiers."[121]

During the 18th and 19th Centuries Africans enslaved some 1.5 million whites. This group of four newly enslaved Caucasian males, two females, and an infant, have been shackled and are being driven by whip to a slave market in Algiers.

WHAT YOU WERE TAUGHT: Even if there were white slaves in Africa at one time, Africans would have treated them with kindness and respect, completely the opposite of how white Confederates treated their blacks slaves.

THE FACTS: Surviving records reveal that Africa's black slave owners treated both their black and white slaves with absolute savagery, daily subjecting them to appalling forms of abuse and even torture that included whipping, branding, starvation, exposure, and beheading. One example of how they handled their personal African slaves will suffice:

> On the death of a king, or a distinguished [African] chief, hundreds of their courtiers, wives, and slaves are put to death, in order that they may have the benefit of their attendance in the future world. It often happens, that where the sword of the rude warrior is once drawn in such cases, it is not again readily sheathed; whole towns may be depopulated before the thirst for blood is satiated.

Thus in 1800 the funeral of Ashanti King Quamina was accompanied by the ritual murder of 200 African slaves. On another occasion the African Ashanti people slaughtered some 2,600 African slaves at a single public sacrifice. In 1873, when the British seized Kumasi, a city in southern central Ghana, they discovered a huge brass bowl five feet in diameter. In it the Ashanti had collected the blood of countless thousands of sacrificed African slaves and used it to wash the footstools of deceased African kings.

African kings were the largest buyers and sellers of African slaves. The reluctant man kneeling on the left is being selected by a tribal leader for enslavement. His life will most likely be short and brutal and will end violently, as was customary for African slaves whatever their race.

Once, when the mother of a certain Ashanti king died, 3,000 African slaves were sacrificed at her tomb, and for two months afterward 200 additional slaves were put to death every week "in her honor." Did anything in the American South ever compare to such horrific savagery?[122]

WHAT YOU WERE TAUGHT: America never had white slaves or white servants. African slavery in the American South was the first and only form of slavery in the U.S.

THE FACTS: The vast majority of white immigrants who came to America's original 13 English colonies—at least two-thirds—came as white servants. Made up primarily of English, Germans, Irish, and Scots, some 400,000 whites formed the first non-American servant population in the region's history, working as unskilled laborers on the budding nation's large new plantations.

White indentured servitude, being much preferred over African slavery (Africans were considered "alien" by early white colonialists), *was the institution that paved the way for black slavery in America*; or as the late 19th-Century New England historian Jeffrey R. Brackett put it, white slavery made "a smoother pathway for the growth of [black] slavery." In 1698, as just one example, not only were there more white servants in Virginia than there were Africans, but white indentured servants were being imported in far greater numbers than blacks at the time.[123]

WHAT YOU WERE TAUGHT: The American slave trade got its start in the South under the Confederate Flag.

THE FACTS: Contrary to what our progressive—and therefore, historically inaccurate—schoolbooks say, America's black slave trade was not born in the South. It was a product of the North. This is why the only slave ships to ever sail from the U.S. left from Northern ports, this is why all were commanded by Northern captains and funded by Northern businessmen, and it is why all of them operated under the auspices of the U.S. flag.

The South, on the other hand, did not own slave ships and never traded in foreign slaves. Her slavery was strictly domestic. This is one of the reasons she banned the foreign slave trade in the Confederacy's new Constitution, penned by the Confederate Founding Fathers in 1861. Thus, while no slave ship ever flew under the Confederate Flag, it is this very flag that is today universally viewed as a "symbol of slavery"!

Though white settlers in the colony of Massachusetts began brutally enslaving Native-Americans as early as 1637, the true official start of the American slave *trade* took place the following year, in 1638, when the New England ship *Desire* brought a number of Africans into Massachusetts and sold them. In 1866 historian George H. Moore noted that "this first entrance into the [American] slave-trade was not a private, individual speculation. It was the enterprise of the authorities of the Colony."[124]

By 1790 Massachusetts possessed some 6,000 African slaves. And these slaves, wrote Benjamin F. Grady in 1899, "were treated as cruelly, and sold with as little regard for paternal, maternal, conjugal, or filial love, as they ever were in any other Colony or State." An advertisement in the May 1, 1732, edition of *The New England Weekly Journal* read:

> A likely negro woman about 19 years and a child of about 6 months of age to be sold together or apart.[125]

Like *all* American slave ships, the *Nightingale* had a purely Northern provenance. Constructed in Maine and outfitted in New Hampshire, she sailed from Massachusetts under the command of a New York captain. With some 1,000 African slaves in her hull, in 1861 she became famous for being the last slave ship to be seized by the U.S. government. Note the large U.S. Flag flying from her stern.

Public slave auctions were still taking place in the city of Cambridge, Massachusetts, as late as 1793. A Yankee eyewitness from this period remarked that "negro children [of slaves] were considered an incumbrance in a [white] family; and, when weaned, were given away like puppies," and advertisements announcing the availability of free black babies were a common item in New England papers. Like most of the other Northern states, Massachusetts never officially abolished slavery within her borders.[126] She simply emancipated her slaves slowly and gradually over the decades, pushing them southward on the unwilling populace of Dixie. But up until 1776 at least, there were far more slaves in the North than in the South.[127]

Early Northern politicians were well aware that they could not fool the public about the origins of slavery simply by deflecting the entire issue onto the South. One of these was U.S. Representative Jonathan Ogden Mosely of Connecticut. When, in the late 1700s, the idea of executing slave ship owners by hanging came up before a congressional committee on abolition, the Yankee politician remarked:

> We have been repeatedly told, and told with an air of triumph, by gentlemen from the South, that *their citizens have no concern in this infamous traffic; that people from the North are the importers of negroes, and thereby the seducers of Southern citizens to buy them*. We have a right to presume, then, that the citizens of the South will entertain no particular partiality for these wicked traffickers, but will be ready to subject them to the most exemplary punishment. So far as the people of Connecticut are concerned, I am sure that, should any citizen of the North be convicted under this law, so far from thinking it cruel in their Southern brethren to hang them, such a punishment of such culprits would be acknowledged with gratitude as a favor.[128]

Now we can better understand the words of U.S. Senator Jefferson Davis, soon to become the Southern Confederacy's first and—so far—only president, who, in 1848, rightly chastised his Northern brethren on the Senate floor for their abolitionist hypocrisy:

> You were the men who imported these negroes into this country; you enjoyed the benefits resulting from their carriage and sale; and you reaped the largest profit accruing from the introduction of slaves.[129]

In 1885 a Confederate woman, Mrs. Allie Travis of Conyers, Georgia, wrote similarly:

> Let our [Yankee] brother in Blue tell of his exploits during the war, but let him feel and express only respect and admiration for those [Confederates] who wore the Grey, and who fought so long and so well for what they believed to be a just cause. *And when he speaks of the sin of slavery let him not forget that he once owned negroes himself and that his ships brought the race from their native land*. The North and the South can never be cemented into a real union until each respects the other and is willing to admit that in "the late unpleasantness" each was actuated by love of country and guided by honest convictions of duty.[130]

The cover of the sheet music of "The Conquered Banner," one of the most inappropriately named Southern songs in history! Early on Confederate veterans themselves took umbrage to the title, and quickly asserted that the songwriter, Confederate chaplain Abram Joseph Ryan, had been mistaken in his choice of words. In 1920 they responded in writing under the heading, "The Unconquered Banner":

> "Time, which alone can furnish us true estimates, has rendered its verdict that the Confederate flag was never a conquered banner; that it never stood for an ignoble cause; that it has never been trailed in the dust. Fifty years of history have immortalized the principles for which it stood and the heroes who fought for those principles—love of country, love of hearthstone, love to God, and faith in God. . . . A conquered banner? Not while true patriotism burns within our breasts."

WHAT YOU WERE TAUGHT: American black slavery began in the Southern Confederacy, whose descendants are still ignorantly flying the Confederate Flag.

At one time slave auctions, like this one in Boston, Massachusetts, were a common sight throughout the American Northeast.

THE FACTS: Actually, the ignorance is all on the side of those who associate our flag with slavery, as this chapter makes patently clear. Like the American slave trade (which is connected to but is distinct from American slavery), American slavery also got its start as a legal institution in the North. Its birthplace was, of course, none other than Massachusetts, the very *first* of the original 13 states (colonies) to legalize it in 1641. In contrast, the *last* of the original 13 colonies to legalize slavery was a Southern one, Georgia, which officially sanctioned it 108 years later, in 1749.[131]

WHAT YOU WERE TAUGHT: The American abolition movement was born in the North.

THE FACTS: While Northern colonies like Massachusetts were busy legalizing slavery and expanding the slave trade, Southern colonies—who considered anything connected to human bondage as an "evil"—were busy trying to put a stop to both.

Indeed, America's first voluntary emancipation took place in a Southern colony, Virginia, in 1655, the same state that launched the American abolition movement. This occurred as early as 1753, at which time Virginia began issuing official statutes in an attempt to block the importation of slaves. In 1732, when English military officer James Edward Oglethorpe founded the Southern colony of Georgia, it became the first to place a prohibition against commercial slave trafficking into her state constitution, calling the institution "unjust and cruel." North Carolina and South Carolina both passed restrictions on the trade in 1787, as did Tennessee in 1805.

In point of fact, at one time or another *all* of the antebellum Southern states tried to stop both the importation of slaves and the kidnaping and selling of slaves within their borders. In other words, the reality is that *up until the year 1800, nearly all Southerners were abolitionists.*

As all of this was transpiring, the Northern states were busy bringing in as many African slaves as possible through their seaports. In 1776 alone, for example, the year the Declaration of Independence was issued, New Hampshire imported 627 slaves; Massachusetts imported 3,500; Rhode Island, 4,376; Connecticut, 6,000; New Jersey, 7,600; Delaware, 9,000; New York, 15,000; and Maryland, 80,000.

In 1835, when Yankee tourist Professor Ethan Allen Andrews told a Virginia slave owner that "the whole public sentiment of the North is decidedly opposed to slavery," the Southerner replied sharply: "So also is that of the South, with but a few exceptions." After visiting Dixie in the early 1800s, British-American scientist George William Featherstonhaugh wrote:

> All Christian men must unite in the wish that slavery was extinguished in every part of the world, and *from my personal knowledge of the sentiments of many of the leading gentlemen in the Southern States, I am persuaded that they look to the ultimate abolition of slavery with satisfaction.*[132]

There were a number of good reasons for the near universal abolitionism across Dixie:

> At the South . . . humanitarianism though of positive weight was but one of several factors. The distinctively Southern considerations against the trade were that its continuance would lower the prices of slaves already on hand, or at least prevent those prices from rising; that it would so increase the staple exports as to spoil the world's market for them; that it would drain out money and keep the community in debt; that it would retard the civilization of the negroes already on hand; and that by raising the proportion of blacks in the population it would intensify the danger of slave insurrections.

Of the 143 abolition societies established in the U.S. before 1827 by Northern abolitionist Benjamin Lundy, *103, comprising three-*

fourths of the total membership, were in the South.[133] Southern Quakers were among the first to protest the spread of the institution. Other Southerners of note who came out against the "peculiar institution" were Bishop William Meade, Christopher Gadsden, Nathaniel Macon, Samuel Doak, Gideon Blackburn, John Rankin, David Nelson, James H. Dickey, James Gilliland, Samuel Crothers, Dyer Burgess, James Lemen, Edward Coles, William T. Allan, James A. Thome, William Ladd, James G. Birney, and George Bourne, cofounder of the "American Anti-Slavery Society" in 1833.

One of the world's most renowned abolitionists, Southerner George Washington.

America's most famous early Southern abolitionists included George Washington, Patrick Henry, James Madison, St. George Tucker, and Thomas Jefferson, the latter whose complaints regarding England's tyrannical laws forcing slavery on the original 13 colonies, helped lead to the American Revolution and secession from Britain.[134]

WHAT YOU WERE TAUGHT: America's first known official slave owner was, no doubt, a Southern white man living in the Confederacy.
THE FACTS: America's first known official slave owner was a black man named Anthony Johnson, an Angolan who came to the colonies as an African servant nearly 250 years before the formation of the Southern Confederacy. After his arrival in 1621, he worked off his term of indenture and began purchasing human chattel in Virginia, where he accrued great wealth and a large plantation. Later, in the chronicles of Northampton County, there is record of a suit brought by Johnson "for the purpose of recovering his negro servant."

This being the first civil case of its kind, Johnson, who owned both black *and* white slaves, actually helped launch the American slave trade by forcing judicial authorities to legally define the meaning of "slave ownership." In 1652 his son John Johnson imported and bought eleven white slaves, who worked under him at his Virginia plantation, located on the banks of the Pungoteague River.[135]

WHAT YOU WERE TAUGHT: There was no such thing as "Northern slavery." Slavery in the U.S. existed only under the Confederate Flag.
THE FACTS: In 1776, at the time of the formation of the *first* Confederate States of America, the U.S.A., of the 500,000 slaves in the 13 colonies, 300,000 (or 60 percent) were possessed by Northern ones, only 200,000 (or 40 percent) by Southern ones. It was only later, when Yankee slave traders pushed slavery south, that Dixie came to possess more slaves than the North.[136]

The main reason *Northern* slavery is virtually unknown and unacknowledged today is because the Left has suppressed much of the evidence, including physical, civil, legal, and literary data. Your local public library, school libraries, and bookstores, for instance, have been thoroughly cleansed of most if not all works pertaining to Yankee slavery by their Liberal administrators and owners.

Along with this is the problem of time: slavery got its start in the 17th-Century North, while it only arose in the South centuries later. Scientifically speaking, this means that archaeological evidence of Southern slavery is more recent, closer to the earth's surface, and thus easier to discover, while physical evidence of Northern slavery, being older, lies deeper in the ground, and its artifacts are less well preserved and more difficult to find.

Despite these issues, archaeological proof of Northern slavery is being brought to light like never before. Near Salem, Massachusetts, for instance, scientists have uncovered traces of a 13,000 acre plantation once owned by a Yankee named Samuel Browne. Near Browne's farm, one that traded its products for Caribbean rum and molasses, a massive slave cemetery was discovered, the final resting place of some 100 African-American slaves who worked there between the years 1718 and 1780.

An 8,000 acre plantation was also recently found at Shelter Island, Long Island, New York. The enormous homestead, which supplied products for slave plantations in Barbados, itself used slave labor: some 20 black servants lived in bondage here in the late 1600s.

With a conservative estimate of about 40,000 slaves living in New York, New Jersey, Delaware, and Pennsylvania alone in 1780, it is not surprising that an African burial ground with 420 skeletons was recently uncovered in what is now Lower Manhattan, New York. It has been estimated that between the 1690s and 1794, as many as 20,000 Yankee African slaves (including some free blacks), were buried at the site, which has since been added to the National Register of Historic Places. Today the history and recollection of those buried in this particular New York black cemetery have been preserved with a large public memorial: the "African Burial Ground National Monument."

Because it is older, archaeological evidence for Northern slavery is less obvious than for Southern slavery. As such, Northern slave artifacts are covered by more layers of dirt and more deterioration has taken place. Despite this, diligent scientists are discovering hundreds of sites throughout the Northern states which reveal a once thriving Yankee slave industry.

More and more Northern slave cemeteries and slave plantations like those discussed here are being discovered and excavated each year, making it more and more difficult for the anti-South movement to hide the truth about the Confederate Flag and slavery.[137]

WHAT YOU WERE TAUGHT: In the 1800s *every* Northerner was an abolitionist who loved African-Americans.

THE FACTS: *Authentic* abolitionism—which I define as the belief that slave owning is *wrong*, that slavery should be *abolished*, and that blacks should be accepted in society as *equals*—was extremely rare in the Old North (if not almost unheard of), while white racism was the norm. Thus *true* abolitionists never represented more than the tiniest percentage of the Northern population. Even then, what little abolitionist sentiment there was in Yankeedom was not based on sympathy for the black man so much as it was on the self interest of the white man, which Lincoln would later go on to prove so overtly as America's sixteenth chief executive.

In 1858 Lincoln himself admitted as much when he discussed abolition with an Illinois audience. After emancipating America's black servants, what then? he asked rhetorically:

> *Free them, and make them politically and socially, our equals? My own feelings will not admit of this*; and [even] if mine would, we well know that those of the great mass of white people will not.[138]

As the future U.S. president intimates here, *abolitionists were detested by nearly all Northern whites*, who saw them as troublemakers, malcontents, agitators, and revolutionaries who threatened white Yankee hegemony. This is why, after all, fellow Northerners gave them the name "radicals"; it is why a furious New England mob attacked abolitionist William Lloyd Garrison in Boston, Massachusetts, threatened to tar and feather him and then tried to lynch him, dragging him through the streets with a noose around his neck; and it is why he was arrested in 1829, tried and convicted by a Northern jury and sent to a Yankee prison for several months for libeling a Northern slave trader.

As hard evidence for the widespread existence of anti-abolitionist sentiment in the North prior to Lincoln's War, we need look no further than the doleful story of Prudence Crandall.

Crandall was a white New England teacher who founded the "High School for Young Colored Ladies and Misses" in Canterbury, Connecticut, in 1834. One would think that fellow Yanks, had they been true non-racist egalitarians, would have applauded her efforts. Instead, for trying to offer blacks a free education in New England, Crandall, a Quaker and abolitionist, was harassed, persecuted, arrested (three times), imprisoned, and had her home burned down, while Northern white mobs attacked and stoned her school, tore it from its foundations using a team of 100 oxen, then physically drove her out of the state.

None of Connecticut's white population shed a tear for Crandall. Instead, the state, and in particular her politicians, were quite happy to see her, and her school, disappear. Their smug parting comment sums up the North's feelings perfectly during this period: "Once open this door, and New-England will become the Liberia of America," they shrieked as Crandall left Connecticut for the last time. New Hampshire whites followed suit by destroying their state's own black schools.

More proof that abolitionists were widely detested in the North comes from the grim tale of white abolitionist publisher Elijah Parish Lovejoy, who was shot to death in Alton, Illinois, by a white gang. Prior to Lovejoy's murder at the hands of his fellow Illinoisans, his printing office had been destroyed three times by Northern anti-abolitionists. He died trying to protect it during their fourth attempt.

This early illustration shows white racist New Englanders attacking the "School for Colored Girls" at Canterbury, Connecticut, in 1834, founded and operated by Yankee Quaker and abolitionist Prudence Crandall. Crandall herself was attacked and jailed, had her house burned down, and was forced from the state. Her school faired no better. After being pillaged it was ripped from its foundation by a team of 100 oxen and destroyed. Such acts were typical in a highly racist region where anti-black sentiment was the norm and the small minority of abolitionists were derogatorily labeled "nigger lovers" and "subversive troublemakers." Despite the mountain of evidence to the contrary, anti-South writers continue to pretend that the Old North was a bastion of "racial tolerance and abolitionism"!

We should not be surprised at the Prairie State's attitude toward blacks. Illinois, Lincoln's adopted home state, became one of the most anti-black states in the nation, in great part, as we will see, because of Lincoln himself. Indeed, Illinois was widely known, even to Southerners, as the place "where they mob and lynch niggers for seeking to make an honest living."[139]

Illustrations of the Old North's hatred of both abolition and black Americans could fill volumes, but we only have room for a few more examples.

In 1827 a citizen of Chillicothe, Ohio, spoke for "all" of the whites in his city when he wrote:

> In most of the towns of Ohio, there are a number of *free blacks*, who with few exceptions, are little less than a nuisance and their numbers are every year increasing by immigration, as well as other causes. *All of the whites* would willingly do something to free themselves from *this evil*.[140]

Nine years later, on July 12, 1836, a white mob in New Richmond, Ohio, broke into the printing office of antislavery advocate James G. Birney, the founder and publisher of the abolitionist publication, *The Philanthropist*—a mouthpiece for the Ohio chapter of the Anti-Slavery Society. Fortunately, Birney, a former Southern slave owner who had traveled North hoping to convert racist Yankees to abolitionism, was not onsite at the time, and the gang merely destroyed some of his printing equipment. But the matter did not end there.

The town called a large meeting, where an appointed committee (that included former speaker of the Ohio House of Representatives David T. Disney) passed several anti-abolitionary resolutions. Birney was warned of more potential mob violence and ordered to cease publication of his paper. He refused, then fled for his life.

Not to be discouraged, violent anti-abolitionist gangs soon resumed their search for Birney. On July 30, after tossing his printing press into the Ohio River, they set about ransacking the homes of the city's blacks, whom they tormented and ill-treated. Unable to find Birney himself (who was still "out of town"), the dangerous mob dispersed, leaving a taint of menace in the air for weeks after.

On March 2, 1835, Northern abolitionist and antislavery speaker Theodore D. Weld, himself a former Yankee slave owner, wrote to his friend Elizur Wright about his experiences in the town of Circleville, Ohio:

> Went next to Circleville, the capitol of Pickaway Co. *I had long heard of Circleville as violent in the extreme against abolition.* Found two decided and open abolitionists and a few others in a state of transition. *The Presbyterian minister, Mr. Benton, said among his people, that I was a rebel, had made all the mischief at Lane Seminary, and surely a man should not be countenanced who was such a disturber of the peace. Further, he said, as I was told, that the distinguished faculty of Lane Seminary had felt themselves impelled from solemn sense of duty to warn the public against me, declaring in their official capacity that I was*

> *a remarkable instance of monomania* [one who is mentally ill due to a single object, in Weld's case, abolition]. *Through his influence the Presbyterian church was shut against me.* Finally, the vestry room of the Episcopal church was procured.
>
> *At the second lecture, the mob gathered and threw eggs and stones through the window. One of the stones was so well aimed that it struck me on the head and for a moment stunned me.* Paused a few minutes till the dizziness had ceased, and then went on and completed my lecture. Meanwhile, some of the gentlemen had hung their cloaks up at the window, so that my head could not be so easily used as a target. The injury was not serious, though for a few days I had frequent turns of dizziness.
>
> *The next day the mob were so loud in threats that the trustees of the church did not feel at liberty to grant the use of the vestry*, but some of them very cheerfully united with other friends, and procured a large room in the centre of the village, recently fitted up for a store and counting room. This would hold comfortably one hundred persons. The next night I lectured there. Room full. *Stones and clubs flew merrily against the shutters. At the close as I came out, curses were showered in profusion. A large crowd had gathered round the door. Lamp black, nails, divers pockets full of stones and eggs had been provided for the occasion, and many had disguised their persons, smeared their faces to avoid recognition.* But the Lord restrained them and not a hair of my head was injured.
>
> *Next evening same state of things, with increase of violent demonstrations. The next, such was the uproar that a number of gentlemen insisted upon forming an escort and seeing me safe to my lodgings, which they did. This state of things lasted till I had lectured six or seven times,* then hushed down and for the latter part of the course had a smooth sea.[141]

When abolitionists John W. Alvord and James A. Thome tried to lecture at the Methodist Church in Willoughby, Ohio, they were met by the angry pastor, who promised to stand in the doorway with a club, if necessary, to prevent them from entering. They decided to try their luck at Middlebury, Ohio, but a mob gathered and threw eggs and glass bottles at them, forcing them to retreat.

Weld was not allowed to lecture at Zanesville, Ohio, and in the county of Putnam not only was he attacked by a mob, but because he had invited blacks to attend his speeches, white Northern gangs attacked them as well. Soon Ohio passed a series of laws prohibiting the hiring of blacks. Whites who ignored these statutes were arrested and jailed.

In 1836 Northern abolitionists sought to hold the Ohio Anti-Slavery Convention at Granville, but the schoolhouse at which James A. Thome was to lecture was torn down by angry white mobs before he could appear. The townspeople purposefully brought in hooligans and bullies to scare off the abolitionists. When they refused to budge, a violent riot broke out, resulting in a number of injuries. Eventually the antislavery group was driven out of the area, riding for their lives on horseback amid a hail of eggs and expletives.

Scores of other examples could be given. For instance, in New York anti-black mobs stormed the home of abolitionist Lewis Tappan. After robbing the house of its valuables, what was left was thrown out into the street and burned. In the ensuing melee the church, home, and store of Reverend A. L. Cox were nearly destroyed, along with the church of Reverend H. G. Ludlow, the homes of 20 black families, a black school, and three black churches.

James G. Birney, a Southern abolitionist who traveled North to try to convert the populace, got the same reception as Yankee abolitionists: he was hounded, harassed, had his printing equipment destroyed, received constant death threats, and was finally forced to flee for his life, chased from the region by violent anti-abolition gangs.

A black parade honoring emancipation in the West Indies was dispersed by a raging white mob in 1839 in Pittsburgh, Pennsylvania. Dozens of blacks were hurt and the Presbyterian Church and the African Hall were torched. In August 1834 an anti-abolition riot erupted in Philadelphia, Pennsylvania. Known as "the Passover Riot," the three-day rampage left 45 black homes and a black Presbyterian church in ruins. On May 16, 1838, just two days after it opened, Philadelphia's Pennsylvania Hall was broken into by a furious anti-abolition gang, which ransacked the interior then set fire to the building, leaving nothing but a smoldering pile of ashes. Why? They objected to the presence of the Female Anti-Slavery Convention that was in session at the hall.

A few decades earlier, around 1800, the Pennsylvania Abolition Society had introduced a proposition calling for "the immediate and total abolition of slavery." It failed to pass for lack of support. Pennsylvania abolitionists got the same result in 1804 when they tried to push through an act that would have freed all slaves over the age of 28. In 1805, when Congressman James Sloan of New Jersey proposed a bill that would free the children of slaves in Washington, D.C., the bill was rejected by a vote of 77 to 31.

Prior to 1840, New England abolitionist Henry B. Stanton (husband of New York's famed women's rights activist, Elizabeth Cady Stanton) was attacked 150 times, while Weld grew so accustomed to hecklers and mob violence that he came to regard it as a routine part of his job.

In Ohio all of this led up to the Cincinnati Riots of 1842, in which roving gangs of white anti-abolitionists set out to destroy the town in protest. So aggressive, brutal, and massive was their force that neither city officials or the military could stop them. The purpose behind the riots? Northern whites wanted to discourage blacks from moving to or even visiting the state. Thus they passed a law requiring all blacks "who could not give guaranties of their good behavior" to be evicted from the city. As this was an impossibility, Cincinnati was able to appreciably whittle down its black population.

Yet, there was a more significant and even simpler reason for the North's open animosity toward abolitionists: not only was racism toward blacks at its deepest and darkest in the North, but, as we have discussed, the slavery business itself began and was headquartered in the North.

New York City, the capital of the North's economy, was also the capital of American slavery right up to the end of Lincoln's War, and for good reason: the two were inextricably linked. And it was for this very reason, that is, pure economic interest, that the North was far more interested in maintaining the institution than the South. As one wealthy New York businessman said to Boston abolitionist Reverend Samuel J. May in 1835:

> Mr. May, we [New Yorkers] are not such fools as not to know that slavery is a great evil, a great wrong. But it was consented to by the founders of our Republic. It was provided for in the Constitution of our Union. A great portion of the property of the Southerners is invested under its sanction; *and the business of the North* as well as the South *has become adjusted to it. There are millions upon millions of dollars due from Southerners to the merchants and*

mechanics of New York alone, the payment of which would be jeopardized by any rupture between the North and the South. We cannot afford, sir, to let you and your associates succeed in your endeavor to overthrow slavery. It is not a matter of principle with us; it is a matter of business necessity. We cannot afford to let you succeed; and I have called you out to let you know, and to let your fellow-laborers know, that we do not mean to allow you to succeed. "We mean, sir," said he with increased emphasis,—"we mean, sir, to put you Abolitionists down— by fair means if we can, by foul means if we must."[142]

A few decades later both Yankee anti-abolitionism and Northern white racism were, if anything, even more unyielding and firmly established; which is why it has been truly said that on the eve of Lincoln's War "the negro was safer in South Carolina than New York, in Richmond than in Boston."

This 1873 illustration of the "New York Draft Riots," published ten years after the rampage, reveals the true focus of the white mobs—and it was not the draft, as Yankee historians still claim. The original caption reads: "Hanging and burning a negro in Clarkson Street."

Here is an illustration. When Lincoln illegally instituted the first military draft in U.S. history, 50,000 Northerners took to the streets in New York in protest. They did not vent their anger in peaceful demonstrations against the government, however. These so-called Northern "humanitarians and abolitionists" turned on the blacks of their state, chasing, beating, and even lynching them. Many were hanged from trees and lampposts, while the bodies of dead blacks were burned in the streets. At least 100 people were killed and damage was estimated to be at least $1.5 million ($33.5 million in today's currency).

So deep was the racism of white New Yorkers that these same mobs attacked and flogged white abolitionists, even destroying their homes and businesses. The "New York Draft Riots," as they are still deceptively called by Northern and New South historians, lasted five days (July 12-16, 1863) and were finally only quelled when Lincoln sent in Union troops returning from the Battle of Gettysburg (fought July 1-3, 1863).

During his tourist visit to Richmond, Virginia, famed Yankee landscape architect Frederick Law Olmsted (the designer of New York's Central Park) heard about a Southern black slave who had bought his freedom so he could go and live with his brother in Philadelphia, Pennsylvania. However, he returned abruptly a short time later. When his former owner asked him why, he replied:

> *Oh, I don't like dat Philadelphy, massa; ain't no chance for colored folks dere.* Spec' if I'd been a runaway de wite folks dere take care o' me; but I couldn't git anythin' to do, so I jis borrow ten dollar of my broder an' cum back to old Virginny.

In his 1913 book, *The Color Line in Ohio: A History of Race Prejudice in a Typical Northern State*, Frank U. Quillin writes:

> John Randolph, of Roanoke, [Virginia] before his death in 1833 set free 518 slaves and bought for them a large estate in Mercer County, Ohio. It was arranged that each one was to have 40 acres and a cabin. *The white inhabitants of the county rose en masse against the influx of the negroes, and Judge Leigh distributed them around Troy, Piqua, Sidney and Xenia.*[143]

Confederate nurse Kate Cumming wrote the following in her diary while working at a Southern hospital in the fall of 1863. She had been given some "relics" from the battlefield of Chickamauga, among which included a letter penned by a South-hating girl from Illinois to a Yankee soldier:

> In reading it I could not but wonder how she could sit down and encourage her [Northern] friends to come here as *murderers and robbers, for they are nothing else.* She raves about the Union as I have heard the men do. I think they must all be demented to even talk of such a thing now. *They speak of us as if we did not have common sense, and had to be dictated to by them.*
>
> . . . She then says she knows it [abolition] is the Lord's doing, and ere long the fetters will be broken and the negro set

> free. I should like to know what kind of freedom she means; if it is *the hatred and contempt which is generally shown the negro by these dear lovers of the race [in the North], excepting when they wish to use them in politics . . .*
>
> If the negro should be set free by this war, which I believe he will be, whether we gain or not, it will be the Lord's doing. The time has come when his mission has ended as a slave, and *while he has been benefitted by slavery the white race has suffered from its influence.*
>
> . . . *Who is it that can not relate story after story of the degradation of the [free] negro in the North . . . ? Why, slavery [in the South] is heaven to it in comparison.*[144]

WHAT YOU WERE TAUGHT: Northern slaves were guarded by numerous humanitarian laws.

THE FACTS: Yankee slave owners had complete freedom to discipline their chattel in any manner they saw fit, and various barbarities—from whipping and branding, to public torture and burning slaves at the stake—were legal, routine, and socially accepted in the North.

In New York, for example, where a 1702 law authorized masters to chastise their human property at their own discretion, slaves convicted of heinous crimes, such as murder, were subject to all manner of hideous fates. These included being "burned at the stake," "gibbeted alive," and "broken on the wheel." This is precisely what occurred in 1712, when New York authorities hanged 13 slaves, burned four of them alive (one over a "slow fire"), "broke" one on the wheel, and left another to starve to death chained to the floor.

In 1741 alone the Empire State executed 31 blacks: 13 were burned at the stake, 18 were hanged, while another 71 were transported out of state. On another occasion a New York slave named Tom, found guilty of killing two people, was ordered to be "roasted over a slow fire so that he will suffer in torment for at least eight to ten hours." Such executions were performed in public, in full view of ordinary New Yorkers, men, women, and children.[145]

This dearth of legal protection stemmed, of course, from the Yankee's lack of sympathy for the black man; or more correctly, from his outright loathing of African-Americans. And it was for this same reason that later, during Lincoln's War, Union soldiers treated blacks so terribly. Indeed, white racism was so severe among Federal troops that most white Yankee officers refused to lead black troops, while the average white Yankee soldier said he would not fight side-by-side with blacks.

Northern white racism in the U.S. army often manifested in far more serious and diabolical ways, however. Southern diaries, letters, and journals are replete with reports of incredible Yankee brutality against not only white Southern women they came across, but black Southern women as well, even against those that had at first cheered them on as liberators. Yankee soldiers' crimes against black females included robbery, pillage, beatings, torture, rape, and even murder.

The racist Old North provided few protective laws for her black slaves. Yankee slave owners, for example, could punish their black chattel at their own discretion, often resulting in appalling and inhumane treatment. Unlike in the Old South, in civil disputes between a Yankee slave owner and his slaves, the courts nearly always sided with the owner. Thus, as this 19th-Century illustration shows, a favorite family pastime in New York was the public slave burning, once a routine spectacle on the streets of Manhattan.

Southern black males were often treated even worse by their Northern "emancipators." Those who survived such crimes were taken, against their will at gunpoint, from their relatively peaceful, healthy, and safe lives of service and domesticity on the plantation, to the filth, hardships, and dangers of life on the battlefield, where at least 50 percent of them died alone in muddy ditches fighting for the Yanks against their own native land: the South.

Those blacks who resisted "involuntary enlistment" into Lincoln's army were sometimes shot or bayoneted on the spot—which is exactly why Belle Boyd referred to this particular type of African-American as "the reluctant victim of Federal conscription."[146] When black soldiers rebelled against the abuse of white Yankee soldiers, they were whipped. Both white and black Union soldiers were known to abuse Southern slaves who remained loyal to Dixie, entering their homes, shooting bullets through the walls, overturning furniture, and stealing various personal items.

Is this appalling? Not when we realize that this was all merely a continuation of Lincoln's policy of coercion, the same one he had used to invade the South in an attempt to destroy states' rights to begin with.

Many newly "freed" black males were used as Yankee shock troops, sent first into battle in conflicts usually known beforehand to be hopeless, where they would draw fire and take the brunt of the violence, sparing the lives of Northern whites. This is almost certainly what Lincoln was intimating in his letter to James C. Conkling on August 26, 1863, when he wrote:

> . . . whatever negroes can be got to do as soldiers, leaves just so much less for white soldiers to do in saving the Union.

Naturally, this included receiving cold Confederate lead and steel.

White Yankee racism flowed from the U.S. White House down. For it was from the office of white supremacist President Lincoln that all racist military orders originated. This is why for the first two years of his war he refused to allow black enlistment, despite the fact that thousands of African-Americans were keen to join. This only changed on January 1, 1863, when he issued his Emancipation Proclamation. Not due to a civil rights necessity, but for what he called a "military necessity"; that is, for the purpose of freeing then enlisting blacks due to the appalling reduction in his white soldier population.

Blacks who now eagerly enlisted in the Union army, however, were in for a rude surprise if they expected to don a fancy new blue uniform and fight next to whites on the battlefield. For at the beginning of black enlistment, Lincoln turned nearly all freed black males into common workers who performed what can only be described as "forced labor"; in other words, slavery. Their work, in fact, was identical to the drudgery they had experienced as servants and slaves. Black military duties under Lincoln included construction, serving officers (known in the South as "body servants"), cooking, washing clothes and dishes, tending livestock, and cleaning stables.

Black Union soldiers line up to receive their monthly pay packet, which as this illustration shows, did nothing to engender good will toward the U.S. government. President Lincoln had ordered that his black soldiers receive half the pay of his white soldiers, infuriating both his African-American enlistees and Yankee abolitionists. When blacks complained about the disparity and obvious racism in the U.S. military they were punished; some were even executed by firing squad.

Not surprisingly, after finally allowing official black enlistment in 1863, Lincoln ordered all of his black troops to be racially segregated, led by white officers, and paid half that of white enlistees, infuriating both his black soldiery and Northern abolitionists.[147]

Confederate nurse Cumming lived amid the savage racism of white U.S. soldiers, and speaks of it often in her hospital diary. On April 30, 1865, for example, she wrote:

> [One Southern man] informed me that the tales which had been told him of the enemy's atrocities in Mississippi, were truly awful. It was a common thing for them [Union soldiers] to *kill negro children*, so as to carry off the parents with greater facility; and that *many a negro child had been left to starve in the woods*. . . . [A white woman from Macon, Georgia, told me that the soldiers of Union General James H. Wilson] use the negroes shamefully, and *kill them on the least provocation*.[148]

A month later, on May 29, 1865, while staying in Mobile, Alabama, Cumming made the following comment about Southern blacks:

> . . . they have behaved much better than we had any right to expect, as *they have been put up to all kinds of mischief by the [Yankee] enemy*. Many of them seem to despise *the Federals*, and it is not much wonder, as *they treat them so badly*.[149]

WHAT YOU WERE TAUGHT: Southern slaves had no human rights laws to protect them.

THE FACTS: In the Old South black servants were protected by a litany of rigorous rules and regulations, crimes against slaves were punishable by law, and cruel slaveholders, though rare, were harshly penalized (even executed) when caught. In 1866 Cumming spoke of this topic in her diary. Referring to Simon Legree, a fictitious cruel slave owner in Harriet Beecher Stowe's fantasy novel, *Uncle Tom's Cabin*, she expressed the typical Southern attitude toward barbaric slaveholders:

> As for Mr. Legree, few southerners deny having such among us. I know of one, a Scotchman. He whipped a negro child to death; *was tried and put in the penitentiary. Hanging would have been too good for such a man*, so *all said. The wife of this wretch died of a broken heart, from ill treatment*. The latter crime, I believe, is not rare among the "unco guid" [self-righteous] and their neighbors, if we are to believe their own papers. I never take up one but I read about some half dozen men being tried for wife-beating. Such a thing is rarely heard of here. *I know of a few more Legrees. Two are New Englanders and one a Dutchman. They beat their negroes, but they are despised by all who know them*. They are no worse than [Wackford] Squeers [a fictitious sadistic schoolmaster in Charles Dickens' novel *Nicholas Nickleby*], *who, we are told, is a true representative of many a man in England*. If we are to judge of Britons from Squeers, and others I have spoken about, *we may all pray to be delivered from coming in contact with such a race of wife-beaters and monsters as they must be. But we all know that atrocities committed by wicked men are no standard by which to judge the nation to whom they belong*.
>
> I have often alleged as *a reason for foreigners and northerners ill-treating negroes so much more than the southerners*, that the negro, like his master, is not over-fond of work. The foreigner is accustomed to have white servants work from daylight till dark, and many of them after dark; they expect the same work from the negro, but all in vain, for the darky has no such ideas of life—eat, sleep, and no work, is his motto. These people, not understanding the character of the negro, lose patience with him, and try by

whipping to get the same amount of work from them as they have been in the habit of getting from white servants. Many a time, while we have listened to the tales about the work done by white servants [slaves] in Scotland, we have said, who could live in a country where such things are done, and where there was such slavery. *The southern people do not respect any one who overworks his servants. . . . And as soon as we have peace, I am told that the first thing our people will do is to improve their condition.*[150]

As this 19th-Century photo reveals, the typical Southern servant ("slave") did not live the harsh and brutish lifestyle described by anti-South writers. Pictured here are George and Susan Page, two of the servants of the Smedes family of Mississippi. Well-dressed, well-fed, well-educated, well-paid, and well-cared for, like all Southern servants they received lifelong *free* food, clothing, health care, and housing, and were protected by a myriad of strict humanitarian laws.

The result of this universal detestation of cruel slavers across the South, as well as the plethora of Dixie's protective slave laws, was that the vast majority of Southern slaves lived lives of comfort, safety, health, and security from birth to death—which is why so many of them, when given a choice, preferred servitude to emancipation.[151]

In 1900 Dr. Henry A. White, history professor at Washington and Lee University, made the following astute comments; words that should be permanently enshrined in granite in the capitol building of every Southern state:

> The [Southern slavery] system produced no paupers and no orphans; food and clothing the negro did not lack; careful attention he received in sickness, and, without a burden [care] the aged servants spent their closing days. The plantation was an industrial school where the negro gradually acquired skill in the use of tools. A bond of affection was woven between Southern masters and servants which proved strong enough in 1861-'65 to keep the negroes at voluntary labour to furnish food for the armies that contended against [Lincoln's] military emancipation.[152] In the planter's home the African learned to set a higher value upon the domestic virtues which he saw illustrated in the lives of Christian men and women; for, be it remembered, the great body of the slave-holders of the South were devotees of the religious faith handed down through pious ancestors from [John] Knox, [Thomas] Cranmer, [John] Wesley, and [John] Bunyan. With truth, perhaps, it may be said than no other economic system before or since that time has engendered a bond of personal affection between capital and labour so strong as that established by the institution of [Southern] slavery.[153]

WHAT YOU WERE TAUGHT: When offered a choice blacks would have preferred life as a Yankee slave rather than as a Confederate slave.
THE FACTS: The opposite is true. Unlike in the North, in the South slaves were paid a weekly salary and were given Sundays, rainy days, and holidays off. Southern servants were also permitted time to hunt, fish, and visit loved ones on neighboring farms and plantations.

On Saturdays, the day traditionally set aside for Southern servants to work their own land, they labored either a half day, or had the entire day free. Each year they also had several week's worth of work-free holidays (such as Christmas, Good Friday, Independence Day, and the post harvest period), with odd days off as rewards.

On many Southern plantations there was a servant-only party held every Saturday night, complete with whiskey, a barbeque, music (items often contributed by the white owners), and dancing. Southern slaves worked from sunrise to early afternoon (eight hours) five days a week, with one to three hours off for lunch. Thus their average work week was 25 to 40 hours long, far below the 75 hour work week of free whites and blacks at the time.

Southern slaves worked 25 to 40 hours a week (far less than free whites and blacks at the time), were given rainy days, weekends, and holidays off to do whatever they liked, and were treated like actual family members by their white owners. Slave pastimes in the South included hunting, fishing, visiting friends on nearby farms, hosting slave parties (with dancing and drinking late into the night), working in their gardens, and selling their own products at market. Many were given important jobs that required great responsibilities, but which also provided enormous freedom and an excellent salary. Little wonder that when they were asked which they preferred, being owned by a Yankee or a Southerner, the vast majority chose the latter. This was borne out the day the Emancipation Proclamation was issued: January 1, 1863. At least 95 percent of Southern African-American servants chose to remain on their owner's plantation rather than try freedom, despite the pleas of their masters. *True* emancipation did not occur until eight months after the War ended, in December 1865, to be exact, with the passage of the Thirteenth Amendment.

The life of the Southern slave was indeed easy and secure compared to the far more difficult life of the Yankee slave. This is why, when asked, nearly 100 percent of American blacks said they would rather be owned by a Southern slaveholder than a Northern one.[154]

WHAT YOU WERE TAUGHT: No one had it as bad as slaves living in the Old South.

THE FACTS: This is incorrect, and the eyewitness accounts of thousands of individuals prove it. After living in the American South for several years, Scotsman William Thomson, for instance, favorably compared Southern agricultural slavery to the industrial slavery experienced by the millions of free white "wage slaves" working in the world's factories and mines:

> I have seen children in factories, both in England and Scotland, under ten years of age, working twelve hours a-day, till their little hands were bleeding. I have seen these children whipped, when their emaciated limbs could no longer support them to their work; and I believe there is not a planter in America whose blood would not rise, and whose arm would not be lifted up to defend even the negroes from such cruelty; *especially the native [Southern] planter, who is much better to his negroes than the planters that have been brought up in free [Northern] states. This is an acknowledged fact, and therefore I need not illustrate it.* If I were to look for the cause of the comparative kindly feeling of the native [Southern] planter, it would partly be found in his having been nursed and tended in infancy by some careful negro, and having made playmates of the little black fellows of his father's house. I acknowledge that the miserably degraded state of the [white] factory slave, or the equally unnatural condition of the [white] miners, is no apology for the continuance of negro slavery; and I only make the comparison to show how difficult it is, under the present irrational state of society, to render pleasant the condition of the "hewers of wood and drawers of water." *I consider myself in some degree qualified to make this comparison, for I have witnessed negro slavery in mostly all the slave-holding states in America; having lived for weeks on cotton plantations, observing closely the actual condition of the negroes; and can assert, without fear of contradiction from any man who has any knowledge of the subject, that I have never witnessed one-fifth of the real suffering that I have seen in manufacturing establishments in Great Britain.*[155]

WHAT YOU WERE TAUGHT: The North was a tolerant region, which is why there were no Jim Crow laws there. But the Southern Confederacy, which was extremely racist, had numerous Jim Crow laws.

THE FACTS: Wherever the various races have the least amount of contact, racism tends to increase—no matter what the skin color of the dominant or majority race.

And this is precisely the situation we find in the Old South and the Old North, for in the latter region most whites had little if any interaction with blacks, making racism far more ingrained. Thus the truth is that Jim Crow laws, along with both legal and customary segregation, were "universal" in all of the Northern states, but were "unusual" in the South.[156]

WHAT YOU WERE TAUGHT: The racially unbiased North never had segregation. It was found only in the Confederacy.
THE FACTS: Since Jim Crow laws in the South were scarce (and seldom enforced where they existed), it is not surprising that racial segregation was also rare. In fact, during the antebellum period there is not a single known case of segregation anywhere in Dixie. Conversely, it was endemic to America's northeastern states right up to, and far beyond, the 1860s.

This white Yankee schoolmaster, blocking a black mother from bringing her two children to school in Rhode Island, is acting under a New England law that prohibited African-Americans from attending educational institutions.

The North's onerous Black Codes forbade, among many other things, black immigration and black civil rights, and even banned blacks from attending public schools. Little wonder that those blacks who managed to survive in the North were generally less educated and less skilled than Southern blacks. Up to 1855 it was this very type of oppression that prevented blacks from serving as jurors in all but one Northern state: Massachusetts.

Even after Lincoln's fake and illegal Final Emancipation Proclamation was issued (on January 1, 1863), literally nothing changed for African-Americans living north of the Mason-Dixon Line. When former slaves managed to make economic progress there, they found themselves blocked at every turn by a hostile racist Northern government, the very body that had supposedly "emancipated" them. As mentioned, this blockage was accomplished not only by Black Codes, by also through the implementation of severe Jim Crow laws and public segregation laws, both which were unconditionedly and widely supported by the white Yankee populace.[157]

WHAT YOU WERE TAUGHT: The type of slavery found in the North was actually servitude. The type found in the Confederacy was real slavery.

So-called "Southern slavery" was not slavery. It was involuntary servitude, one that could be terminated at any time by the servant himself, simply by paying the owner the cost of his original purchase. True slaves cannot buy their freedom. Only servants have this right.

THE FACTS: Two of the key indicators of *authentic* slavery are that 1) a slave has no rights of any kind, and 2) he or she cannot purchase their freedom. Both of these rights, however, are available under a much milder form of bondage known as servitude, making it completely different than true slavery.

Contrary to the myths of Northern anti-South propagandists, from slavery's first appearance in the South, black servants were accorded a myriad of civil and personal rights, and also could purchase their freedom at any time. In fact, the first blacks in the American South came to this country as indentured servants, just as most white colonists did at the time, not slaves, as uninformed Liberal educators teach.

The truth is that it was in the colonial North, where there were few laws protecting blacks and where slaves could not buy their liberty, that *genuine* slavery was practiced. What North and New South writers conveniently and slanderously call Southern "slavery" then was actually, as Edward A. Pollard rightly asserts, a "well-guarded and moderate system of negro servitude." As he wrote during Lincoln's War:

> In referring to the condition of the negro in this war, we use the term "slavery" . . . under strong protest. *For there is no such thing in the South; it is a term fastened upon us by the exaggeration and conceit of Northern literature*, and most improperly acquiesced in by Southern writers. *There is a system of African servitude in the South; in which the negro, so far from being under the absolute dominion of his master (which is the true meaning of the vile word "slavery"), has, by law of the land, his personal rights recognized and protected, and his comfort and "right" of "happiness" consulted, and by the practice of the system, has a sum of individual indulgences, which makes him altogether the most striking type in the world of cheerfulness and contentment.* And the system of servitude in the South has this peculiarity over other systems of servitude in the world: that it does not debase one of God's creatures from the condition of free-citizenship and membership in organized society and [which] thus rest on acts of debasement and disenfranchisement, but [instead it] elevates a savage, and rests on the solid basis of human improvement. *The European mind, adopting the nomenclature of our enemies, has designated as "slavery" what is really the most virtuous system of servitude in the world.*[158]

WHAT YOU WERE TAUGHT: It was because the South was all about slavery and the North was all about abolition, that Yankees were the "true friends of the black race" and Southerners were the "true enemies of the black race." Thus it is the Confederate Flag, not the U.S. Flag, that is racist.

THE FACTS: A statement like this is sure to get a laugh in the traditional South. Why? As this very book demonstrates, the contrary is true. How could the North be the "friend of blacks" when this is where both the American slave trade and American slavery got their start, where white racism was at its most acute, and where New York served as the slave trading capital of the U.S. for decades?

Conversely, how could the South be the "enemy of blacks" if this is where the American abolition movement was born, where white racism was the least severe, and where Southerners were emancipating their slaves as early as 1655—at which time the Northern states were increasing both their slave trade and their slave ownership? In addition, as we just discussed, there was no such thing as authentic slavery in the South. Instead, what was practiced was a mild form of paid servitude in which servants could purchase their freedom whenever they wished.

In the 17th Century, while Northerners were importing as many African slaves as possible, Southerners were busy freeing theirs. The earliest recorded Southern emancipation occurred in 1655 in Virginia, the birthplace of the American abolition movement. Unlike in the Old North, where there were laws against freeing slaves, the Old South had no such regulations. In 1798, at great financial loss, this Tennessee slave owner freed his entire staff of African-American servants—62 years before the election of Abraham Lincoln and the start of the American "Civil War."

Intelligent Victorian Southerners were highly aware of these facts, even if many Yankees were not. During Lincoln's War, for instance, Confederate nurse Kate Cumming commented on the subject of why Great Britain was withholding its support for the Southern Confederacy. "It certainly was not due to Southern slavery," she said:

> . . . I have given up that notion, for I know that the Britons are endowed with judgement enough to see through *the mask worn by [Yankee] abolitionists, and to know that we [Southerners], not they, are the true friends of the negro*.
>
> Mr. [James Alexander] Lindsay, [British] M. P., made a speech lately in Middlesex, England, in which he says he has conversed with [explorer] Dr. [David] Livingstone on the condition of the negro in Africa, and *Dr. L. had told him it was not possible to*

> *conceive any thing like the degradation of the race in that country.*
>
> If people would only think, they would see, even taking Mrs. [Harriet Beecher] Stowe's book [*Uncle Tom's Cabin*] for their standard, that *there are no negroes on the face of the earth as happy as those who are slaves in this country [Dixie].* Mrs. S. drew a true picture when she drew Uncle Tom [a civilized black], for we have many such among us; and from all we can learn *such characters are rare in the North and other countries where the negro race is.*[159]

WHAT YOU WERE TAUGHT: All Confederate military officers were slave owners and anti-abolitionists.

THE FACTS: The vast majority of Southerners, as well as Confederate militiamen and politicians, were longtime advocates of not only abolition, but of black enlistment as well. One of these was General Robert E. Lee, just one of the many reasons he is still so loved in the South.

On December 27, 1856, five years before Lincoln's War, Lee—who unlike General Grant and many other Northern officers, never owned slaves in the literal or technical sense, and who had always been opposed to slavery—wrote a letter to his wife Mary Anna in which he stated that slavery is a "moral and political evil," worse even for the white race than for the black race.

Lee's sentiment is just what one would expect from a Virginian, the state where the American abolition movement began, and whose native sons, most notably U.S. Presidents George Washington and Thomas Jefferson, struggled for so long to rid America of the institution; and this while the North was sending hundreds of slave ships to Africa, and whose main port cities, like New York, Providence, Philadelphia, Baltimore, and Boston, were functioning as the literal epicenters of slave trading in the Western hemisphere.

But Lee was far from being the first prominent Confederate to advocate emancipation and the recruitment of Southern blacks. Another example was my cousin Confederate General Pierre G. T. Beauregard, the "Hero of Fort Sumter," and an important decision maker in the development of the Confederate Battle Flag.

Yet another well-known Southerner was Louisiana governor and commander-in-chief Thomas O. Moore, who, on March 24, 1862, commissioned the first black militia in the Confederacy (the Native

Guards of Louisiana). Moore called on the all-black unit, one that had already been protecting New Orleans for several months, to "maintain their organization, and . . . hold themselves prepared for such orders as may be transmitted to them." Their purpose? To guard homes, property, and Southern rights against "the pollution of a ruthless [Northern] invader."

Another noteworthy pro-black white Confederate officer was General Patrick R. Cleburne, known as the "Stonewall Jackson of the West" for his bold tactics on the battlefield. A native of Ireland and a division commander in the Army of Tennessee, at an officers' meeting on January 2, 1864, the Irishman disclosed a written proposal that would soon become known as the "Cleburne Memorial." Calling for the immediate enlistment and training of black soldiers, it promised complete emancipation for *all* Southern slaves at the end of the War.

Confederate General Patrick Ronayne Cleburne, just one of thousands of Rebel officers who supported black enlistment and emancipation.

In early 1865 Southern Congressman Ethelbert Barksdale stated before the House that *every* Confederate soldier, whatever his rank, wanted and supported black enlistment. This sentiment was backed up by such establishments as the renowned Virginia Military Institute, which agreed, if called upon, to train Southern blacks in the art of soldiering.[160]

WHAT YOU WERE TAUGHT: All Union military officers were non-slave owners and abolitionists.

THE FACTS: Thousands of Yankees are known to have owned slaves right up to and through Lincoln's War. Among them were the families of Union General George H. Thomas, Union Admiral David G. Farragut, Union General Winfield Scott, and the family of Lincoln's wife, Mary Todd.

Arguably the most famous Yankee slaveholder was Union

General Ulysses S. Grant, an Ohioan who evinced no sympathy for the situation of American blacks, never discussed the Underground Railroad, and as an officer in the Mexican War, was waited on by servants—one, a Mexican man named Gregorio, whom he took home with him after the War to entertain his family. Grant never showed any personal interest in his colored servants—except perhaps those who attended him while he was slowly dying in New York in 1885.

Upon his marriage to Julia Boggs Dent in 1848, Grant inherited a small army of 30 black Maryland slaves that belonged to her family. Later, in 1858, he was known to still own "three or four slaves, given to his wife by her father," Colonel Frederick Dent. Grant leased several additional slaves and personally purchased at least one, a 35 year old black man named William Jones. Never once did he reveal a desire to free either his own slaves or Julia's. Instead, like Lincoln, his wife, and most other Northerners at the time, Grant assumed that the white race was superior to non-white races, and that this was simply the natural order of things.

On the eve of Lincoln's War in early 1861, Grant grew increasingly excited over the possibility that a conflict with the South would greatly depreciate black labor, then, he happily exclaimed, "the nigger will never disturb this country again." In an 1862 letter to his father, Jesse Root Grant, General Grant wrote honestly:

> I have no hobby of my own with regard to the negro, either to effect his freedom or to continue his bondage.

This apathy for the black man continued throughout Lincoln's War. In 1863 Grant penned: "I never was an abolitionist, not even what could be called anti-slavery." Even after the issuance of Lincoln's Emancipation Proclamation, Grant maintained the same sentiment, noting sourly that white Americans were now still "just as free to avoid the social intimacy with the blacks as ever they were . . ."

Since Lincoln's bogus and illicit Emancipation Proclamation on January 1, 1863, did not liberate slaves in the North (or anywhere else, for that matter), Grant was permitted to keep his black chattel—which is precisely what he did. In fact, he did not free them until he was forced to by the passage of the Thirteenth Amendment on December 6, 1865, which occurred eight months *after* Lincoln's death and the War had ended.

And what or who was behind the Thirteenth Amendment? It was not Grant, Lincoln, Garrison, or any other Northerner. It was proposed by a *Southern* man, John Henderson of Missouri.

The Union's highest ranking military officer, Ulysses S. Grant, was a well-known Yankee slave owner who only freed his slaves when he was forced to by the Thirteenth Amendment in December 1865.

But the amendment seemed to have little meaning to Grant or his wife Julia, the latter, who as late as 1876, still looked upon all blacks as slaves. We should not be shocked by any of this. It was the celebrated Yankee General Grant who, in the midst of Lincoln's War, said that the only purpose of the conflict was to "restore the union," and if he ever found out it was for abolition he would immediately defect to the other side and join the Confederacy.[161]

WHAT YOU WERE TAUGHT: Probably 100 percent of Confederates were slave owners.

THE FACTS: Pro-North writers would have us believe that "every Southerner was once a slave owner." However, as with all of their other anti-South propaganda, this too is false. In 1860 the South had reached its highest rate of slave ownership. According to the U.S. Census that year, with a white population of 7,215,525, only 4.8 percent, or 385,000, of all Southerners owned slaves, the other 95.2 percent did not. Of those that did, most owned less than five.

Correcting for the mistakes of Census takers—which would include counting slave-hirers as slave owners and counting more than once those thousands of slave owners who annually moved the same slaves back and forth across multiple states—this figure, 4.8 percent, is no doubt too large. Either way, at the time Southerners themselves believed that only about 5 percent of their number owned slaves, which is slightly high, but roughly accurate.[162]

Let us allow a Victorian Virginian to speak on the matter. The year is 1860, as mentioned, the peak period of Southern slave owning:

> . . . the census this year gives Virginia one million and fifty thousand white people, and of these the fifty thousand hold slaves and the one million don't. The fifty thousand's mostly in the tide-water counties . . .[163]

Calculating these figures we find that Virginia's 50,000 white slave owners represented *slightly less than 4.8 percent* of the state's total population of 1,050,000. Less than five out of every 100 individuals.

WHAT YOU WERE TAUGHT: Old South Southerners viewed slavery as the "cornerstone" of the Confederacy.
THE FACTS: Anti-South writers enjoy excoriating Confederate Vice President Alexander H. Stephens for his March 21, 1861, speech at Savannah, Georgia, in which he made this statement:

> [The] corner-stone [of the Constitution of the Southern Confederacy] rests upon the great truth, that the negro is not equal to the white man; that slavery, subordination to the superior race, is his natural and normal condition.

Before discussing the facts behind these words, let us compare them with those of Yankee President Abraham Lincoln, delivered publicly a few years earlier on July 17, 1858, at Springfield, Illinois:

> My declarations upon this subject of negro slavery may be misrepresented, but cannot be misunderstood. *I have said that I do not understand the Declaration [of Independence] to mean that all men were created equal in all respects. . . . Certainly the negro is not our equal in color—perhaps not in many other respects . . .*[164]

A few months later, on September 18, 1858, at Charleston, Illinois, Lincoln made the following statement:

> *I will say then that I am not, nor ever have been, in favor of bringing about in any way the social and political equality of the white and black*

> *races*—that I am not, nor ever have been, in favor of making voters or jurors of negroes, nor of qualifying them to hold office, nor to intermarry with white people; and I will say in addition to this that *there is a physical difference between the white and black races which I believe will forever forbid the two races living together on terms of social and political equality*. And inasmuch as they cannot so live, while they do remain together there must be the position of superior and inferior, and *I as much as any other man am in favor of having the superior position assigned to the white race.*[165]

My point here is that Vice President Stephens' racism was no different than President Lincoln's. Both men were products of a 19th-Century white society that saw blacks as an "inferior race," as Lincoln nearly *always* referred to African-Americans. Thus, if critics of the South wish to avoid being called hypocrites, Northerner Lincoln must be denounced just as heartily as Southerner Stephens. As the "Great Emancipator" Lincoln himself said of "nearly all white people" living in the North at the time:

> There is a *natural disgust* in the minds of nearly *all white people*, to the idea of an indiscriminate amalgamation [mixing] of the white and black races.[166]

As for Stephens, he turns out to be far less bigoted than Lincoln; as for Stephens' Cornerstone Speech, it turns out to be far less vicious and racist than modern South-loathers have asserted—and in fact Stephens was widely known as "a true benefactor of the negro."[167]

For one thing, during his address the vice president was engaging in hyperbole to get his point across, a common enough practice among politicians. Second, the speech we read today is not a literal translation of the original, but an "interpretation" by journalists in the audience, who introduced their own biases and mistakes into the final transcription.

Third, Stephens himself repeatedly maintained that his words were misinterpreted, and for good reason. When he made his comment about slavery being the "cornerstone" of the Confederate Constitution, he was merely repeating the words of a *Yankee* judge, Associate Justice of the U.S. Supreme Court, Henry Baldwin of Connecticut who, 28 years earlier, in 1833, had said:

> *Slavery is the corner-stone of the [U.S.] Constitution*. The foundations of the Government are laid and rest on the rights of property in slaves, and the whole structure must fall by disturbing the corner-stone.[168]

As Richard M. Johnston noted later in 1884, all Stephens did during his Cornerstone Speech was accurately point out the fact that "on the subject of slavery there was no essential change in the new [Southern Confederate] Constitution from the old [the U.S. Constitution]."[169]

Unlike white supremacist, white separatist Abraham Lincoln, Confederate Vice President Alexander H. Stephens treated African-Americans with dignity and respect and they treated him the same in return. Even the alleged "racism" of his Cornerstone Speech has been completely misrepresented. And yet it is Stephens not Lincoln who is regularly eviscerated by the anti-South movement. After the War Stephens and one of his black servants posed for this photograph, something we can be sure neither would have done had the great Southern statesman been a true racist.

WHAT YOU WERE TAUGHT: There was little or no slavery ever practiced in the American North, and what little there was lasted only a couple of years.

THE FACTS: Southern slavery lasted from 1749, when Georgia became the first Southern state to legalize slavery, to 1865, the year the Thirteenth Amendment was ratified and American slavery was officially abolished, a mere 116 years.

In contrast, Northern slavery lasted from 1641, when Massachusetts became the first Northern state to legalize slavery, to 1865, a span of 224 years. This period increases if we count from 1626, the year New York imported the first black slaves into North America, a span of 239 years—ending in 1865.

Either way, the North practiced slavery for over a century longer than the South did, between 108 and 123 years longer.[170]

WHAT YOU WERE TAUGHT: Abraham Lincoln was both the true friend of the black man and the Great Emancipator.

THE FACTS: According to not only his party members but his own words, U.S. President Abraham Lincoln stalled emancipation, blocked black civil rights, promoted American apartheid, and spent his entire adult life pushing for the deportation of blacks. Furthermore, he was a lifelong supporter and onetime leader of the racist Yankee organization, the American Colonization Society, whose stated goal was to make America "white from coast to coast" by shipping out as many blacks as possible to foreign lands.[171]

As his own writings and speeches attest, few people in early America were less interested in *true* abolition than Abraham Lincoln.

As if this were not enough, if Lincoln's goal was truly to "free the slaves" we must ask ourselves why he waited so long to attempt to emancipate them. From the first day of his inauguration, both white and black civil rights leaders—men like Horace Greeley, Benjamin F. Wade, Thaddeus Stevens, John C. Frémont, David Hunter, John W. Phelps, Theodore Tilton, Wendell

Phillips, Frederick Douglass, Henry Ward Beecher, and George B. Cheever—put constant pressure on the president to abolish slavery. Yet time and time again he refused.

First the year 1861 passed. Then 1862. Nearly two years into the War, Lincoln still would not be moved to liberate America's slaves, earning him the well deserved nicknames the "tortoise President" and the "slow coach at Washington."

As occurred with a number of other Union officers, General David Hunter attempted to free slaves in the South, but was stopped by Lincoln.

As further proof of Lincoln's apathy toward blacks, during the War several abolitionist Yankee officers tried to issue emancipations, but were forbidden by their anti-abolitionist Yankee president. One of these was the famous "Pathfinder," Union General John Charles Frémont, who declared martial law, then freed slaves in Missouri. Lincoln rescinded both orders, had the slaves returned to their owners, and relieved Frémont of his command—despite a tearful face-to-face plea from Frémont's famous wife Jessie (Ann Benton).

Frémont's successor, abolitionist General David Hunter, also bucked Lincoln's racism by trying his own hand at emancipation. Hunter's "General Order No. 11" declared all slaves in the Union-held territories of South Carolina, Georgia, and Florida "forever free." Lincoln was not amused and again revoked the proclamation.

But the slavery-hating Hunter continued to disobey the chief executive. When Hunter formed the 1st South Carolina Regiment, made up of blacks he had (illegally) enlisted in that state, Lincoln promptly ordered him to disband the group, reaffirming that he would not free the slaves until "it shall have become a necessity indispensable to the maintenance of the Government . . ."

Others in Lincoln's cabinet and military who tried to abolish slavery were also blocked by the racially intolerant president, among them Simon Cameron, John W. Phelps, and Jim Lane.[172]

Naturally Lincoln was heartily despised for such actions by abolitionists, but idolized by white supremacists, many who continue to revere him into the present day. Individuals from the latter category include: William P. Pickett, author of *The Negro Problem: Abraham Lincoln's Solution*; James K. Vardaman, the popular Mississippi politician known as the "the Great White Chief"; and Thomas Dixon, Jr., the playwright who inspired D. W. Griffith's controversial film, *The Birth of a Nation*.

In point of fact, Lincoln was not just a callous Leftist with socialist leanings, he was also a publicly avowed white racist, white supremacist, and white separatist whose plans for African-Americans included corralling them in their own all-black state and exiling the rest back "to their own native land," as he phrased it in a speech at Peoria, Illinois, on October 16, 1854.

Not only that, Lincoln's Emancipation Proclamation did not actually free a single slave. This was because his edict only liberated slaves in the Confederate States, a sovereign nation where he had no legal authority, while leaving slavery intact in the United States, where he had full legal authority. For these reasons alone—and there are many others—Lincoln cannot be considered either the "friend of the black man" or the "Great Emancipator."[173]

WHAT YOU WERE TAUGHT: Jefferson Davis was a Confederate racist and the enemy of blacks.

THE FACTS: While Lincoln was plotting the exile of all blacks from America's shores, Confederate President Jefferson Davis and his wife Varina (Howell) adopted a young black boy named Jim Limber, who they raised as their own in the Confederate White House.

During the War they always treated their black servants equitably and with the greatest respect, as part of their family in fact. And after Lee's surrender, during the Davis family's escape southward, their coachman was a free and "faithful" African-American man.

Later, after the War, the one-time Rebel president and his wife sold their plantation, Brierfield, to a former slave. Davis even spoke once of a time when he led "negroes against a lawless body of armed white men . . .," something we can be sure that white separatist Lincoln never did—or would have even considered.

Finally, Davis was against black colonization (preferring that blacks remain in the South, where they had been since the 1500s), banned the foreign slave trade in the Confederacy four years before the Union did, and committed the C.S. to complete abolition in January 1865, almost a year before the U.S. implemented the Thirteenth Amendment. For these reasons alone Davis must be considered not only the real friend of blacks, but the true Great Emancipator.[174]

C.S. President Jefferson Davis is called a "racist" by Liberals, yet U.S. President Abraham Lincoln is referred to as the "Great Friend of the Black Man." Why? It was Davis who adopted an orphaned black boy during the War and planned on ending slavery in the South 11 months before the North issued the Thirteenth Amendment. It was Lincoln who barred blacks from entering the White House, promised not to interfere with slavery in his First Inaugural Address, supported the 1861 Corwin Amendment, stalled emancipation for three years, refused to grant equal pay to black Yankee soldiers, blocked black civil rights, referred to blacks as an "inferior race," and spent his entire political career trying to deport African-Americans to foreign countries.

WHAT YOU WERE TAUGHT: The American Civil War was a fight over slavery, just as the North and the South said it was.

THE FACTS: Yes, this is what we have been taught by pro-North mainstream historians who possess a hatred for the South and the facts, and most who were not even at the scene, or who lived decades or even over a century or more after the fact. In any event, merely making this statement does not make it true. In fact, coming from such sources you can be sure that it is altogether false. Those who actually participated in the War concur. And indeed the alleged connection between the Civil War, the South, the Confederate Flag, and slavery completely evaporates when one looks at the authentic record.

For one thing, if slavery had been the "cause," the War would have ended on September 22, 1862, when Lincoln issued his Preliminary Emancipation Proclamation, or at least by January 1, 1863, when he issued his Final Emancipation Proclamation. Yet, the bloody, illegal, and unnecessary conflict continued for another two years.

Furthermore, it would have cost ten times less to simply free America's slaves than to go to war. Not even the megalomaniacal Lincoln, with all of his psychological problems and emotional disabilities, was mentally unbalanced enough to overlook this important fact.

However, contrary to Yankee claims, the most damning evidence against the Yankee myth that "Southern slavery caused the Civil War" comes from the top political and military leaders of *both* the Confederacy and the Union. Here is how C.S. President Jefferson Davis put it:

> *The truth remains intact and incontrovertible, that the existence of African servitude was in no wise the cause of the conflict*, but only an incident. In the later controversies that arose, however, its effect in operating as a lever upon the passions, prejudices, or sympathies of mankind, was so potent that it has been spread like a thick cloud over the whole horizon of historic truth.[175]

In the Fall of 1864, when a Yankee asked Davis, "why not simply stop fighting?" he replied:

> I desire peace as much as you do; I deplore bloodshed as much as you do; but I feel that not one drop of the blood shed in this War is on my hands—I can look up to my God and say this. *I tried all in my power to avert this War. I saw it coming, and for twelve years I worked night and day to prevent it; but I could not. The North was mad and blind; it would not let us govern ourselves*; and so the War came: and now it must go on till the last man of this generation falls in his tracks, and his children seize his musket and fight our battle, unless you acknowledge our right to self-government. *We are not fighting for Slavery. We are fighting for Independence*; and that or extermination we will have.[176]

Seventeen years on, in his landmark work, *The Rise and Fall of the Confederate Government*, Davis made this famous remark:

> . . . the war was, on the part of the United States government, one of aggression and usurpation, and, on the part of the South, was for the defense of an inherent, unalienable right.[177]

That "unalienable right" was the constitutional promise of states' rights, or self-government, guaranteed to us by the Founding Fathers.

This fact was understood by every Southerner, and in particular, Confederate officials. After Davis' death in 1889, H. W. Bruce, a former member of the Confederate Congress and a friend of the Rebel president, said of him:

> [Jefferson Davis] believed the people of each State should rule its own affairs; in other words, he believed in the people of each State governing themselves without dictation or even interference from the people of other States or countries. *It was the violation of this principle, you know, that brought on the war. The Southern States refused to yield to such dictation and interference with their domestic affairs. War was waged against them in consequence. They resisted.* The world, not understanding the issue, sided against them, and they were defeated. States' rights seemed to go down in this defeat. But *our great leader said the cause was not lost. It will rise again. The people of this great country cannot afford to surrender the rights of the States, and will not do so permanently.* The assertion of those rights hereafter, however, will not be impeded by the incubus of slavery as it was in 1860-1865, and *the principle for which our hero and chief led the hosts of the Confederacy will ultimately prevail.*[178]

In 1903 Robert E. Lee's major of artillery, Robert Stiles, glanced backward in time and wrote of his Confederate soldiers and the true cause of the War:

> What now of the essential spirit of these young volunteers? Why did they volunteer? For what did they give their lives? We can never appreciate the story of their deeds as soldiers until we answer this question correctly.
>
> *Surely it was not for slavery they fought. The great majority of them had never owned a slave and had little or no interest in the institution.* My own father, for example, had freed his slaves long years before; that is, all save one, who would not be "emancipated,"—our dear "Mammy," who clung to us when we moved to the North and never recognized any change in her condition or her relations to us. *The great conflict will never be properly comprehended by the man who looks upon it as a war for the preservation of slavery.*[179]

All Southerners, even Southern children, understood that the

Confederate Cause was "not for the slavery of the colored race, but for the freedom of the white race from the abuses of the majority."[180] In 1865 Confederate heroine Belle Boyd commented on the real reason the North invaded the South: the desire to accrue and centralize political power at Washington, D.C.

> . . . it will be admitted that *the emancipation of the negro was not the object of Northern ambition*; that is, of the faction which *grasps exclusive power in contempt of general rights.*[181]

Robert E. Lee and two of his military staff a week after the Confederate surrender. From left to right: General George Washington Custis Lee (eldest son of R. E. Lee), General Lee, and Lieutenant Colonel Walter Herron Taylor. You will never learn the truth in any mainstream history book, but all three of these men supported the ideas of African-American enlistment in the Confederate army, as well as complete Southern emancipation. Slavery was simply of no interest to them. Taylor, for example, wrote a 200 page book on the War in 1878 without using the words slave, slaves, slavery, negro, negroes, or even servant.

The everyday Confederate soldier too was keenly aware of why he was fighting—and it was not over slavery. He knew as well as both Presidents Davis and Lincoln that the "peculiar institution" had nothing remotely to do with the conflict. Indeed, this is why, after the War, so many of the memoirs written by Rebel officers contained nothing on the subject. One of these men, Colonel Harry Gilmor, for example, who served under the great Confederate chieftain Turner Ashby, wrote a 300 page book on his wartime exploits without ever once mentioning either slavery or slaves.[182]

Another, Walter Herron Taylor, Adjutant General of the Army of Northern Virginia under Robert E. Lee, authored a 200 page book on his experiences, but never once used the words slave, slaves, slavery, negro, negroes, or even servant.[183] Yet pro-North propagandists continue to preach that slavery was at the center of every Southerner's life, especially Confederate military officers—most who, as history shows, were non-slave owners and pro-abolition!

Confederate First Lieutenant Albert Theodore Goodloe did not fight to preserve Southern slavery. He went to war to prevent *all* Southerners from becoming slaves of the tyrannical North.

The reason so many 19th-Century Southern autobiographies and memoirs lack any reference to the "peculiar institution," is because the real issue was never black agricultural and domestic slavery under Davis and the South. It was always about white economic and political slavery under Lincoln and the North, who, through a declaration of war, made it plain that Dixie was to be subdued and shoved under the boot heel of an all-powerful, anti-Constitution, anti-South Yankee government. In 1893 First Lieutenant Albert T. Goodloe, of Company D, Thirty-Fifth Regiment Alabama Volunteer Infantry, commented on this very reality:

> Nothing was farther from my mind throughout my boyhood and early manhood days than the thought of going to battle, my very dreams of war being oppressive and frightful; and there is no probability that any occasion other than the one that did occur could ever have induced me to volunteer for military service.

> To *Abraham Lincoln, who inaugurated and perpetuated the bloody era of our country, as Confederates all believed*, is due the credit of my becoming a soldier. *His original call for seventy-five thousand troops to subdue "the rebellion,"* so called, not only transformed me from a Unionist into a Secessionist, but also engendered within me the warrior spirit. I was never as brave as I wished to be, but I fought him with what courage and vehemence I could command, because *he placed before me the alternative, as I understood him, of becoming his bond-servant [slave], or of defying his self-constituted authority at the point of the bayonet.*
>
> That I did rebel against such authority as Mr. Lincoln assumed, and defy his armies on the field without reference to cost, *I not only do not regret, but consider that occasion was thus furnished me for great personal gratification. I regard, indeed, this act of mine as not only altogether justifiable in every sense, but as constituting the most momentous and loftiest movement of my life or that is possible to any man. To have been a Confederate soldier in the true sense is to have done the sublimest thing that could have been done. The children of Confederate soldiers rise up and call them blessed, as will also the generations which are, in succession, to follow.*[184]

In 1882 Sam Watkins of the famed "Maury Grays," Company H of the First Tennessee Infantry, spoke for Johnny Reb, the everyday Confederate soldier, on the cause of the War:

> . . . I am as firm in my convictions to-day of the right of secession as I was in 1861. The South is our country, the North is the country of those who live there. We are an agricultural people; they are a manufacturing people. They are the descendants of the good old Puritan Plymouth Rock stock, and we of the South from the proud and aristocratic stock of Cavaliers. *We believe in the doctrine of State rights, they in the doctrine of centralization.*
>
> John C. Calhoun, Patrick Henry, and [John] Randolph, of Roanoke, saw the venom under their wings, and warned the North of the consequences, but they laughed at them. *We only fought for our State rights, they for Union and power. The South fell battling under the banner of State rights, but yet grand and glorious even in death.*[185]

One of Jeb Stuart's artillery men, George M. Neese, noted what was apparent to all Southerners: whatever one thought of states' rights, the Constitution, or the right of secession, the South had no choice but to pick up arms when, on April 15, 1861, Lincoln inexplicably and illegally called for 75,000 troops to invade Dixie:

> I am individually opposed to war, and intend to go slow to get there. . . . *When imperative duty calls me to the field of actual war to resist the onward march of an invading foe*, then, and not until then, will I respond to the demands of patriotism voluntarily.
>
> I have always looked upon war as a dangerous and desperately destructive affair, especially when it is well played on both sides, therefore battle-fields have no charms for me. *But if our pious friends in the North, whose sham philanthropy for Southern slaves is excelled by avaricious envy and legislative meanness, still refuse to listen to the pleadings of reason, and mock at the offerings of Justice, then all that is left for the South to do is to cry, like a certain people of old once did, "To your tents, O Israel!"*[186]

In 1907 Confederate General Edward Porter Alexander, chief of artillery under General James Longstreet, wrote:

> As to the causes of the war, it will, of course, be understood that *every former Confederate repudiates all accusations of treason or rebellion in the war, and even of fighting to preserve the institution of slavery*. The effort of the enemy to destroy it [slavery] without compensation was practical robbery, which, of course, we resisted. The unanimity and the desperation of our resistance—even to the refusal of Lincoln's suggested compensation at Fortress Monroe [in February 1865], after the destruction had already occurred—*clearly show our struggle to have been for that right of self-government* which the Englishman has claimed, and fought for, as for nothing else, since the days of King John.
>
> *It has taken many years for these truths to gain acceptance against the prejudices left by the war, even though it has been notorious from the first that no legal accusation could be brought against any one, even Mr. [Jefferson] Davis.*[187]

General Alexander is referring to the fact that not even the U.S. government itself could find an attorney to represent it in a court battle against President Davis after the War. Why? Because everyone knew, and by then were forced to admit, that the South had seceded in an effort to preserve the constitutional right of self-government, and that secession was perfectly legal. Thus the prosecution would not have a leg to stand on.[188] In 1912 Confederate author Robert M. Howard wrote:

> The United States Government, after keeping Jefferson Davis in prison two years (a portion of the time in manacles) liberated him without trial. And why? Because *it knew a trial would result in acquittal, which would forever prove and establish the right of secession under the Constitution and history will so record it. Every decision of the United States Supreme Court from its foundation down to the present time where States' Rights and States' Sovereignty were the questions for adjudication, has sustained the principle and doctrine*, and I challenge denial and refutation of this fact.[189]

Confederate veteran Robert Milton Howard in 1912, with four of his granddaughters, whom he called my "bright, beautiful sunbeams." Howard confirmed the truth known to all Southerners then and now: the Southern Confederacy took up arms to preserve constitutional freedom, not slavery.

The average Union soldier had no pretenses about fighting for black civil rights or even abolition. He believed he had gone into battle to honor the U.S. Flag, "put down the rebellion," and "preserve the Union." "This is a white man's war, and that's the way we want to keep it. We will never fight for or alongside the nigger," thousands of Yankee soldiers were heard to exclaim during the War. This Northern antipathy toward African-Americans is precisely why, when Lincoln finally allowed black enlistment (with the issuance of the Emancipation Proclamation on January 1, 1863), his white soldiers hissed and booed, desertions increased, and a general "demoralization" set in across the entire U.S. military.[190]

Months before Lincoln released his unlawful edict, individuals much smarter than he had warned him about the probable negative reaction of his soldiery—but he unwisely ignored them. One of these men was the Honorable Edson Baldwin Olds, a medical doctor and politician from Ohio who, on July 26, 1862, gave his celebrated "Berne Township Speech," for which he was imprisoned by Lincoln. Why?

As we will discuss shortly, halfway through the conflict the Yankee president decided to change the character of his war from a political one ("preserving the Union") to a moral one ("destroying Southern slavery"). Though the intention was only superficial not actual, he believed this word trickery would help draw the support of Europe, as well as accrue abolitionist votes for his upcoming reelection in 1864.

Lincoln had a habit of illegally arresting and imprisoning fellow Northerners who disagreed with him. One of the thousands of unfortunate souls who suffered this fate was Yankee Conservative Dr. Edson B. Olds, who spent several months in a Union gulag for trying to expose Lincoln's linguistic skullduggery.

The president's nefarious idea, however, to *pretend* to fight for abolition, was so disliked in the North that it would drive away potential recruits, eventually requiring a military draft, with all of its accompanying negative after-effects. Additionally, since the plan was not meant to *permanently* overturn slavery or ensure black civil rights (neither issue which was of great importance to Lincoln, as his own words prove),[191] the Emancipation Proclamation would not be issued for the benefit of African-Americans. It was purely for the purpose of self-aggrandizing political expediency, and reasonable and intelligent individuals such as Dr. Olds were justifiably against the idea, and he said so in his address.

A Northern conservative, Ohio Representative Olds maintained that the focus of the latter half of the War should continue to be for the purpose of preserving the Union rather than abolition, for abolition was an idea that was roundly detested by the vast majority of Yankees of both the major parties in 1862. If Lincoln went ahead with his plan, the outcome could only damage his political aspirations, intensify sectional hostilities, and prolong the War. Olds, who yearned for a Union victory but who, like most white Northerners, had little concern for Southern slaves or the institution itself, turned out to be right.

But dictator Lincoln either did not grasp the underlying message of the Berne Township Speech, or he did and chose to ignore it. Instead, he felt that the Ohio senator had "discouraged enlistments" and "encouraged resistance to the draft," and had him illegally arrested.

What follows are excerpts from Dr. Olds' oration. They are important because they show the Northern apathy toward, even abhorrence of, abolition at the time and, in consequence, that slavery could not have been the cause of the War. There was simply no support for this idea in the North:

> These warnings, time and again, the Democracy [that is, the Democrats, the Conservatives of the day] have [been] held up to the view of our Republican friends [that is, the Liberals of the day]; but we have been met only with taunts and derision. . . . I call God to witness here to-day, in the presence of the Republicans, that if I, by sacrificing myself, could restore this Union to what it was *before the Abolitionists destroyed it*, I would lay myself upon the altar a sacrifice, and give the very last drop of my heart's blood to *repair the evils Abolitionism has brought upon my ruined country*. . . . I say . . . that *if this war ceases to be a war for the suppression of the rebellion; if it is no longer to be prosecuted for the maintenance of "the Constitution as it is," and the restoration of "the Union as it was," and is to become an Abolition war; if your battle-cry, henceforth, is to be, "Throw down your arms, you damned rebels, and free your negroes," Democrats [that is, Conservative Yankees] will refuse to volunteer; and, in order to raise these six hundred thousand soldiers, the Administration will be driven to the draft.*
>
> . . . I see what must be the inevitable consequences of *a fraudulent draft*. Every man who feels himself cheated, who feels that he has been unfairly dealt by in this draft, will refuse to be mustered into service, and such refusal will cause the shedding of blood; a file of soldiers will be sent for him, and he will resist even at the point of the bayonet. If the President wishes to avoid such fearful results; if he wishes to avoid bringing civil war and bloodshed into our peaceful cities and villages [in the North], let him make some proclamation, by *which we may know that this war is not prosecuted for the abolition of slavery*, and this draft will become unnecessary.
>
> Let him proclaim that this war, in the future, will be

> prosecuted for the sole object of putting down the rebellion, for the maintenance of the Constitution and the Union, and he will find strong arms and willing hearts ready to rally round the old Star-spangled Banner.
>
> Let him do this, and this same old [Conservative] Democratic party [to which Olds belonged], that the [Liberal] Republicans are denouncing as disunionists and secessionists—this same old Democratic party, that rallied around his standard, *so long as they believed him devoted to the Union and the Constitution*—will again fill the ranks of his army to overflowing; they will, as heretofore, more than count life for life, bone for bone, and blood for blood, with the Republicans, upon all your battle-fields.[192]

(Contrary to Dr. Olds' words, the North was not fighting for "the maintenance of the Constitution," or even for the "preservation of the Union," two Yankee myths that I debunk throughout this book.)

As further proof of the real reason the North fought, let us go directly to one of our more significant sources: the common Union soldiery. What follows is a revealing eyewitness account of a Southern woman whose home was illegally invaded and pillaged by a Union regiment:

> Now we heard hoofs approaching, and the servants ran off towards their quarters in haste and terror. I entreated my mother and sister to follow and to go around to the back door, so the house would not be empty, and thus the more liable to be fired [burned]. This fresh company of Yankees then reined up beside me.
>
> "Hi! looks as if Yankees had been along here to-day!" the leader shouted, looking down at me.
>
> I replied with another question, without stopping to think: "Are you not Yankees?"
>
> He gave me a savage glance, spurred up his horse, and trotted towards the house, followed by his band. I, too, followed rapidly and was on the front steps as soon as they.
>
> "There is food on our breakfast table," I said, "If you and your men are hungry, come in," and I led the way.
>
> He looked through the piazza window at the table, then whistled to the men, who shouted to the others coming up and they crowded in; others rushed through the house and yard to the back premises and some tramped upstairs. . . .
>
> [One of our black servants] Nelly then pushed through

> the crowd, and pulling my arm said, "Please, Mam, letch de key uf de smoke-house. Dem Yankee gwine brok open de door."
>
> I followed, thankful that I had this key in my pocket.
>
> . . . The yard was filled with the lawless soldiery, but with an unusually steady hand I put the large brass key into its curious hole, unlocked the door and throwing it wide open said, "all our meat is here." Like hungry wolves they rushed in, and some climbing like monkeys pulled down piece after piece, while others carried it off or handed it to their comrades on mule or horseback in the yard. Then, with satisfaction and thankfulness, I saw some sitting on the benches cracking the walnuts they gathered from under the shelves, just as we had hoped they would do.
>
> While watching this my attention was diverted by one demanding the key of an out-house nearby. In this we had tried to hide our soldier boys' trunks and some other precious things, putting empty boxes before and on them and then purposely leaving the door unlocked. This key had also been carried off by the miscreants who looked the doors and trunks in the house. I told the man I did not have the key, but as it was a padlock he was able to remove the hasp with his bayonet [so he could] search that room. The hasp was soon off and his bayonet thrust aside my boxes. I was so unwilling to have my boys' clothes and little treasures stolen that I stood before them till the little room was crowded with Yankees. I slipped out and saw them force the trunks open. At the sight of a uniform coat once worn by my son-in-law in the Citadel Academy and given to my youngest son, they set up another Indian yell or war-whoop. Then one garment after another they took, piling them on their arms. They were chiefly boys' summer clothing and some few other things very precious from tender associations.
>
> "Those are my sons' clothes," I said, "which they do not need, but we expect to give them to our negro boys" [that is, the children of her adult servants].
>
> *"What do we care for the negroes?" one [of the Yankee soldiers] answered.*
>
> *"Are you not fighting for the negro?" [I asked.]*
>
> *"No, we are fighting for the [U.S.] flag.* Your boys are lying on some battle field," and, carrying his armful off, he sang: "Who will care for mother now?"[193]

Violating every rule of civilized warfare, the sarcastic and unruly Union soldiers proceeded to unlawfully and needlessly dismantle the woman's beautiful Southern home, taking everything they could carry away, destroying everything they could not.

If the War was over slavery, or even preserving the Union, why did Yankee soldiers routinely pillage and burn down Southern homes and abuse, rape, and even murder their innocent occupants? This angry, clench-fisted Union officer (right) is threatening to torch the beautiful home of a genteel, harmless woman living in Columbia, Tennessee, whose husband is off fighting with Confederate General Nathan Bedford Forrest. Her pleas to spare the house went unheeded. After taking her valuables, the immoral invaders drove her family into the street and set the home on fire. The question the South is still asking is why?

As this Victorian photograph shows, the warm relations between Southern whites and their black servants was not a secret. Indeed, both races continually boasted of the love and respect they shared for one another. It was 19th-Century pro-North propagandists who tried to hide the fact, and they are still doing so today. Why? Because the truth about white-black relationships in the Old South would undermine and destroy the entire myth of the Civil War and the Confederate Flag.

Note that at the sound of the approaching Union army the house servants ("slaves" to Yankees) did not welcome the soldiers as conquering heroes or run into their arms as righteous emancipators, which is what one would expect if the War had been about slavery and abolition. Instead, according to their own mistress, the black staff fled to "their quarters in haste and terror," the typical reaction of "slaves" across the Southland.

During a similar Yankee invasion of a Confederate household in South Carolina, a group of Union soldiers had kidnaped the home's black servants, bringing forth screams and tears, both from their owners and the servants themselves. As he was wheeling his horse around to leave with the captured "slaves," a Union colonel said to Timonah, the white mistress of the house: "I do not see why you care so much for those old negroes." The Southern belle was too distraught to respond at the time, but later penned her feelings about the incident in her diary:

> There is just where the difference lies. *We really care for them*, and the Yankees only want to make us suffer through them.[194]

After the War a Confederate woman, Annie E. Johns of Leaksville, North Carolina, wrote about her experience working in a hospital where many of the patients were Union soldiers. As she went from bed to bed one day, she came upon a sickly Yankee who made it a point to say to her:

"I am from East Tennessee . . . and *did not go into the war for slavery, but for the Union.*"

"Is there anything I can do for you?" I asked, not wishing to discuss the subject.

"Will you send me some milk?" he said pleadingly.

I promised to do so and . . . left the hospital.[195]

If the War had been an effort by the North to rid the South of slavery, why did millions of Southern blacks voluntarily remain with their white owners, protecting them and caring for them throughout the conflict? They were free to leave at any time. After the War a Confederate woman from South Carolina wrote about her own "slaves":

> I cannot refrain here from saying something of *the devotion of our servants during the entire war*. We have now among our relics a ten-dollar bill of Confederate money, which our old [black servant] nurse brought my mother when we were homeless in Sumter, saying, "Missis, please let me help you." She would take no refusal, and although it could never be used [for Lincoln's War had rendered Confederate money valueless by then], yet it speaks even now of *her love and unselfishness. It is wonderful, when we consider that our men were in the service, only women, children and old men at home, and in many cases whole households left under the care of the [black] family servants, and yet through the length and breadth of our land you heard of nothing but kindness and protection from these people, whom our Northern friends would tell us we oppressed and treated like slaves—a term I never heard applied to them until now*. We never locked our doors, and the key to the outer door was always kept by the [black] butler, so that he could come in early without disturbing the family. Can the Northerners live thus with their white servants? The family of one of our friends was told that their servants held nightly meetings in their kitchen, and they thought that their servants were making arrangements to desert them for the Yankees. One night a low, earnest sound was heard from the kitchen, so two of the young ladies crept softly down to hear what the conspiracy might be. Judge of their feeling as they saw the entire group of servants kneeling in prayer, while one of their number was offering up an earnest petition to his "Fader in Heben to bless dere Missis and children, partickler dere young masters in de wah."[196]

Mrs. S. A. Crittenden of Greenville County, South Carolina, wrote of the "loyal and noble negroes," one named Peter, whose humility prompted him to refer to himself in the third person:

> *To the eternal honor of the [Southern] negroes be it spoken, that many of them aided and sustained their former owners in these trying times, with a devotion as surprising as it was noble.*
>
> One old fellow brought a store of provisions and laid it before his [destitute] former master, saying: "Massa, it nearly breaks my heart to see you in dis old shanty, but it would break entirely to know you were hungry and couldn't get nothing to eat."
>
> "But, Peter, my good fellow," returned his master, "I cannot take these things from you and leave you and your children to starve."
>
> "No danger of dat. Peter's used to helpin' hisself, and dat, massa, you never could do, you nor ole miss neither."
>
> "Peter," said the master with a suspicious moisture about his eyes, "we have fallen upon evil days; but, perhaps, I might live to repay you."
>
> "You's done dat already, massa; you's took care of Peter a good many years, and I's sure it's his time to take care of you and ole miss."[197]

Here is a question that no South-hater has ever been able to adequately answer: If the War was indeed over slavery, why did the man who started the conflict promise not to interfere with the institution in his First Inaugural Address?

These are facts of the War, facts you will never read in pro-North versions of the fratricidal fight. Why? Because the Yankee view is based on popular opinion, personal beliefs and feelings (for example, "justice" and "fairness"), socioeconomic ideologies, and political correctness, and so comes nowhere close to the truth.

No one was more definitive about the true purpose, and thus the true cause, of the "Civil War" than the man who started it: U.S. President Abraham Lincoln. In his First Inaugural Address, March 4, 1861, only four weeks before the conflict, he declared:

> *I have no purpose, directly or indirectly, to interfere with the institution of slavery in the States where it exists.*[198]

Liberal Ohio politician Thomas Corwin, for whom the pro-slavery Corwin Amendment was named. The proposed resolution, which was passed by the 36th Congress in March 1861 with the wholehearted blessing of President Lincoln, was a failed Northern attempt to entice the seceding Southern states to rejoin the Union. If "the North fought to *abolish* slavery," why did Lincoln and his constituents offer to add an amendment to the Constitution that would permanently ban Congress from abolishing or even interfering with the institution just one month before the start of the conflict? And if "the South fought to *preserve* slavery," why did she reject the offer of the Corwin Amendment, which would have allowed her to continue to legally practice slavery in perpetuity under the Constitution? Why indeed!

In this same speech Lincoln gave his full backing to the Corwin Amendment, which would have allowed American slavery to continue in perpetuity without any interference from the Federal government.[199] "I have no objection to its being made express and irrevocable," he stated emphatically before the country on his first day as president. Had hostilities not exploded between the South and the North at Fort Sumter a month later, what I call Lincoln's "proslavery amendment" would have been signed into law, and Northern and Southern slavery would have continued indefinitely.[200]

In the Summer of 1861, with the War now in full swing, Lincoln told Reverend Charles E. Lester:

> I think [Massachusetts Senator Charles] Sumner, and the rest of you [abolitionists], would upset our apple-cart altogether, if you had your way. . . . *We didn't go into the war to put down Slavery, but to put*

> *the flag back . . .*[201]

On August 22, 1862, Lincoln sent this public comment to Horace Greeley, owner of the New York *Tribune*:

> My paramount object in this struggle is to save the Union, and *it is not either to save or destroy slavery. If I could save the Union without freeing any slave, I would do it . . .*[202]

Impatient over misunderstandings on the topic, on August 15, 1864, Lincoln clarified his position yet again:

> *My enemies pretend I am now carrying on this war for the sole purpose of abolition. So long as I am President, it shall be carried on for the sole purpose of restoring the Union.*[203]

In 1862 Lincoln told Yankee newspaperman Horace Greeley that "my paramount object in this struggle is not to destroy slavery."

Indeed, it was so well-known that Lincoln was not interested in destroying slavery, that many Yankee Christian abolitionists refused to vote for him, or even support him, lest they commit a biblical sin. In 1862 one Northern abolitionist insisted

> *that the policy of the President, in prosecuting the war, was to restore the Union as it was, and that, if successful, it would leave slavery unabolished*; that therefore no Christian, in any way, could give aid to the [Lincoln] Administration in the prosecution of the war against the rebels, without sinning against God.[204]

Until the end of his life Lincoln never changed his mind about allowing slavery to continue indefinitely. All he asked was that the South return to the Union and pay its taxes. We know this because on February 3, 1865, just two months before his death, he attended the

Hampton Roads Peace Conference (the one and only time the imperious U.S. president agreed to meet with Confederate peace delegates), where he reiterated that his primary concern was "preserving the Union." And he would go to nearly any length to do so, he told the Southern representatives, Vice President Alexander H. Stephens, Senator Robert M. T. Hunter, and Assistant Secretary of War John A. Campbell.

These lengths included allowing the South to continue practicing slavery after it rejoined the U.S.[205] According to those present that day, Lincoln's

> . . . own opinion was, that as the [Emancipation] Proclamation was a *war measure*, and would have effect only from its being an exercise of the war power, *as soon as the war ceased, it would be inoperative for the future.* It would be held to apply only to such slaves as had come under its operation while it was in *active* exercise. This was his individual opinion . . .[206]

Attorney John Archibald Campbell of Georgia. As Confederate assistant secretary of war under Jefferson Davis, Campbell attended the Hampton Roads Peace Conference in February 1865, where Lincoln reemphasized that the Emancipation Proclamation was a "war measure," and thus would cease to be effective if and when the South laid down her arms and rejoined the Union.

Some Confederate military officers reported that Lincoln's "war measure," which he also revealingly called his "military emancipation," was actually deactivated in some parts of the South immediately after the War. On April 21, 1865, for example, just nine days after the Confederate surrender, Rebel Brigadier General Johnson Hagood, later governor of South Carolina, recorded the following in his journal. Still in the field with his men, he penned:

> [Confederate] General [Robert Frederick] Hoke [just] returned from Greensboro [North Carolina] with various items of news. *We are to return to the Union under the status of 1860, the rights of property to be respected, and property as defined in each State to be recognized.* All laws passed since 1860 to be submitted to the Supreme Court, *negro slavery to be untouched*, the troops to be marched to their respective State capitals, and there ground their arms; at the capital, too, each soldier is to take an oath of allegiance to the United States.[207]

Thus there were regions in the postwar South where the Emancipation Proclamation ceased to be active, just as Lincoln had promised when the South rejoined the Union. Why is this fact never discussed in our mainstream history books? Because it would expose one of the great lies of what I call "The Great Yankee Coverup"; namely that the War was *not* over or about slavery, preserving it or destroying it. For the South, at least, it was about constitutional rights and principles.[208]

In fact, the highest ranking military officers on *both* sides said as much. According to one of the South's most admired generals, Robert E. Lee:

> All the South has ever desired was that the Union as established by our forefathers should be preserved; and that the government as originally organized should be administered in purity and truth.[209]

The North's most famous general, Ulysses S. Grant, made these remarks on the topic of slavery and the cause of the War:

> The *sole object* of this war is to restore the union. Should I be convinced it has any other object, or that the government designs using its soldiers to execute the wishes of the Abolitionists, I pledge to you my honor as a man and a soldier, *I would resign my commission*

and carry my sword to the other side.[210]

The average Union soldier was of the exact same mind, as Confederate nurse Kate Cumming noted during the conflict:

> I have conversed with a number of [Yankee] prisoners [recovering in my hospital]; *they all express the same opinion as the others, that they dislike Lincoln and the abolitionists as much as we do,* but they are fighting for the Union.[211]

Midway through the War Yankee slave owner and Union General Ulysses S. Grant said that if he had been told that the North was fighting for abolition, he would have resigned and joined the Confederacy.

An everyday Confederate soldier serving in the Eastern Theater described the Southern Cause like this: "We struck for the God-given right of freedom and liberty . . ."[212] Countless more quotes like these could be given—from men and women in both the Confederacy and the Union.

The South as a whole summed up its feelings on the matter years later on February 8, 1898, at the Constitutional Convention of the State of Louisiana in New Orleans. Here, Dr. C. H. Tebault, Surgeon General of the United Confederate Veterans, proposed the following resolutions, laying down the true cause of the War as seen from the South's perspective:

> Resolved, That the following history of the last three amendments to the Constitution of the United States [the Thirteenth, Fourteenth, and Fifteenth], which was taken down by an experienced stenographer while being delivered in connection with a law lecture before the Tulane law class by a distinguished statesman, lawyer, and professor of the Tulane Law School, is deserving of preservation. The history is succinctly and briefly stated as follows:

"There were no more amendments until the civil war. Mr. Lincoln issued his [Emancipation] proclamation of 1863 as a war measure for the emancipation of the negroes. Nobody believed that he had the power to emancipate slaves, but he did it.

"As soon as we were subjugated, in 1865, they adopted what is called the *Thirteenth Amendment*. The adoption of this amendment ratified what had been done by Mr. Lincoln, and made constitutional what had been unconstitutional, and abolished slavery in the United States. That was the immediate result of our subjugation.

"In 1866 they adopted what is called the *Fourteenth Amendment* to the Constitution, which declares that all persons born or naturalized in the United States [are citizens], etc. Why did they do it? It was to override the celebrated Dred Scott decision. In that case a free negro had instituted a suit in the courts of the United States in Missouri against a citizen of another State, claiming that he was a free man. The question was whether a free negro was a citizen of the United States.

"The Supreme Court of the United States decided that a free negro was not and never had been regarded as a citizen either of the colonies or of the State previous to the formation of the United States; and, therefore, never could be a citizen of the United States. The Chief Justice [Roger B. Taney] went into the history of the African race in this country. Mr. [Charles] Sumner [of Massachusetts] and Mr. [William H.] Seward [of New York], in the Senate, denounced this decision. The North rose up in arms.

"The [newly created Liberal] Republican party, when it assembled [in 1860] to nominate a candidate, adopted as a part of its platform that the decision of the Supreme Court of the United States was not binding upon the country on such a question. And they would not recognize it.

"Mr. Lincoln was elected upon that

platform, and when he was elected the South thought that as the people of the North had claimed for half a century that the Supreme Court of the United States was the arbiter of this constitutional question, that as they had undertaken to repudiate this decision and elect a President on a platform which repudiated the authority of the United States Supreme Court, and that if there was ever a time to go to war that was the time, they went to war upon it. *That is the origin of the civil war.*

"It was not that Mr. Lincoln was elected upon a free-soil platform [as Yankee myth still claims], but a *platform which repudiated a decision of the United States Supreme Court on this subject in contradiction to which they had contended for up to that time, simply because it was in favor of the South.* Slaves were after that made citizens, in 1865-66.

"Then came the last amendment [*the Fifteenth*]: The right of citizens of the United States to vote shall not be denied, etc. They [the Yanks] thought they had secured the predominance of the [Liberal] Republican party in the South, because the negroes in many of the States were in the majority. Note: 'That the right shall not be abridged on account of race, color, or previous condition of servitude.'

"*The Supreme Court, when this article came up for consideration, said that this did not give anybody the right to vote.* It is true, negroes were citizens, but the State could discriminate as to what citizens should or should not vote for any other cause than race, color, or previous servitude. *This did not secure to the negroes the right to vote, but merely secured to them that they should not be discriminated against on account of race, color, or servitude.*"

Resolved, That this valuable and instructive legal history be spread on the journal of this convention.

The resolutions were adopted.[213]

The truth of the matter is that Lincoln's War would have taken place whether slavery existed or not. Why? Because *the real cause of the conflict was the Liberal Yankee's lust for power, money, and domination.*

WHAT YOU WERE TAUGHT: Not only is the Confederate Flag racist, but there's not even any reason to wave it anymore. The Civil War wiped out the North-South boundary, making us one democracy again, with one flag: the U.S. Flag.

THE FACTS: To begin with, we are not a democracy—a country ruled by the majority, as Left-wingers and socialists like to believe. We are a republic—a country ruled by law.

Second, though one of Liberal Lincoln's primary goals was to Northernize the leisurely, religious, agrarian South and turn her into a mirror image of the fast-paced, agnostic, industrial North, he and his socialistic South-hating descendants have been unsuccessful in the endeavor, despite the rise of the so-called "New South" and her scallywag and migrant Yankee population. This is because "Southerness" is a state of being, a lifestyle, a generational heritage that dates back over four centuries to the founding of Jamestown, Virginia, in 1607.

In 1862 Lincoln told Interior Department official T. J. Barnett that he planned to change the character of the War to one of "subjugation . . . The South is to be destroyed and replaced with new propositions and ideas," the president avowed determinedly.

Those progressive cultural cleansers, like Lincoln, who believe that Southerness, along with our flags, can be permanently wiped out, are fooling themselves. This was, after all, the purpose of "Reconstruction" (1865-1877), which, as history demonstrates, was a miserable failure. Victorian traditional Southerners were not about to let meddlesome Northerners come down South and transform their homeland into a playground for Yankees. Even many Yanks themselves realized the futility of trying to Northernize the South, correctly calling it "a fool's errand." One of these, Ohio carpetbagger Albion W. Tourgee, put it this way:

> *The North and the South are simply convenient names for two distinct, hostile, and irreconcilable ideas,—two civilizations they are sometimes called, especially at the South.* At the North there is somewhat more of intellectual arrogance; and we are apt to speak of the one as civilization, and of the other as a species of barbarism. *These two must always be in conflict until the one prevails, and the other falls.* To uproot the one, and plant the other in its stead, is not the work of a moment or a day. That was *our mistake.* We [Yankees] tried to superimpose the civilization, the idea of the North, upon the South at a moment's warning. *We presumed, that, by the suppression of rebellion, the Southern white man had become identical with the Caucasian of the North in thought and sentiment; and that the slave, by emancipation, had become a saint and a Solomon at once.* So we tried to build up communities there which should be identical in thought, sentiment, growth, and development, with those of the North. It was a fool's errand.[214]

In other words, the South will always be the South, the North will always be the North, the Confederate Flag will always be on display here in Dixie, and the well-marked, geographical and cultural dividing line between the two regions will never disappear. Anyone who thinks otherwise is either deluded or mad. Robert M. Howard had this to say on the topic:

> The so-called apostles of progress and commercialism tell us that the war forever obliterated Mason and Dixon's line, that there is now no North, no South, no East, nor West, but one grand brotherhood of peace, harmony and mutual good will between all sections of the government. *The assertion is an infamous lie; bayonets don't make brothers.* That line was a geographical one marked by degrees and minutes of the compass. *It is now traced by a line of innocent blood so wide and so deep that time can never bridge it nor can all of ocean and mountain billows ever submerge it.* There is no new South as claimed by those who fain would sacrifice our glorious heroic past upon the altar of Mammon [materialism]. *The old South still lives and will yet Phoenix-like rise from her ashes and become the greatest, best portion of the Government, developing the highest, purest civilization of the world.* Grand, glorious old South; God made your dirt, your men and your women!—made your history which will remain unsullied as long as Heaven's glittering dewdrops shall kiss the blushing rose to bring forth her spotless beauty and matchless fragrance.[215]

Southern patriot Mrs. Ridgely Brown with an eleven-star parade version of the Stars and Bars. In the early 1900s, according to Northern women, Southern women were far more "hostile," "resentful," and "unkind" toward former Yankee soldiers and the U.S. Flag than Southern men or even former Confederate soldiers.

As late as 1909, in an effort to halt Northernization and preserve the South's Southerness, many Southern schools were banning the flying of the U.S. Flag above their campuses. That year the following speech was given before the largely anti-South members of a Chicago branch of the G.A.R., or "Grand Army of the Republic," the forerunner of today's Sons of Union Veterans, a pro-North group dedicated to the memory of the Yankee soldier. Though she should not be, the female speaker is particularly shocked about the "hostile spirit," "unkind feelings," and "resentment" evinced by Southern *women* toward the North and the U.S. flag:

> *Startling charges* were laid before the Southside Association of G. A. R. this afternoon, when Mrs. Myrtle McGowan, National Patriotic Instructor of the Woman's Relief Corps, stated to the veterans at a picnic held in Jackson Park that *there were many schools in the South where the American flag is not allowed to fly over the public schools.* She said she had just returned from a trip to Andersonville, Georgia, and that the principal of the school at Bainbridge, Georgia, *not only refused the gift of a [U.S.] flag to his school, but had vehemently declared that not so long as he should be principal of the school would he allow the Stars and Stripes to be flown from the school mast.* But this is not the only schoolhouse in the South that has refused to fly the American flag, declared Mrs. McGowan. Time and time again we have offered flags to the schools in the Southern States and *have been told our [U.S.] flags are not wanted*, that their schools do not use flags. It is my duty to promote patriotic [that is, pro-North!] education, of course. It came into my province to inquire into these things. *You would be surprised at the hostile spirit felt toward the North in some of their hot-blood districts*; *I must confess that this unkind feeling is felt more among the [Southern] women than it is among even the old Confederate veterans themselves. These old veterans have passed upon old scores and are true and loyal citizens. It is the daughters and granddaughters of the veterans who stir up things and hold resentment still against the North.*[216]

If Northerners only knew that, if it were legally possible, millions of Southerners would still like to ban the U.S. Flag from being flown over their public schools!

Yes, the South is here to stay, and the presence of thousands of brightly colored Confederate Flags waving across Dixie—from trucks and cars, from house windows, from flag poles—is a testament to the fact. Indeed, Confederate Major Innes Randolph's song is still one of the most popular Southern anthems in Dixie, and always will be:

O, I'M A GOOD OLD REBEL
O, I'm a good old Rebel, now, that's just what I am;
For the "Fair Land of Freedom" I do not care a damn;
I'm glad I fit against it, I only wish we'd won;
And I don't want no pardon for anything I done.

I hates the Constitution, this Great Republic, too;
I hates the Freedman's Buro' in uniforms of blue;
I hates the nasty eagle, with all his brags and fuss;
The lyin', thievin' Yankees, I hates them wuss and wuss.

I hates the Yankee Nation and everything they do,
I hates the Declaration of Independence, too;
I hates the glorious Union—'Tis dripping with our blood—
I hate their striped banner, I fit it all I could.

I followed old Mars' Robert for four year, near about,
Got wounded in three places and starved at Point Lookout.
I cotch the roomatism a campin' in the snow.
I killed a chance o' Yankees, I'd like to kill some mo'.

Three hundred thousand Yankees is stiff in Southern dust;
We got three hundred thousand before they conquered us;
They died of Southern fever and Southern steel and shot;
I wish they was three million instead of what we got.

I can't take up my musket and fight 'em any mo',
But I ain't going to love 'em, now that is certain sho';
And I don't want no pardon for what I was and am,
I won't be reconstructed, and I don't care a damn.

At a Confederate Reunion in 1917 two aging Confederate veterans from Georgia proudly display their battle flag, torn, faded, shot through, and tattered from four years of life on the battlefield. A half century later their eyes are still filled with the spirit, determination, courage, and fire that animated the Southern Cause in 1861.

WHAT YOU WERE TAUGHT: Under the U.S. Flag Lincoln's military troops were racially integrated. Under the C.S. Flag, Davis' military troops were racially segregated.

THE FACTS: This is pure Yankee myth and a complete misrepresentation of authentic history.

Lincoln, a dyed-in-the-wool white separatist, was literally obsessed with the idea of American apartheid (the geographical segregation of the races), which is one reason why, when he was a member of the Illinois legislature, he asked for funds to expel all free blacks from the state. This was also the reason he became a manager of the Illinois chapter of the American Colonization Society, which one day hoped to make the entire U.S. "as white as New England."

This 19th-Century illustration reveals what no Liberal wants you to know: quite unlike the segregated units in the Union army, throughout Lincoln's War white and black Southerners fought side-by-side in integrated regiments. These two Rebel infantryman (a white soldier upper left, a black soldier center front) are surveilling a Union encampment in Virginia.

Not surprisingly, after finally allowing official black enlistment in 1863, Lincoln ordered all of his black troops to be racially segregated, led by white officers, and paid half that of white enlistees, infuriating both his black soldiery and Northern abolitionists.

Naturally, in the far more racially tolerant South, the birthplace of the American abolition movement, President Davis simply integrated blacks directly into his army and navy—usually without even listing their race on their enlistment forms. As in Southern society itself, *where segregation was nonexistent*, there was no need for a separation of the races among the South's military forces. Unlike in the racist North, Southern troops, both white *and* black, did not want it or require it.[217]

WHAT YOU WERE TAUGHT: There was no such thing as a "black Confederate soldier."

THE FACTS: The truth that you will never read in pro-North Civil War histories is that not only were there black Confederate soldiers, but far more blacks fought for the Confederacy than for the Union. The Union possessed about 3 million soldiers. Of these about 200,000 were black, 6 percent of the total. The Confederacy had about 1 million soldiers. Of these an estimated 300,000 were black, 30 percent of the total. Simply put: 30 percent of Davis' army was black, but only 6 percent of Lincoln's army was black.

Silas Chandler (right), photographed here with Confederate Sergeant Andrew M. Chandler (left), was just one of hundreds of thousands of blacks who served in the Confederate military. Enemies of the South would ban this photo if they could.

And these numbers are conservative if we use the definition of a "private soldier" as determined by German-American Union General August Valentine Kautz in 1864:

> In the fullest sense, *any man in the military service who receives pay, whether sworn in or not, is a soldier*, because he is subject to military law. Under this general head, laborers, teamsters, sutlers, chaplains, etc., are soldiers.[218]

Using Yankee General August V. Kautz's definition of a "private soldier," at least 1 million African-Americans officially served in the Confederate army and navy in some capacity, five times more than served in the Union military.

By Kautz's definition of a "private soldier," some 2 million Southerners fought for the Confederacy: 1 million whites and perhaps as many as 1 million blacks. As most of the 4 million blacks (3.5 million servants, 500,000 free) living in the South at the time of Lincoln's War remained loyal to the Confederacy, and as at least 1 million of these either worked in or fought in the Rebel army and navy in one role or another, Kautz' definition raises the percentage of Southern blacks who defended the Confederacy as real soldiers to as much as 50 percent of the total Confederate soldier population—five times or 500 percent more than fought for the Union.[219]

WHAT YOU WERE TAUGHT: Southerners claim there were black Confederate soldiers, but where's the proof to back it up?
THE FACTS: There is plenty of evidence for the existence of black Confederate soldiers, beginning with both the eyewitness testimonies of white Confederate soldiers—many who took their African-American servants into the War with them (men like General Nathan Bedford

Forrest)—and the accounts of numerous black Confederate soldiers themselves. As Yankees had the malicious habit of illegally and unnecessarily torching Southern courthouses (where thousands of records were kept), a great deal of this evidence has literally gone up in smoke.[220] Nonetheless, much remains.

One of the better known African-American Rebel soldiers was "Uncle" Mack Dabney,[221] who served for the entire War with "one of the best of the Tennessee regiments": the Third Tennessee Regiment under General John C. Brown. In 1913, nearly 50 years later, Uncle Mack could still vividly remember fighting in such battles as Vicksburg, Missionary Ridge, Chickamauga, and Franklin II. Surrendering on May 10, 1865, at Gainesville, Alabama, he was one of the last Confederate soldiers to lay down his arms. Known to white Southerners as a "faithful servant and negro soldier," of him Confederate Captain Andrew P. Gordon wrote:

"Uncle" Mack Dabney of Cornersville, Tennessee, black Confederate soldier.

> "Old Uncle" Mack Dabney was born and reared three miles south of this place (Cornersville, Tenn). His old master, the late J. O. Dabney, one of Giles County's best citizens, *sent five noble boys to the Confederate army and also Uncle Mack to cook and wait upon them, which he did well and faithfully to the end.* He was with us in all the marches from Fort Donelson to Atlanta and on to Gainesville, Ala., where we all surrendered. [After the War he] . . . came home with us and went to work to try to make an honest living for himself and family, and in all these long fifty years just passed I have never heard one single thing against Uncle Mack Dabney. *He is true and faithful to his family and the old [Confederate] soldier.* He is now, and has been for years, sexton at the Methodist church. All the young masters that he went out with have passed away, except one, Sam D. Dabney, who lives here.[222]

Two other black Confederates of note were William Johnson and "Uncle Ned" Hawkins, both who were written up in the September 1900 issue of *Confederate Veteran* magazine in a special section called "Tributes to Faithful Servants":

While the race problem creates serious concern for the welfare of both races and for the country, *it behooves the [white] Southern people, who are, and ever have been, their best friends [i.e., blacks], to be on the alert for opportunities to influence all classes for the general good. The* Veteran *improves its opportunities to pay tribute to faithful slaves, and it bespeaks the cooperation of our people in sending concise contributions to the honor of those who have ever been faithful.* Two illustrations are here given.

William Johnson (colored) lives by Nolensville, Tenn., near his birthplace. He was a slave, and the property of Mr. Ben Johnson, as was also his mother.

In 1862 a part of the army commanded by Gen. [Nathan Bedford] Forrest was stationed at Nolensville, and young William Johnson (fifteen years old) drove one of the wagons with provisions for the army. Capt. B. F. White, who had been assistant adjutant general on the staff of Gen. Forrest, had been detached, and was in command of a battery of artillery captured at Murfreesboro. Seeing the boy William, he liked him, and proposed to buy him. Mr. Johnson sold him to Capt. White for $1,200, and *he went with Capt. White in the regular field service.*

William Johnson of Nolensville, Tennessee, black Confederate soldier.

Soon after his purchase of William, the great battle of Murfreesboro was fought; and while on the battlefield, during the battle, Capt. White was attacked suddenly with inflammatory rheumatism. His servant William was with the wagon train, and did not reach him until the next day. The day following, the Confederates retreated, and the Federals, who also had been falling back, retraced their movements and occupied the area in which

> Capt White was left in that painful and awful predicament, attended only by his servant William. For three months Capt. White was guarded by the Federals in a house on Thomas Butler's plantation, near the village of Salem. One bitter cold night the [Yankee] guard went to his camp some distance away, when the Captain asked William if he couldn't get him away from there. It was soon arranged for him to take a spring wagon and a broken-down army horse on the Butler farm. He put his charge in the wagon, and by a circuitous route got away without apprehension. Late in the night the horse so nearly gave out that William walked in water and ice over his boots, and would lift the wheels of the vehicle out of the mire, and moved on until they were safe in the Confederate lines. A better horse was procured, and the afflicted officer was taken to Shelbyville, and from there he was permitted to visit Mobile, where he recuperated, William of course going with him. This faithful servant remained with Capt. White, who went back into field service, but his health failed, and when his constitution gave down he was put on post duty, and at the end of the war he was paroled at Albany, Ga. He brought William back to Nashville, leaving him with an uncle when he left to reside in Memphis. He afterwards moved to California. They never met again.
>
> When the notice of Capt. White's death appeared in the December *Veteran* for 1899, *William saw it, and asked to pay tribute to his memory. That desire becomes the occasion for the Veteran to pay just and well-merited tribute to William Johnson.*
>
> . . . William has lived all these years in the neighborhood of his birthplace, and *has maintained a reputation as an honest, upright man—such as will ever have the devoted friendship of the white people, and who will prove it if later in life misfortunes should render him unable to support himself.*
>
> During the time of Capt. White's confinement in the Federal lines he allowed William to carry three young ladies through the lines to Shelbyville. They were Misses Sallie J. McLean and Lizzie and Julia Lillard. After his return from that trip, Capt. White gave him [William] permission to visit his mother, at Nolensville, before *they escaped to the South*.[223]

The second "faithful" Confederate servant mentioned in this article, "Uncle Ned" Hawkins, is described like this:

> Comrade C. L. Kalmbach, of Cobb's Legion (Ga), procured through Samuel L. Richards, a nephew of Uncle Ned's mistress, a sketch of his labors in the [eighteen] sixties. The scouts

generally of the Northern Virginia army knew him, and will gladly recognize his kindly face after these many years. The data furnished is as follows:

"Uncle Ned" Hawkins of Culpepper County, Virginia, black Confederate soldier.

Living on the banks of the Rappahannock, in the county of Culpeper, is a venerable old colored man, known by all near him as "Uncle Ned." *His fidelity to his old [white] mistress, his loyalty to the Confederacy, and his devotion to our soldiers were truly remarkable. He risked his liberty and his life more than once for the safety of our citizens and soldiers.* On one occasion some of our scouts called at the house of his mistress—*knowing they were always welcome there*—and while she and her sister, assisted, of course, by "Uncle Ned," were busily engaged in preparing for them a much-needed breakfast, the dreaded cry was heard: "The Yankees are coming!" They were guided by *the ever-faithful* "Uncle Ned" to the pines near by, and he returned to the house. After the Yankees left, he took the breakfast in an old haversack, with a few ears of corn on top, and told our [Confederate] scouts if all was right when approaching them he would raise his hat and scratch his head, and if not, his hat would remain on his head: and should he meet the Yanks, with those ears of corn, his excuse would be that he was hunting his sheep. *Many, many such acts he did for the safety of our soldiers, and now he and his aged companion are struggling hard for a living; and—O that some brave Confederate could assist them in their good old age!* He is certainly worthy of notice.[224]

As I am a Tennessean let us continue with a few more examples of notable African-American Confederate soldiers from the Volunteer State. The obituary of Bill King, of the Twentieth Tennessee Infantry, was written up in the June 1910 issue of *Confederate Veteran*:

> BILL KING, A BLACK CONFEDERATE—Bill King is dead. Members of the 20th Tennessee (Battle's) Regiment will remember him. *No more faithful negro ever served a cause than did Bill King serve the boys of the old 20th. He went into the war as the body servant of the sons of Mr. Jack King, of Nolensville, Tenn., but he became the faithful servant of every member of this regiment. He went with the brave boys into the heat of battle, he nursed and cared for them in sickness, and assisted in burying the dead on the battlefields. He was as true to the cause of the South as any member of that gallant band* under the intrepid leadership of Col. Joel A. Battle. In Shiloh's bloody affray Colonel Battle was captured, and the leadership fell to young Col. Thomas Benton Smith.
>
> When one of his young masters was killed in battle, *Bill was one of the escort which tenderly bore the body back to his mother and father*.
>
> *Since the war Bill King had been classed as an unreconstructed Rebel. He was a true and loyal Confederate until his death. He affiliated with old soldiers, attending every gathering within his reach. He was a member of Troop A, Confederate Veterans, Nashville. He lived on his old master's farm, near Nolensville*; but he died in Nashville at Vanderbilt Medical College, where he underwent a serious surgical operation.
>
> Mr. William Waller, an undertaker, took the body back to Nolensville for burial. *The body was clad in the Confederate uniform which he had during the past few years worn on all reunion occasions, according to his request*. The funeral service was conducted in Mount Olivet Methodist Church (white) by the pastor, Rev. H. W. Carter.
>
> Bill King was seventy-three years old, and leaves a wife and ten or eleven children. He was a Baptist; but as there is no church of this denomination near his home, his friends decided to have the funeral in the Methodist church. He was buried in the Nolensville Cemetery.[225]

Another black Confederate Tennessee soldier was "Uncle" Jerry Perkins of the Thirty-First Tennessee Infantry. The September 1903 issue of *Confederate Veteran* provides the following information on him:

"Uncle" Jerry Perkins of Tennessee, black Confederate soldier.

Charles Perkins enlisted at Brownsville, Tenn., under Capt. H. S. Bradford, who was afterwards Col. Bradford, of the 31st Tennessee Infantry. He was killed in the battle near Atlanta July 22, 1864. The boy Jerry went with him as a body servant. Before leaving, Charley's mother told Jerry that he must bring his "Marse Charley" back to her, and he promised that he would do it; that he would take him back alive or dead.

On that fateful July 22 young Perkins was killed; and when the regiment fell back to bivouac for the night, Jerry was alarmed not to see Marse Charley, and, upon being told that he was dead, said, "Here's your supper. I'm going to find Marse Charley," and away in the darkness he went.

In a short while he returned, carrying the dead body of his young master on his back. He carried it a mile or so farther to a farmhouse, got some plank, borrowed a saw, hatchet, and nails, made a box, dug a grave, and buried him in the farmer's yard. He walked from Atlanta to Brownsville, Tenn., and reported the sad news. He was supplied with a farm wagon and a metallic coffin, went back to Georgia, disinterred the body of Charley Perkins, and hauled it home to Brownsville.

Jerry is a favorite with the Hiram S. Bradford Bivouac, and attends all of their [Confederate] Reunions. The foregoing data comes from J. W. McClish, of Brownsville.[226]

From the same issue comes this next story of a black boy named Jim Battery, whose time with the Confederate army is as revealing as it is educational. From it the attitude of the typical Southern black toward both the Confederates and the Yankees is made apparent:

> CASE OF A NEGRO BOY DURING THE WAR. By W. H. Strange. Gift, Tenn., June 23, 1900: "While at Holly Springs [Earl] Vandorn's [Van Dorn] Cavalry went to the enemy's rear and captured that place one morning about daybreak. A negro boy was making his way out, and, being dressed in blue and in the early twilight, I took him to be a Federal and halted him. After finding that he was only a negro boy, *I would have let him go on, but he wanted to go with me for protection [from Union soldiers]* and, picking up an old mule, I put him on it and let him go with us. He said he was thirteen years old and was waiting on an artillery officer, Maj. Mudd, I think. The boy said he lived near Huntsville, Ala., and went with the Federals from there to Memphis.
>
> "After taking Holly Springs, our command continued to go north, and, crossing Little Hatchie at Davis's Bridge, we had quite a skirmish with the enemy in getting across the river. The lame horse crowd being in the rear and one of my neighbor friends being in the crowd, I let the little negro stay with him. They got cut off from the command and went home, in Tipton County, Tenn., and the boy went with him. After getting home, the boy went to my father's and remained there during the war. *Although the Federals were frequently at my father's after that, he never wanted to go with them, but stayed at home and would help to hide the [live] stock.* On one occasion he got one horse back from them after they had it in their possession. *After I got home from the war, he lived with me for several years.*
>
> "He was a bright boy, and *I taught him to read and write.* He took a great interest in learning and progressed rapidly, finally *becoming a Methodist preacher.* He got a country circuit, and after three or four years was made presiding elder. Since that time I have not known much of him, but think he has quit preaching and *is running a large farm in Arkansas. He was always Democratic [the Conservative Party of that day] in politics, and would sometimes take an active part in trying to get the negroes to vote for some of his white friends.* He has always gone by the name of Jim Battery. I do not remember who he belonged to before emancipation."[227]

One of the more illuminating stories of a black Confederate concerns Jerry W. May:

An interesting figure at the Louisville reunion was Jerry W. May, colored. Jerry is a mail carrier at Macon, and has been in the service for over twenty years. *Each year when the time for the Confederate Reunion rolls around Jerry asks for his vacation and accompanies Camp Smith to the rendezvous of the old Confederates. This is the fourteenth reunion he has attended.*

Jerry W. May of Macon, Georgia, black Confederate soldier.

During the war Jerry was the body servant of William Wynn, of Georgia, who enlisted and served throughout the long contest as a private. His master [Wynn] was a member of the 7th Georgia Regiment of Harrison's Brigade. After the war, his master, who had lost everything by the ravages of the Federal army, moved to Prescott, Ark, leaving Jerry in Macon. A few years later he died, and his widow was left alone with nothing on which she might rely for a support. *Jerry began the task of securing a pension for her, and after several years of hard work he was successful. Through his efforts she was enabled to live comfortably.*

The *Veteran* wrote to Jerry in regard to the above, and he responded promptly, stating:

> "My old master, William Wynn, was born and reared in Monroe County, Ga. He enlisted in the 7th Georgia Regiment, as stated, Company D. He took me as body servant; and after the war, everything was lost to him—even I myself came near being lost to him, but not quite. After the war, he moved to Prescott, Ark, and began farming; but he was quite old

> and feeble, so he could do but little at it. Later he wrote me that he could get a pension under the Arkansas laws, but he was too feeble mentally and physically, and he wanted me to do it for him. *I replied that I would do anything in my power on earth for him and his wife as long as they lived. I went at once to [U.S.] Gen. C. M. Wyley, the Ordinary for Bibb County, got application blanks, took one to every member of the old company that I could find, got them signed with affidavits before proper officers, made oath myself, and had seals put on where seals could be found. Sad but true, he died just before I got the papers ready. I then went back and got other blanks, and did the same work for his widow. I paid every cent of money necessary without any cost to her. I sent all the papers for him and her both, and the committee put her on the pension list. She wrote me her sincere thanks for what I did, and said she was all the more grateful because I had been one of her slaves.*"[228]

WHAT YOU WERE TAUGHT: Southern slaves hated the Confederacy and were happy the Civil War came, so that they could be free to escape North into the welcoming arms of the non-racist Yankee.
THE FACTS: We have already disproven every one of these absurd statements. But as there is nothing like a stone monument to offer up as solid evidence, let us examine the example of a Southern memorial set up by whites in honor of "faithful servants." In 1899 it was described in the following manner:

> Four steps of masonry support a marble pedestal, on which is a square shaft for inscriptions.
>
> On the south side is inscribed:
>
> 1860
> Dedicated to
> the faithful Slaves
> who, loyal to a sacred trust,
> toiled for the support
> of the army with matchless
> devotion, and with sterling

fidelity guarded our defenseless
homes, women, and children during
the struggle for the principles
of our Confederate States of America.
1865

On the east side, in a receding panel, appears a log under a shade tree, whereon rests one of the faithful slaves, his hat on the ground, shirt open in front, with a scythe and at rest. Before him are shocks of grain.

On the north side is the following:

> "1895. Erected by Samuel E. White, in grateful memory of earlier days, with the approval of the Jefferson Davis Memorial Association."

There are added names of some faithful slaves.

On the west side, in a receding panel, appears a farmer's mansion, and on the front steps sits an "old black mammy" with a white child in her arms, both of whom are in loving embrace, while in the foreground are the baby's wagon and other playthings. Above this square shaft is a tall obelisk of pure white marble.[229]

A Confederate reunion of the men of General Nathan Bedford Forrest's Escort, about 1890. One of the most dangerous and successful military outfits ever organized, this specialized racially integrated cavalry unit was both respected and feared by Yankee troops. Near the center a woman is holding up a large Confederate Third National Flag with the words "Forrest's Escort" on it. Three of Forrest's 65 black Confederate soldiers are in attendance. No signs of racism here.

A photo of a section of the famous Confederate Memorial at Arlington National Cemetery that has been banished from our mainstream history books. Why? Because it shows an armed black Confederate soldier (center) proudly marching off to war, side by side with his white Southern brothers. Proof in stone of the African-American Confederate!

The truth is that despite the North's effort to destroy, suppress, and expunge them, thousands of records of black Confederate soldiers have been preserved. These include courageous African-American servicemen like Joe Warren, Fielding Rennolds, Henry Love, Hiram Kendall, and Dan Humphreys, all of the Fifth Tennessee Infantry.

Then there was Monroe Gooch of Davidson County, Tennessee, who served in the Forty-Fifth Tennessee Infantry under Confederate Captain William Sykes. On one occasion during the War Gooch was given a pass to return home, where he could have remained had he so desired. But being true to the Confederate Cause, he returned to his infantry until the final surrender in 1865. After the conflict it is said that Gooch was proud to be a Confederate veteran.

Confederate Private Louis Napoleon Nelson, the only known black chaplain in the Rebel army, fought in numerous battles and attended 39 Confederate reunions after the War. At his funeral in 1934 his coffin was draped with a Confederate Battle Flag.

I have a personal connection to one black Rebel soldier: Private Louis Napoleon Nelson, whose grandson, African-American educator Nelson W. Winbush, M.Ed., wrote the foreword to my bestselling book, *Everything You Were Taught About the Civil War is Wrong, Ask a Southerner!* Private Nelson was born March 15, 1847, and served with Company M, Seventh Cavalry, Tennessee, for the entire duration of the War. He worked in various capacities, from body guard and cook, to forager and armed soldier. He fought in some of the War's most momentous battles, including Shiloh, Lookout Mountain, Brice's Cross Roads, and Vicksburg.[230]

Like nearly all Southern "slaves," Nelson returned to live with his former white owners (in his case, the Oldhams in Lauderdale County, Tennessee) after the War. The only known official black chaplain in the C.S. army, he belonged to the John Sutherland Camp, United Confederate Veterans, and attended 39 postwar Confederate reunions proudly dressed in his uniform and medals. He died on August 25, 1934, at the age of 87, a true Confederate-American patriot.[231]

Along with an abundance of military records and photos of black Confederates dating back to the War itself, entire books have been written on this subject. Do we really need to continually go over this ground just to placate South-haters? At this point only mean-spiritedness and ignorance can account for individuals who are unaware of the reality of the Confederacy's 1 million African-American soldiers.

WHAT YOU WERE TAUGHT: The South would never have abolished slavery had it not been for Lincoln and the Civil War.
THE FACTS: Wrong on all counts. Beginning in the 1600s we have numerous records of Southerners seeking the abolition of both the slave trade and slavery. Indeed, as we have discussed, the American abolition movement got its start in the South, in Virginia, to be exact, where, in 1655, the first known voluntary emancipation in the American colonies took place. In the 1700s some of the more famous of the Virginia abolitionists were George Washington, Thomas Jefferson, James Madison, and George Mason. According to a Virginian speaking in 1860, Virginia's

> House of Burgesses used to try to stop the bringing in of negroes, and . . . the colony was always appealing to the king [George of Britain] against the traffic. . . . in 1778, two years after Virginia declared her independence, she passed the statute prohibiting the slave trade. . . . *she was the first country in the civilized world to stop the trade*—passed her statute thirty years before England! . . . . *all of the great Revolutionary men hated slavery and worked for the emancipation of the negroes who were here . . .*[232]

The following comments, written in 1910, are by former Confederate officer Randolph H. McKim:

> Let me here state a fact of capital importance in this connection: *the sentiment in favor of emancipation was rapidly spreading in the South in the first quarter of the nineteenth century.* [President Woodrow] Wilson acknowledges that *"there was no avowed advocate of slavery" in Virginia at that time.* . . . So strong was the sentiment in

Virginia for emancipation that, in the year 1832, one branch of her Legislature came near passing a law for the gradual abolition of slavery; and I was assured in 1860 by Col. Thomas Jefferson Randolph, who was himself a member of the Legislature that year, that emancipation would certainly have been carried at the next session but for the reaction created by the fanatical agitation of the subject by the Abolitionists, led by [Yankee busybody] Wm. Lloyd Garrison. Though emancipation was defeated at that time by a small vote, yet the Legislature passed a resolution postponing the consideration of the subject till public opinion had further developed. The *Richmond Whig* of March 6, 1832, said: "The great mass of Virginia herself rejoices that the slavery question has been taken up by the Legislature, that her legislators are grappling with the monster," etc. A Massachusetts writer, George Lunt, says: "*The States of Virginia, Kentucky, and Tennessee were engaged in practical movements for the gradual emancipation of their slaves. This movement continued until it was arrested by the aggressions of the Abolitionists.*"

Of the nearly 150 American abolition societies founded by Yankee Benjamin Lundy before 1827, the majority of them were located in the South, a fact never mentioned in our Northern-slanted history books.

These facts are beyond dispute: 1. That *from 1789 down to 1837 slavery was almost universally considered in the South a great evil*; 2. That public opinion there underwent a revolution on this subject in the decade 1832-1842. What produced this fateful change of sentiment? Not the invention of the cotton gin, for that took place in 1793. No, but the abolition crusade launched by Wm. Lloyd Garrison, Jan. 1, 1831. Its violence and virulence produced the

> result that might have been expected. It angered the South. It stifled discussion. It checked the movement toward emancipation. It forced a more stringent policy toward the slave. The publication of Garrison's "*Liberator*" was followed, seven months later, by Nat Turner's negro insurrection in which sixty-one persons—men, women, and children—were murdered in the night. President [Andrew] Jackson, in his message of 1835, called attention to the [Yankees'] transmission through the mails "of inflammatory appeals addressed to the passions of the slaves, in prints and various sorts of publications, calculated to stimulate them to insurrection, and to produce all the horrors of a servile war."
>
> *The conclusion is irresistible that but for that violent and fanatical movement slavery would have been peaceably abolished in Virginia, and then in other Southern States [decades before Lincoln took office].*[233]

As we have seen, by the early 1800s the American abolition movement was at its peak across Dixie. Some 143 abolition societies had been set up across the U.S. before 1827 by Northern abolitionist Benjamin Lundy. Of these, 103, three-fourths of the total membership, were in the Southern states.[234] North Carolina, as one example, had a number of well-known "forceful" antislavery leaders, such as Benjamin Sherwood Hedrick and Daniel Reaves Goodlow. And in South Carolina the famed Quaker sisters Sarah and Angelina Grimké were just two among millions of Southerners fighting for the cause of abolition. The Southern abolition movement involved so many Southerners, so many Southern states, and covered such a large span of time, that the latter Grimké sister wrote an entire book on the subject.

Reverend Dyer Burgess, another well-known Southern abolitionist that the anti-South movement does not like to talk about.

We have already named some of the other esteemed Southerners who came out against the "peculiar institution," for example: James G. Birney, John Rankin, James A. Thome, Dyer Burgess, David Nelson, Samuel Doak, James H. Dickey, James Gilliland, Samuel Crothers, James Lemen,

Edward Coles, Christopher Gadsden, William T. Allan, Bishop William Meade, William Ladd, Nathaniel Macon, Gideon Blackburn, and George Bourne, the cofounder of the "American Anti-Slavery Society" in 1833. On August 14, 1776, South Carolina rice planter and slave owner Henry Laurens wrote the following to his son John, who was also antislavery:

> You know, my dear son, *I abhor slavery. I was born in a country in which slavery had been established by British Parliaments and the laws of the country for ages before my existence.* I found the Christian religion and slavery growing under the same authority and cultivation. I nevertheless dislike it. In former days there was no combating the prejudices of men, supported by interest [money]. The day I hope is approaching when from principles of gratitude and justice every man will strive to be foremost in complying with the golden rule. £20,000 sterling [about £2.5 million, or $4 million in today's currency] would my negroes produce if sold at auction tomorrow. *I am not the man who enslaved them; they are indebted to Englishmen for that favour. Nevertheless I am devising means for manumitting many of them and for cutting off the entail of slavery.*[235]

What our Yankee biased history books do not teach is that from the 1600s on, every year thousands of Southerners simply emancipated their slaves, all without any prompting from the supercilious North. Among them were slave owners like Nathan Bedford Forrest, who liberated his slaves even before Lincoln's War in 1861, and Robert E. Lee, who freed his wife's servants before the Emancipation Proclamation was issued in 1863. Unlike in the North, there were no laws against manumission in Dixie, so Southerners gave full vent to their humanitarian instincts.

Southerner U.S. President Thomas Jefferson, one of America's earliest and most fervent abolitionists.

Thomas Jefferson had been working on Southern abolition from his first days as an American statesmen, and was responsible for prohibiting the

American slave trade after January 1, 1808 (tragically, Yankee slave traders ignored the ban, continuing to sail to Africa right into the Civil War period). Indeed, it was Jefferson's criticism of Britain for imposing slavery on the 13 original American colonies that helped instigate the American Revolution, which in turn led directly to the first "Confederate States of America"—as the U.S.A. was known in the 1700s and 1800s.

The South was still grappling with precisely how to initiate full abolition, or what Jefferson aptly compared to holding "a wolf behind the ears," when Lincoln tricked the South into firing the first shot of his war at the Battle of Fort Sumter on April 12, 1861.[236]

WHAT YOU WERE TAUGHT: The American South was the first region in the West to practice slavery and the last to try and abolish it.
THE FACTS: The opposite is true. In 1749 Georgia became the last of the 13 British-American colonies to legalize slavery. This was long after every Western nation had already adopted the institution. Seventeen years earlier, in 1732, Georgia became the first colony to place a prohibition against commercial trafficking in slaves into her state constitution, making the American South the first Western region to move toward abolition.

Around the same time, dozens of abolition societies began to spring up across Dixie, with Virginia leading the way in white America's tireless attempt to end slavery—which began in the Dominion State with, as noted, the first voluntary emancipation in 1655.[237]

WHAT YOU WERE TAUGHT: The American South has always been more racist than the North, which is why it is right to hate the Confederate Flag.
THE FACTS: If that is the basis for your dislike, you should be focusing it on the U.S. Flag, not the C.S. Flag. Scores of eyewitness accounts, both domestic and foreign, reveal that the Old North far surpassed the Old South when it came to racial intolerance. As early as 1831 individuals like French aristocrat Alexis de Tocqueville, who toured the South and the North that year, noticed that Southerners were "much more tolerant and compassionate" toward blacks than Northerners. This is why, while visiting America in the 1850s, Englishman Sir Charles Lyell observed that the Southern states justifiably "make louder professions

French historian, writer, and traveler Alexis de Tocqueville was only one of many early visitors to the U.S. who noted that white racism was much worse in the North than in the "more tolerant and compassionate" South.

than the Northerners of democratic principles and love of equality."

The racial discrepancy between the South and the North was also remarked on by British journalists, even in the middle of the Civil War. In 1862 the *North British Review* noted that in the North, "where slavers are fitted out by scores . . . free Negroes are treated like lepers." This was the same year Union President Lincoln issued his Preliminary Emancipation Proclamation, which, of course, called for continued efforts to deport all freed blacks out of the U.S.

After his travels across the U.S. in 1831 and 1832, Tocqueville summed up his observations this way:

> Whosoever has inhabited the United States must have perceived that in those parts of the Union in which the negroes are no longer slaves, they have in no wise drawn nearer to the whites. On the contrary, *the prejudice of the race appears to be stronger in the States which have abolished slavery than in those where it still exists; and nowhere is it so intolerant as in those States where servitude never has been known.*[238]

Thousands more eyewitness testimonials like Tocqueville's could be given. They would fill many volumes.

WHAT YOU WERE TAUGHT: All American slave owners were white Southerners.

THE FACTS: Liberal historians carefully hide the fact from the general public, but the reality is that *there were tens of thousands of black slave owners in early America*, most who were not counted in the U.S. Census (viewing them as unimportant—for under the Constitution they were not considered American citizens—Census takers were prone to vastly underreporting blacks, free and enslaved). Additionally, some black slaveholders abused and whipped their African servants, another fact that you will seldom find in pro-North, anti-South history books.

In 1830 some 3,700 free Southern blacks owned nearly 12,000 black slaves, an average of almost four slaves a piece. That same year in the Deep South alone nearly 8,000 slaves were owned by some 1,500 black slave owners (about five slaves apiece). In Charleston, South Carolina, as another example, between the years 1820 and 1840, 75 percent of the city's free blacks owned slaves. Furthermore, *25 percent of all free American blacks owned slaves, South and North*.

It is important to remember that in 1861 the South's 300,000 white slave owners made up only 1 percent of the total U.S. white population of 30 million people. Thus, while only one Southern white out of every 300,000 owned slaves (1 percent), one Southern black out of every four owned slaves (25 percent). In other words, far more Southern blacks owned black (and sometimes white) slaves than Southern whites did: 25 percent compared to 1 percent.

In early America 25 percent of all free blacks owned slaves, a statistic our Liberal educators refuse to teach our children. This affluent African-American slaveholder in South Carolina owned both black *and* white slaves.

Most Southern black slave owners were not only proslavery, they were also pro-South, supporting the Confederate Cause during Lincoln's War as fervently as any white Southerner did. At church each Sunday thousands of blacks would pray for those blacks, both their own slaves and their free friends, who wore the Rebel uniform. Their supplications were simple: they asked God to help all African-American Confederates kill as many Yankees as possible, then return home safely. Often, as was true all across the racially tolerant Old South, blacks themselves would lead the white congregations in prayer. "There was not even a shadow of an objection," Alabamian Parthenia A. Hague wrote in 1888, "to the negro slave's occupying the pulpit."[239]

In 1887 Reverend John William Jones, a chaplain in General Robert E. Lee's army, spoke of

> the kindly relations and sympathies between master and slave which

> none can appreciate who did not witness them, but *illustrations of which could be indefinitely multiplied.*[240]

The following incident is but one of them:

> A Texas planter having responded in person to one of the late calls of [Confederate] Colonel [Earl] Van Dorn for service in the West, his negroes were left in the care of the overseer. One night, at a late hour, the overseer was aroused by a noise at the "quarter." He immediately arose and went in the direction of the noise far enough to ascertain that it was the voice of prayer. Drawing still nearer, he discovered that the prayer-meeting was a special occasion, for the benefit of the master who had "gone to the wars." Earnest prayers ascended that his health and life might be spared, and that God would grant him a safe return.[241]

The Metoyers, a black pro-slavery Louisiana family, owned the equivalent of $20 million in slaves in today's currency.

Wealthy blacks bought, sold, and exploited black slaves for profit, just as white slave owners did. The well-known Anna Kingsley, who began life—as was nearly always the case—as a slave in her native Africa, ended up in what is now Jacksonville, Florida, where she became one of early America's many black plantation owners and slaveholders.

Some, like the African-American Metoyers, an anti-abolition family from Louisiana, owned huge numbers of black slaves; in their case, at least 400. At about $1,500 a piece, their servants were worth a total of $600,000, or $20 million in today's currency. This made the Metoyers among the wealthiest people in the U.S., black or white, then or now. Louisiana's all-black Confederate army unit, the Augustin Guards, was named after the family patriarch, Augustin Metoyer.

Black slavery was not just common among blacks. It was also found among America's 19th-Century Indians, who bought and sold African chattel right alongside black and white slave owners. In fact, one of the many reasons so many Native-Americans sided with the Southern Confederacy was that she promised to enforce the fugitive slave law in Indian Territory, making it a legal requirement to return runaway slaves to their original Indian owners.

While the average white slaveholder owned five or less slaves (often only one or two), the average red slaveholder owned six. One Choctaw slaver owned 227. Again, it was *non-white* slave owners who individually owned the most slaves, not whites.

Cheyenne Chief Wolf Robe. Nearly 100 percent of America's aboriginal peoples engaged in one or more forms of slavery, including the Cheyenne.

Slavery was practiced right up until the 1950s by some Native-American tribes, principally the Haida and the Tlingit peoples of the Pacific Northwest. Among the Haida, slaves performed all of the menial labor, ate only food scraps, were refused health care, and could not own property. And since there were no laws of protection, Haida slaves could be purchased, sold, beaten, molested, and even murdered at the whim of their owners. This is *true slavery*, the exact opposite of the much milder *servitude* experienced by Africans in the Old American South.[242]

Native-Americans have been practicing slavery on one another for untold millennia. After the arrival of Europeans in the 1500s, they enslaved whites as well. This white woman has just been captured by a band of Indians. She will be forced to live under one of the world's most brutal forms of bondage, and will most likely die soon from mistreatment or will eventually be ritually sacrificed.

WHAT YOU WERE TAUGHT: The South would have never gotten rid of slavery if it hadn't been for the Civil War.

THE FACTS: In January 1865 Confederate Secretary of State Judah P. Benjamin ordered Confederate commissioner Duncan F. Kenner to England to announce the Confederacy's commitment to full emancipation. This was nearly a year before the U.S. issued the Thirteenth Amendment (on December 6) banning slavery throughout the nation.

Let us note here that, contrary to Yankee mythology, the Northern states *never* officially abolished slavery. Instead they slowly and methodically destroyed the institution through a long drawn out process known as "gradual emancipation," taking over 100 years to complete the process, which finally ended in 1865 with, as noted, the ratification of the Thirteenth Amendment. Tragically, the North refused to grant the South the same privilege, and instead demanded "immediate, complete, and uncompensated abolition," an impossibility at the time.

The Confederacy's motion to abolish slavery across the South had the complete support of the Southern populace, of course, the very people who had inaugurated the American abolition movement in the early 1700s. One of the better known of the great Southern abolitionists was the celebrated antislavery Virginian, Robert E. Lee, who, on December 27, 1856—five years before Lincoln's War—made this comment about the "peculiar institution":

> There are few, I believe, in this enlightened age, but what will acknowledge that *slavery as an institution is a moral and political evil in any country.*[243]

Later, during the War, like *all* Southern civilians and Confederate soldiers and officers, Lee supported the idea of immediate abolition and black enlistment, a fact purposefully left out of our history books.[244]

WHAT YOU WERE TAUGHT: The Confederate military was intentionally all white. So the Confederacy was racist, which is why we should detest the Confederate Flag.

THE FACTS: Yes, we have been taught that the Confederate armies were "100 percent white," this due to the "boundless white racism" that

You are not supposed to know that uniformed, armed, and highly trained black Confederate soldiers, like these two, made up as much as 50 percent of the Rebel military force, proudly serving in a variety of capacities, from hostlers, nurses, and musicians, to spies, infantrymen, and sharpshooters.

existed across the Old South. We have already seen, however, that the integrated South was far less racist than the segregated North, so it is obvious that this charge cannot be true. The South's army and navy, in fact, reflected the region's citizenship, which was made up of every race, creed, and nationality.

Though—thanks to the vicious Yankee custom of burning down Southern courthouses—exact statistics are impossible to come by, Southern historians have determined that the following numbers are roughly accurate. In descending numerical order the Confederate army and navy was composed of about 1 million European-Americans, 300,000 to 1 million African-Americans, 70,000 Native-Americans, 60,000 Latin-Americans, 50,000 foreigners, 12,000 Jewish-Americans, and 10,000 Asian-Americans.

There were so many black Rebels on the battlefield that Northern soldiers, most who were overtly racist, were dumbstruck at the sight. And their fear was justified: Confederate blacks were known to be ferocious fighters, fearless soldiers, and crack shots. Indeed, the first Northerner killed in the War, Yankee Major Theodore Winthrop of the Seventh Regiment, New York State Militia, was brought down by a black Confederate sharpshooter at the Battle of Bethel Church, June 10, 1861.

Some 3,000 blacks served in Confederate General Thomas "Stonewall" Jackson's army alone.

Confederate General Gilbert M.

Sorrel, who served under Longstreet, mentioned blacks serving with his troops.[245] General Stonewall Jackson's army alone contained some 3,000 black soldiers. Clad "in all kinds of uniforms," and armed with "rifles, muskets, sabres, bowie-knives, dirks, etc.," to the shocked Yankee soldiers they were "manifestly an integral portion of the Southern Confederacy." On March 1, 1865, Union Colonel John G. Parkhurst sent a battlefield dispatch to Union General William D. Whipple, reporting that: "The rebel authorities are enrolling negroes in Mississippi preparatory to *putting them into service*."[246]

Sixty-blacks, 45 of them from his own plantations, served under Confederate General Nathan Bedford Forrest. He hand-picked seven of them to be his armed guards. Of his African-American soldiers Forrest later said: "These boys stayed with me, drove my teams, and better Confederates did not live."

If more proof of the black Confederate soldier is needed we need look no further than a letter written by former Northern slave Frederick Douglass to Lincoln in 1862. In it the black civil rights leader uses the example of the overwhelming number of blacks in the Confederate army to urge the president to allow blacks to officially enlist in the Union army (Lincoln had steadfastly refused up until that time). Wrote Douglass:

> *There are at the present moment, many colored men in the Confederate Army doing duty not only as cooks, servants and laborers, but as real soldiers, having muskets on their shoulders and bullets in their pockets, ready to shoot down loyal [Yankee] troops, and do all that soldiers may do to destroy the Federal government and build up that of the traitors and rebels.* There were such soldiers at Manassas, and they are probably there still. There is a negro in the [Confederate] army as well as in the fence, and our Government is likely to find it out before the war comes to an end. *That the negroes are numerous in the rebel army, and do for that army its heaviest work, is beyond question.*[247]

Unfortunately, the reality of the black Confederate soldier does not conform to Northern and New South myths about Southern blacks and slavery, and so it has been disregarded and suppressed. But we are bringing it back into the light of day for all to see.[248]

Black Confederate soldiers, like these three, guarding a railroad in Louisiana, were a fact of history. But because they do not fit the fantasy version of the War that Liberals have invented, they are ignored in our mainstream history books.

True Southerners, of all races, continue to be proud of our region's multiracial history, and of the many contributions made to Dixie by individuals of all colors, religions, and nations.[249]

WHAT YOU WERE TAUGHT: Lincoln's Emancipation Proclamation is what finally ended slavery in the South.

THE FACTS: It is well-known to educated Southerners today that the Final Emancipation Proclamation, issued January 1, 1863, only "freed" slaves in the South, and even then, only in specific areas of the South. Lincoln's edict purposefully excluded Tennessee, for example (the entire state had been under Yankee control since the fall of Nashville, February 25, 1862), all of the Border States, and numerous Northern-occupied parishes in Louisiana and several counties in Virginia.

The Final Emancipation Proclamation, in fact, was issued only in areas of the South *not* under Union control; that is, it only "freed" *Southern* slaves who had sided with the Confederacy. It did not ban slavery anywhere in the North, where thousands of Yankees still practiced it, including Union officers like General Ulysses S. Grant and his family.

As Lincoln states in the proclamation itself, the entire North, as well as those Southern places that were exempted, "are for the present left precisely as if this proclamation were not issued." He could not have made the meaning of this sentence more clear: *slavery was to be allowed to continue in the U.S. (that is, the North) and in any areas of the C.S. (that is, the South) controlled by the U.S. (that is, by the Union armies).*

The question Southerners have been asking Northerners for the past century and a half is why, if Lincoln was so interested in black equality, did he only abolish slavery in the South where he had no jurisdiction but not in the North where he had full control?

Lincoln showing the Final Emancipation Proclamation to his cabinet. The unlawful and duplicitous document is not at all what Liberals teach. In the edict the president himself states that it was issued as a "military necessity," so that freed blacks could "be received into the armed service of the United States to garrison forts, positions, stations, and other places."

The answer is obvious to most Southerners today, just as it was to a majority of them in 1863: the Emancipation Proclamation was nothing more than a clever political illusion, for he did not free slaves where he legally could (in the North and in the Border States), yet he sought to free them (in the South) where he had no legal right to do so. Therefore the entire proclamation was made null and void by its creator himself. This indeed is why the Thirteenth Amendment had to be issued.

If only Northerners had asked themselves this same question at the time, they would have never created the myth of Lincoln the "Great Emancipator" to begin with! In truth our sixteenth president did not issue the Emancipation Proclamation for the specific purpose of trying to establish black civil rights across the U.S. If that had indeed been his intention he would have also banned slavery in the North and in non-Union occupied areas of the South.

Being the penultimate politician, halfway through his war Lincoln decided that it would be politically expedient to shift the character of the conflict from a political issue, "preserving the Union,"

President Woodrow Wilson of Virginia asserted what his fellow Southerners have known all along: midway through his war Lincoln intentionally changed its disposition by issuing the Emancipation Proclamation. Not because he cared about black civil rights or slavery, but in order to "put the South at a moral disadvantage" for the purpose of wining the support of Europe, encouraging enlistments, and insuring votes for his reelection. It was this very type of treachery, not his alleged moral character, that earned Lincoln the sarcastic nickname "Honest Abe."

to a moral issue, "abolishing slavery." Both were rank falsehoods, however, carefully calculated to obtain European support and procure Northern and abolitionist votes in the upcoming 1864 presidential election.

Part of this devilish ruse was the issuance of the Final Emancipation Proclamation on January 1, 1863, which, tellingly, he publicly referred to not as a "civil rights measure," but as a "*war measure*"; not as a "civil rights emancipation," but as a "*military emancipation*." It was nothing more, as he declared in the edict itself, than a "*military necessity*," "*a fit and necessary war measure for suppressing the rebellion*."[250] Thus according to Lincoln himself, his proclamation did not have a single thing to do with black equality or even true abolition.

Yet, what a dastardly brilliant idea it was. For no one could argue against emancipation—not even the most pro-South Northerners (Copperheads) or pro-North Southerners (scallywags)—if Lincoln could prove that freeing the slaves was vital to winning the War. Assuming that he would reap untold benefits from this shift in the character of the conflict from a political basis to a moral one, it did not matter whether or not any Southern slaves were actually freed to not. And thus legally none were.[251]

Our twenty-eighth president, Woodrow Wilson, wrote of this dishonorable and unlawful moment in American history:

> The unexpected scope and magnitude of the war, its slow and sullen movement, its anxious strain of varying fortune, its manifest upheaval of the very foundations of the government, turned men's hopes and fears now this way now that, threw their judgments all abroad, brought panic gusts of disquietude and dismay which lasted a long season through before any steady winds

of purpose found their breath and their settled quarter. For eighteen months *Mr. Lincoln* had waited upon opinion, with a patience which deeply irritated all who wished radical action [on abolition] taken. He knew the hazards of the time as well as any man: feared that at almost any moment news might come of the recognition of the southern Confederacy by the old governments abroad [in Europe]; knew how important success was to hold opinion at home no less than to check interference from without; was keenly conscious how the failures of the [Union] Army of the Potomac offset and neutralized the successes of the federal arms in the West; and *realized to the full how awkward it was, whether for the government of opinion at home or over sea, to have no policy more handsome than that of conquest and subjugation. It was necessary [therefore] to put the South at a moral disadvantage by transforming the contest from a war waged against States fighting for their independence into a war against States fighting for the maintenance and extension of slavery, by making some open move for emancipation as the real motive of the struggle. Once make the war a struggle against slavery, and the world, it might be hoped, would see it a moral war, not a political; and the sympathy of nations would begin to run for the North, not for the South.* But Mr. Lincoln knew also that the thoughts of the people changed more slowly than the thoughts of politicians; that the mass of men, who must fill the ranks of the armies and vote at the polls in the elections, quitted their old ways of thinking stiffly and with reluctance. He waited for their purpose to harden. *He had come into office declaring that the party he led had no intention whatever to molest slavery in the States which had already established it*; and he knew that he must wait for the people at his back to change their temper under the strain of the fighting before he openly turned about to accept a revolution and seek emancipation as the object of the war.

By midsummer, 1862, he was convinced that opinion was ready. He waited only for some show of victory by the Army of the Potomac to put the new, *aggressive policy* he contemplated in countenance. The check given [Confederate General Robert E.] Lee at Antietam served the purpose, in lieu of something better; and on the 22nd of September he issued a proclamation [the Preliminary Emancipation Proclamation] which gave formal notice that unless the southern States returned within a hundred days to their allegiance to the Union he would declare the slaves within their limits free. On the 1st of January, 1863, accordingly, he put forth a definitive proclamation of emancipation [the Final Emancipation Proclamation]. *It was an act which bound no one except commanders in the field. The President had no authority to alter or abolish the laws of the southern States, in open secession though they were. He could do nothing more in actual execution of the proclamation than*

> *command federal officers in the field to set free the negroes who fell into their hands, and keep their freedom secure within the territory actually occupied or controlled by their troops.* That he could do as an act of war, under his authority as commander-in-chief [this view is still hotly debated]. Some of the federal commanders [such as John C. Frémont] had already ventured to set the negroes free in the districts they occupied, but Mr. Lincoln had rebuked them and annulled their acts till he should be ready. *The proclamation, when it came, was no law, but only his deliberate declaration of policy, for himself and for his party; and changed, as he had meant that it should change, the whole air of the struggle, and of politics as well.*[252]

It is important to remember, as discussed earlier, that despite Lincoln's issuance of the Emancipation Proclamation and the subsequent alteration of the *character* of his War midway through the conflict, this did not change his *purpose* in fighting the War, which, until the end, he maintained was an effort by the North to "preserve the Union."

WHAT YOU WERE TAUGHT: Lincoln issued the Emancipation Proclamation for only one reason: to help the black race.

THE FACTS: Despite his cynical backroom conniving, President Lincoln did hope that his Emancipation Proclamation would yield results beyond merely garnering public support. But why did he wait nearly three years before issuing the document? If the War was over slavery *and* he was also concerned about black civil rights, as pro-North and New South advocates claim, why did he dither so long, only succumbing after years of pressure and harassment?[253]

The fact is that Lincoln issued the proclamation with five primary wishes in mind. By changing the character of the War from a political issue to a moral one: 1) He hoped it would secure Europe's support. 2) He hoped it would instigate slave rebellions across the South (as the document itself intimates). 3) He hoped to secure new troops to compensate for his drastically declining white soldiery. 4) He hoped to pick up new voters for the upcoming 1864 election. 5) He needed to legally free American blacks before he could deport them.

Unfortunately for Lincoln, all five reasons were utter failures, for he was widely known among Southern blacks as a white racist who detested the abolitionist movement; who delayed abolition for as long as possible; was a leader in the American Colonization Society; used slaves to complete the construction of the Capitol dome in Washington, D.C.; implemented extreme racist military policies; used profits from Northern slavery to fund his War; referred to blacks as "niggers"; said he was willing to allow slavery to continue in perpetuity if the Southern states would come back into the Union; engaged in a lifelong campaign to deport all American blacks; as a lawyer defended slave owners in court; backed the proslavery Corwin Amendment to the Constitution in 1861; and continually blocked black enlistment, black suffrage, and black citizenship. All of this is, in fact, why Frederick Douglass said that Lincoln's attitude toward blacks lacked "the genuine spark of humanity."[254]

Lincoln used slaves to complete the dome on the Capitol Building, as well as build roads and other structures around Washington, D.C. When the War started, he used profits from the Yankee slave trade to fund it, but he would not allow blacks to enlist in the U.S. army or navy for the first two years. These are just three of the many reasons Southerners will never call Lincoln "the Great Emancipator."

WHAT YOU WERE TAUGHT: Lincoln's Emancipation Proclamation was a well thought out program to free Southern slaves and quickly merge them into white society.

THE FACTS: Lincoln had absolutely no formal plan for dealing with the millions of Southern slaves he intended to suddenly liberate in January 1863. If he truly cared about African-Americans, as we are asked to believe, this makes no sense whatsoever.

The reality is that he cared little for blacks, and he seldom tried to hide the fact. He even banned them from entering the White House, unless they were part of the servant staff—as former Yankee slave, black abolitionist, and women's right advocate Sojourner Truth discovered firsthand. Once, when asked what was to become of liberated slaves after they were "freed" by his Emancipation Proclamation, Lincoln likened them to wild hogs, and said humorously: "Let 'em root, pig, or perish!"—and that is exactly what occurred, as our next entry shows.[255]

Educated African-Americans were incensed by Lincoln's overt racism and apathy. Former Yankee slave Frederick Douglass, for example, declared that the president's approach to dealing with black Americans was missing "the genuine spark of humanity."

WHAT YOU WERE TAUGHT: The Emancipation Proclamation was a great success, allowing former slaves to immediately improve their lives.

THE FACTS: After the issuance of the Final Emancipation Proclamation on January 1, 1863, only three things happened immediately: Union recruitment plummeted, Union desertion skyrocketed (Yankee General Benjamin F. Butler determined that by the end of the War some 177,000 Federal soldiers had deserted),[256] and the quality of life for blacks sank to an all time low, remaining far beneath even former slavery levels for the next 100 years.

After the War, for instance, black life span dropped 10 percent, diets and health deteriorated, disease and sickness rates went up 20 percent, the number of skilled blacks declined, and the gap between white and black wages widened, trends that did not even begin to reverse until the onset of World War II, 75 years later, in 1939. At least one out of four "freed" blacks died in a number of Southern communities.

Of life after January 1, 1863, Adeline Grey, a black South Carolina servant, wrote that when "liberation" came she could still vividly remember it, while slavery was but a dim memory. Why? Because "life was much more difficult and painful *after* emancipation than before."

The "pain" of emancipation was due, in great part, to the fact that Lincoln never pushed through any kind of organized, gradual, or compensated emancipation plan, as nearly every other Western nation had done when it abolished slavery. His proclamation, for example, contained no plans for freed black slaves, no provisions for housing, food, clothing, employment, or healthcare.

Freed slaves were merely "turned loose" to fend for themselves; literally cast out into the streets with no education, no jobs, no shelter, no job training, no grants or loans. The more unfortunate ended up on so-called "government plantations," malodorous squatter camps where poverty, sickness, hunger, thievery, and prostitution reigned.

As seen here, Lincoln devotees enjoy sentimentalizing their idol's Emancipation Proclamation. The truth is that the edict was illegal, unscrupulous, a failure, and one of America's most nightmarish debacles. Lincoln himself called it "the greatest folly of my life."

And Lincoln's promise to freedmen of "forty acres and a mule" was little more than a carrot on the end of a stick, used to lure blacks into a false sense of governmental protection after emancipation. After all, his so-called "black land giveaways" were never meant to be permanent, and what little of these were dispersed went primarily to wealthy white Northerners.

Under what I call Lincoln's "root, pig, or perish emancipation plan," blacks who as servants had lived quality lives equal to and often superior to many whites and free blacks, now found themselves living out in the open or in makeshift tents, begging for food and work. There was now less labor available to them under freedom than there had been under servitude, and thus the once booming Southern black economic system plunged.

Disease, homelessness, starvation, and beggary now became the lot of untold thousands of former black servants. Even many of those who managed to become sharecroppers eventually found themselves in a state of peonage (a debt that tied them to the land), living in crude filthy shacks, suffering from illiteracy, ill health, and malnutrition. All of this was a far cry from the excellent quality of life experienced by Southern blacks when they had lived under servitude. According to eyewitnesses, by 1867, just four years after the Emancipation Proclamation was issued, 1 million, or 25 percent, of all Southern blacks had perished from starvation, neglect, infanticide, corruption, and disease.

Lincoln had no "grand plan" to help the millions of black servants who were set free after his War. This is why so many of them ended up on "government plantations" like this one; hazardous, ghastly, unsanitary camps swarming with vermin, disease, thieves, prostitutes, bummers, and carpetbaggers. Due to what the author calls Lincoln's brutal and inhumane "root, pig, or perish emancipation plan," by 1867 at least 1 million, or 25 percent, of all Southern blacks were dead.

Southerners had warned of these possible problems years before they occurred, but the North did not listen or care. In January 1861, for example, four months prior to the War and two years before the Emancipation Proclamation, Mississippi's official "Declaration of Immediate Causes of Secession" asserted that:

> [The North] seeks not to elevate or support the slave, but to destroy his present condition without providing a better.[257]

A truly accurate prediction, years ahead of its time.

Due to how it was handled, the Emancipation Proclamation was indubitably a national disaster on an epic scale, as Lincoln himself admitted. It was "the greatest folly of my life," he later opined.[258]

WHAT YOU WERE TAUGHT: Not a single Southern black man or woman supported the Confederacy.

THE FACTS: Of the South's 3.5 million black servants, the "vast majority," 95 percent (19 out of 20), remained in the South, all the while maintaining their loyalty to Dixie. Ignoring Lincoln's fake proclamation of freedom, they instead pledged their allegiance to their home states, to the South, and to their white families. Remaining at home they ran their owner's farm, grew food, produced provisions for the Confederate military, and protected their master's family and property while he was away on the battlefield. In 1910 Pastor Benjamin F. Riley noted that the Southern black servant

> *sustained the armies of the Confederacy during the great Civil War; he was the guardian of the helpless women and children of the South while the husbands and sons were at the distant front doing battle . . .*; against him was not a whisper of unfaithfulness or of disloyalty during all this trying and bloody period; *when the land was invaded by the [Northern] armies . . . he remained faithful still, and often at great personal risk of life, secreted from the invader [his owner's] . . . horses and mules, and buried the treasures of the family that they might not fall into the hands of the enemies of the whites . . . . he declined to accept freedom when it was offered by the invading army, preferring to remain loyal and steadfast to the charge committed to him by the absent master, all this and more the Negro slave did.* There was not a day during the trying period of the Civil War when he might not have disbanded the Southern armies. An outbreak on his part against the defenseless homes of the South would have occasioned the utter dissolution of the Southern armies, and turned the anxious faces of the veterans in gray toward their homes. *But no Southern soldier ever dreamed of the possibility of a condition like this. So far as his home was concerned, it was not any apprehension of the unfaithfulness of the slaves which occasioned the slightest alarm.*[259]

In an effort to raise money for the Southern war effort many Southern slaves and freemen bought Confederate bonds. Others held bake sales and auctions, while still others donated clothing and other goods in an effort to help support Confederate soldiers. Those untold thousands of African-Americans who marched off to resist Lincoln and his illegal invaders, proudly stood up for "ole Jeff Davis," wearing placards on their hats that read: "We will die by the South." Among them were tens of thousands who served the Confederacy as teamsters, bridge and road builders, musicians, nurses, carpenters, smithies, couriers, lookouts, and cooks—many from among the last occupation who had been trained by the best culinary schools in Paris.[260]

The following wartime conversation was later recorded by a Confederate woman living in Richmond, Virginia, in 1867:

> An enthusiastic female slave one day said to her master, "*The very next time I meet General Lee on the street, I mean to shake hands with him*. . . . when I do shake hands with him, I am going to tell him that all *I'm sorry for is, that I have not got ten sons to give him to fight for the Confederacy*."
>
> Her master, amused, commended her for her patriotism. The same negress, at the time of the occupation of Richmond by the Federal troops, secured from the wreck of some of the dry-goods stores a lot of gentlemen's collars, which she carefully preserved, to send, as she said,—"Just as soon as I get a chance"—as a present to President Davis. Even to this day, this . . . woman avows the most unqualified devotion to the memory of the Southern Confederacy.[261]

Contrary to Yankee myth, Southern blacks did not hate Southern whites, the Confederacy, or the Confederate Battle Flag. An example: according to scores of eyewitnesses (both white and black), when Confederate General Robert E. Lee rode through town alone or with his soldiers, African-Americans, both free and in servitude, respectfully bowed or saluted him as he went past. In response the general always smiled kindly, touched the brim of his hat, and nodded.

The cover of the sheet music for "The Palmetto State Song." The words at the bottom read: "Music composed and Respectfully dedicated to the Signers of the Ordinance of Secession unanimously passed in convention at Charleston, S.C., Dec. 20th, 1860." Less than 5 percent of the South Carolinians sitting in this audience were slave owners. However, 100 percent of them were freedom lovers.

We not only have copious reports of Southern blacks both supporting the Confederacy at home and fighting in the Confederate army and navy, but also of their amazing valor on the battlefield. Many an eyewitness account has been handed down to us, for example, of brave Southern African-Americans pulling wounded whites from the battlefield at the height of the shooting. Countless blacks lost their lives in just this manner. The following incident occurred during the Battle of Secessionville at Charleston, South Carolina, June 16, 1862:

> Many valuable lives were lost, and much individual heroism was displayed in this short and decisive campaign. . . . [Confederate] Lieutenant John A. Bellinger, of the artillery, was asleep in his quarters some distance from the battery when the roar of [Confederate Colonel T. G.] Lamar's columbiad summoned the garrison to its defense. After he had repaired to his post, his negro servant [Daniel] discovered that in his haste he had left his pistol, and hastened to carry it to him against the remonstrances of his companions, for the approach to the battery was now swept by bullets as with the besom of destruction. *But the faithful servitor could not bear that his young master should be in such deadly conflict without his trusty weapon; and he fell, mortally wounded, in the attempt to bear it to him.* Every attention that affection could suggest to Bellinger soothed poor Daniel's last moments during the week that he lingered. He said to his master just before he died, "Duncan and Normie"—Bellinger's little motherless sons—"Duncan and Normie will be sorry when they hear that I am dead."[262]

Daniel was right. In 1867, just two years after the War, Miss Sarah "Sallie" Ann Brock, a white Virginian, wrote elegantly about the "fidelity" of Southern blacks:

> There is an inherent pride in personal responsibility, and this was fully exemplified in the test of the negro during the war. *It was a matter of infinite gratification with him to take care of his mistress and the little ones, while his master was absent in the field.* The duties of rearing and of training the children of a Southern family were always proudly shared by the domestics known as "house servants." In almost every Southern [slave owning] household there was the "mammy," the "daddy," and aunties and uncles of the senior servants, who *received these appellations from the affection and respect in which they were held by the members of the white family to which they were attached.*

We might cite numerous instances of the fidelity of negroes that came under our notice, but will only refer to one, illustrating the deep attachment of which the negro is capable, and the just sense of responsibility which takes hold of his mind.

Southern servants did not just stay on their respective plantations during the War and idly wait for the conflict to end. They continued working to keep everything running smoothly, even taking over the entire operation of their owner's farm while he was off fighting Lincoln's foreign invaders. In addition, Southern "slaves" also protected the mistress of the home and her children, hid valuables from the Yankees, and produced crops and other much needed products for the Confederate armies. As part of the massive Southern black war effort, many held bake sales and auctions, or donated clothing and canned goods to the Confederate Commissary Department.

A young soldier from Georgia brought with him to the war in Virginia a young man who had been brought up with him on his father's plantation. On leaving his home with his regiment, the mother of the young soldier said to his negro slave: "Now, Tom, I commit your master Jemmy into your keeping. Don't let him suffer for anything with which you can supply him. If he is sick, nurse him well, my boy; and if he dies, bring his body home to me; if wounded, take care of him; and oh! if he is killed in battle, don't let him be buried on the field, but secure his body for me, and bring him home to be buried!" The negro faithfully promised his mistress that all of her wishes should be attended to, and came on to the seat of war charged with the grave responsibility placed upon him.

In one of the battles around Richmond the negro saw his young master when he entered the fight, and saw him when he fell, but no more of him. The battle became fierce, the dust and smoke so dense that the company to which he was attached, wholly enveloped in the cloud, was hidden from the sight of the negro, and it was not until the battle was over that Tom could seek for his young master. He found him in a heap of the slain. Removing the mangled remains, torn frightfully by a piece of shell, he conveyed them to an empty house, where he laid them out in the most decent order he could, and securing the few valuables found on his person, he sought a conveyance to carry the body to Richmond. Ambulances were in too great requisition for those whose lives were not extinct to permit the body of a dead man to be conveyed in one of them. He pleaded most piteously for a place to bring in the body of his young master. It was useless, and he was repulsed; but finding some one to guard the dead, he hastened into the city and hired a cart and driver to go out with him to bring in the body to Richmond.

When he arrived again at the place where he had left it, he was urged to let it be buried on the field, and was told that he would not be allowed to take it from Richmond, and therefore it were better to be buried there. "I can't do it," replied the faithful negro; "I can't do it; *I promised my mistress [Jemmy's mother] to bring this body home to her if he got killed, and I'll go home with it or I'll die by it; I can't leave my master Jemmy here*." The boy was allowed to have the body and brought it into Richmond, where he was furnished with a coffin, and the circumstances being made known, the faithful slave, in the care of a wounded officer who went South, was permitted to carry the remains of his master to his distant home in Georgia. The heart of the mother was comforted in the possession of the precious body of her child, and in giving it a burial in the churchyard near his own loved home.

Fee or reward for this noble act of fidelity would have been an insult to the better feelings of this poor slave; but when he delivered up the watch and other things taken from the person of his young master, the mistress returned him the watch, and said: "Take this watch, Tom, and keep it for the sake of my dear boy; 'tis but a poor reward for such services as you have rendered him and his mother." The poor woman, quite overcome, could only add: "*God will bless you, boy!*"

To allude to an institution which is without the prospect of or a wish for its resurrection, would be like opening the grave and exhibiting the festering remains of our former social system; but *we cannot forbear extracting from an evil*—and only evil morally, not necessarily involving sin [for the Bible sanctions slavery]—*many a beautiful lesson from the relation in which it was held by us. Our slaves were most generally the repositories of our family secrets. They were our*

> *confidants in all our trials. They joyed with us and they sorrowed with us; they wept when we wept, and they laughed when we laughed. Often our best friends, they were rarely our worst enemies. Simple and childlike in their affections, they were more trustworthy in their attachments than those better versed in wisdom. For good or evil, in his present altered condition the negro has the warmest sympathies of his former master, and ever in him will find a "friend in need," who will readily extend to him the hand of kindness and generous affection.*[263]

WHAT YOU WERE TAUGHT: After the end of the Civil War, Southern blacks fled North to get away from their racist former owners. **THE FACTS:** Not only did the majority of Southern blacks stay in the South after the War, but many of them remained with their former owners, or returned to them after a short experiment with freedom. In 1892 Southern writer and newspaperman Thomas C. DeLeon wrote of the latter group:

> Lured from old service for a time, most of them followed not far the gaudy and shining Will-o'-the-Wisp; and almost all—especially the household and personal servants—soon returned to "Ole Mas'r" once more, sadder and wiser for the futile chase after freedom's joys.[264]

Cumming tells of a similar experience after Lee's surrender. While traveling on a road in Alabama, she noted in her diary in May 1865:

> We met hundreds of negro men, women, and children, returning to their homes in Montgomery, where they had been with the Federals [Yankee soldiers], and had had a taste of freedom; and to judge from their looks it had brought them anything else but happiness.[265]

That former "slaves" would stay with their former "masters" after emancipation and war's end is not surprising. After all, relationships between whites and blacks in the Victorian South were better than anywhere else in the world in the 1800s. The mutual respect between the races was such that, according to Southern slaves themselves, white masters would take off their hats and bow, while white mistresses would "make a low curtsey," when greeting their African-American servants.[266]

Do not be deceived by the incongruous word-twisting of the anti-South movement. During the Victorian period race relations were better in the American South than anywhere else in the Western world.

This was not just a mere Victorian courtesy. On most Southern farms and plantations the mutual love and respect was real: whites considered their black servants a legal part of their white family (and registered them as such at the time of purchase), while blacks considered their white owners part of their black family.[267] In 1860 a white citizen of the Old Dominion remarked:

> Ain't anybody ever accused [us] Virginians of not being good to [our] servants! and it don't take more'n half an eye to see that the servants love their white people.[268]

In his *Memoirs*, my close relation Confederate Colonel John Singleton Mosby (from whose ancestral family I descend), wrote:

> My father was a slaveholder, and I still cherish a strong affection for the slaves who nursed me and played with me in my childhood. *That was the prevailing sentiment in the South—not one peculiar to*

> *myself—but one prevailing in all the South . . .*[269]

Not only did white Southerners give Christmas gifts to their black servants, but the reverse was also true. Miss Brock of Virginia noted that in the Old South slaves would often hoard their savings for months in order to purchase Christmas gifts for their master and mistress.[270]

This tender relationship between the Southern races is one of the many reasons white slave owners provided their African-American servants with *free* cradle-to-grave housing, clothing, food, salary, transportation, and health care, frequently even putting their chattel before themselves.[271] In 1888 Parthenia A. Hague of Alabama wrote:

> During the war when bacon was scarce, it often happened that the white household would deny themselves meat to eat, so as to give it to the slaves . . . [and] if a negro was sick, a doctor, who was already paid, was called in all haste, as planters used to engage a doctor by the year, at so much for each slave whether large or small.[272]

Additionally, it is a fact that by 1860, 99 percent of all blacks were native-born Americans, a larger percentage than for whites, with some blacks having American ancestors dating back to the 1600s. This made the South their one and only true home—which is why they considered themselves not "African-Americans," but "Southern-Americans." It was the sunny Southland where generations of their families had been raised, lived, and died, filling countless cemeteries with beloved family members and friends. Why test life in the cold racist North when they were already living comfortably in the warm tolerant South?

Esteemed former Virginia slave and black educator Booker T. Washington spoke for nearly all Southern blacks when he said:

> I was born in the South. I have lived and labored in the South. I wish to be buried in the South.[273]

The bond between Southern whites and blacks was so enduring that neither war, slavery, or even emancipation could break it.

Throughout the antebellum, bellum, and postbellum periods, for instance, we have thousands of stories of warm relations between Southern whites and Southern blacks, and of free blacks and slaves providing various forms of support for both the war effort and for former white slave owners who had been made indigent by Lincoln's War. In 1901 Booker T. Washington made these eyewitness comments on race relations in Dixie after the War:

> *As a rule, not only did the members of my race entertain no feelings of bitterness against . . . [Southern] whites before and during the war, but there are many instances of Negroes tenderly caring for their former masters and mistresses who for some reason have become poor and dependent since the war.* I know of instances where the former masters of slaves have for years been supplied with money by their former slaves to keep them from suffering. I have known of still other cases in which the former slaves have assisted in the education of the descendants of their former owners. I know of a case on a large plantation in the South in which a young white man, the son of the former owner of the estate, has become so reduced in purse and self control by reason of drink that he is a pitiable creature; and yet, notwithstanding the poverty of the coloured people themselves on this plantation, *they have for years supplied this young white man with the necessities of life.* One sends him a little coffee or sugar, another a little meat, and so on. Nothing that the coloured people possess is too good for the son of "old Mars Tom," who will perhaps never be permitted to suffer while any remain on the place who knew directly or indirectly of "old Mars Tom."[274]

Virginian Booker T. Washington loved and understood the South, a region still incomprehensible to most Yankees and Liberals.

4

THE CONFEDERATE FLAG: HISTORY, HERITAGE, AND HONOR

FLAG OF THEIR GLORY

It hangs on the wall,
Where soft shadows fall,
The golden light streaming
From skies that are gleaming,
And seems by its magic the past to recall.

They're marching away,
Those soldiers in gray,
With music's loud pealing,
Their stern thoughts revealing,
And high in the sunshine this banner asway.

At last, filled with woe,
Now homeward they go,
Brave, tattered, undaunted,
Their country fear-haunted.
And see! o'er the silence the old flag bends low.

Ah! soft folds, e'er wave
In sunshine to lave;
Keep fresh thy sweet story,
Flag of their glory,
Who gave of their lifeblood their fair land to save.[275]

GRACE IMOGEN GISH, 1916

CHAPTER 4

WHAT YOU WERE TAUGHT: Southerners themselves are responsible for the terrible reputation of the Confederate Battle Flag.

THE FACTS: Not according to history. Disparagement of the Confederate Battle Flag started in the North, and with the only person capable of conceiving such an evil design: Abraham Lincoln. This occurred on September 11, 1863, when the infamous U.S. president arrested and deported (to the South) a group of Maryland publishers for printing a poem about the Confederate Battle Flag called "The Southern Cross."[276]

In 1861 Southerners wore this secession rosette and badge, with Jefferson Davis' picture on it, to celebrate their new country: the C.S.A.

With this single act monstrous Lincoln launched a false narrative about the flag, imbuing it with a sinister character that it has never possessed. From that day forward it was seen in the North as a negative standard symbolizing treason and, eventually, slavery and racism. But neither Dishonest Abe's villainous machinations or the race-baiting rhetoric of modern South-haters make it so.

WHAT YOU WERE TAUGHT: The official flag of the KKK is the Confederate Battle Flag, which proves that it is a racist symbol.

THE FACTS: Actually, as both early and current photographs of the organization clearly show, the official flag of the modern Ku Klux Klan is not the Confederate Battle Flag. It was, is, and always has been the U.S. Flag, the same banner that flew over every American slave ship!

Perversely, the reason many KKK groups use the Confederate Battle Flag is the same reason that Liberal enemies of the South call it "racist": both get their American history from mainstream pro-North writers and university presses; disingenuous authors and publishers whose books are filled with disinformation and Yankee propaganda, brimming with egregious errors copied from earlier uneducated writers, all with an anti-South, anti-Christian, anti-Conservative agenda.

Just because an individual uses a particular symbol to represent his or her beliefs does not mean that that symbol actually represents those beliefs. If this were true then every symbol, especially flags, would come under the auspices of "racism," for everything has, at one time or another, been used as an emblem by people to represent intolerant bigoted ideas, none more so than the U.S. Flag.

Wrongly believing it to be a product of Aryan (Caucasian) culture, the Nazis assimilated the swastika and proceeded to imbue it with meanings it never possessed. For this prehistoric solar symbol was once used by people of all races in every part of the globe, mainly as an emblem of good luck, health, the Divine Feminine, and eternal life. It was in this way that Hitler and his German socialist organization turned the swastika from a symbol of love into one of hate. Modern day American socialists and Liberals have done the same thing with the Confederate Battle Flag, and, in fact, with all things Confederate. But this does not alter the original and true meaning of our Confederate emblems. It only underscores them while revealing the ignorance and malice of their detractors.

The swastika, for example, was adopted by socialist leader Adolf Hitler and the Nazis, who turned it into a symbol of racism and hate. Yet, this was not the original meaning of the right-pointing or clockwise "whirligig": before recorded history the swastika was used by Paleolithic people as a solar symbol, and since ancient times it has been viewed across Asia, Africa, South America, and Europe as a spinning Sun wheel, bestowing good fortune and health. In Tibet it still serves as a talisman, in China it is the emblem of infinity, and Buddhists see it as the "Key of Paradise" and the "Seal on Buddha's Heart." In traditional folkways the swastika has long been believed to have apotropaic properties, while ancient Norsemen imaged Thor's Hammer as a swastika.[277]

The swastika was used by Native-Americans, ancient Romans and Greeks,

Just because German socialists like Hitler said the swastika is a racial symbol does not make it so. Just because American socialists like Obama say the Confederate Battle Flag is a racial symbol does not make it so.

and early Swedes, the latter who placed the popular regeneration symbol on tombstones. As an archetypal emblem of the number four, ancient Pagans and Gnostic Christians saw it as a symbol of the four seasons and their accompanying four solar festivals: the Spring Equinox, the Summer Solstice, the Fall Equinox, and the Winter Solstice.

Also known as the gammadion or *crux gammata*, in Old Europe the left-pointing or counterclockwise swastika was a feminine lunar symbol representing the Great Mother in her Moon-goddess form. The swastika was even adopted by the early Christian Church as a symbol of Jesus, which it used lavishly both in funerary art and as ornamentation in cathedrals.[278] In Christianity the swastika is, in other words, just another one of the nearly 400 sacred variations of the four-pointed Christian cross.[279]

The word swastika itself has no relation to Hitler, the Nazis, or even the German language. It derives from the Sanskrit word *svastika*, meaning "so be it," making it identical to the Christian word "Amen,"[280] the Hindu "Om," the Egyptian "Amon," the Hebrew "Amam," the Tibetan "Hum," the Greek-Christian "Om-ega," and the solar-name "Sol-Om-On" (Solomon) of the Kabbalah.[281]

It is plain from this single example that symbols have different meanings to different people, and that only the original and earliest meanings are authentic. Imbuing an emblem with meanings it has never had, as Hitler did with the swastika and as modern hate groups do with the Confederate Battle Flag, is therefore not merely historically incorrect, it is wrong, immoral, and unjust. Some believe it should be made illegal. Either way, it is a violence to the symbol, and it is the responsibility of every intelligent individual to educate himself or herself, as well as others, about a particular symbol's *true* historical background.

Because enemies of the South falsely define the KKK as a specifically *Southern*, white supremacist, anti-black organization whose official emblem is the Confederate Flag, it is worth taking a brief look at the facts in order to correct these lies and reestablish the truth.

Above I mentioned the "*modern* KKK." It is important to differentiate between today's Klan and the original Klan of the 1860s, or what I call the "Reconstruction KKK." (I have given it this name because this, the original KKK, would not and could not have arisen without the imposition of the North's "Reconstruction" program, which began immediately after Lincoln's War in April 1865.) The two groups have no connection to one another whatsoever—other than the unfortunate fact that the 20th-Century one took the name of the 19th-Century one.

To begin with, the Reconstruction KKK of the late 1860s was not an anti-black group; it was an *anti-Yankee* one, which quite appropriately described itself as an institution of "chivalry, humanity, mercy, and patriotism." In fact, during the first two years of its existence this social aid organization was comprised of thousands of white *and* black members, for its sole mission was to protect and care for those who had been disenfranchised by Lincoln's War (that is, vets, widows, seniors, children, etc.), *whatever their race*. This explains why *there was an all-black Ku Klux Klan that operated for several years in the Nashville area*.

This illustration from 1868 shows the real focus of the original Reconstruction KKK: not blacks, but carpetbaggers; treacherous Northern whites who came South after the War in order to prey on the ravaged region and its impoverished inhabitants.

The Reconstruction KKK's other primary goal was to help maintain law and order across the South. Though Lincoln's Reconstruction program had called for military rule, its implementation had the opposite effect. Lawlessness and vicious criminal behavior became commonplace, problems exacerbated by the appearance of thick-skinned, greedy carpetbaggers (Northerners) and treasonous, unscrupulous scallywags (Northernized Southerners), both groups which sought to prey on and exploit the long-suffering Southern survivors of Lincoln's War.

In 1869 the social atmosphere in the South changed dramatically.

By this time the government-sponsored black Loyal Leagues and the Freedmen's Bureau had been formed, organizations meant to aid Southern blacks dispossessed by Lincoln's cruel, illegal, and unplanned emancipation (note that no U.S. government leagues were ever formed to aid dispossessed Southern whites specifically). Instead, carpetbaggers and scallywags used the Leagues to inculcate freed slaves in pro-North, anti-South propaganda, training them to use weapons and military tactics to taunt, punish, and even murder their former white owners.[282]

The anti-South movement wants you to believe that the Ku Klux Klan is a specifically Southern movement and that therefore these Klan members (with "KKK" on their hat bands) must be from Dixie. Actually this 1870 photo is of "KKK Watertown Division 289." Not Watertown, Tennessee, or Watertown, Georgia, but Watertown, New York, a state which once served as the epicenter of the American slave trade, and which participated in the institution far longer than any other, North or South.

One of Lee's chaplains, Reverend John William Jones, wrote of this period shortly after the War, as bedraggled Confederate troops walked home (most of the South's railroads had been destroyed by Lincoln and his armies):

> After four years' absence from any industrial pursuit, with fondly cherished hopes all blighted, plans all frustrated,

fortunes swept away, and avenues of business all closed, they returned to their desolated homes. Alas! in many instances blackened ruins marked the spot of their once happy homes, and there were loved ones to tell tales of outrage and wrong which men of Anglo-Saxon blood have not been wont to hear unmoved.

To make matters worse (under the then avowed purpose of [U.S. President] Andrew Johnson to "make treason odious") *there were stationed in every county squads of "blue coats," [Yankee] provost marshals and freedman's bureau agents, who were not always discreet, and not unfrequently did or said things well calculated to provoke serious collisions between these returned soldiers and themselves, or the newly emancipated negroes.* Then followed the "carpet-bag" and "negro rule" of the Southern States [at which time Northern officials intentionally placed blacks into political offices across Dixie—without a single vote being cast—in order to stir up animosity and disrupt the South's attempt to rebuild herself], which is a blot upon our history, at which every true American should blush, and concerning which Dr. John A. Broadus so well said at an educational banquet in Brooklyn four years after the war:

> "You brethren at the North think that you have a great deal for which to forgive the South for the four years of war. I will not discuss that. But I tell you, brethren, we of the South have a great deal for which to forgive the North for the four years since the war."[283]

The Yankee Reconstruction policy of inculcating Southern blacks against their former owners, as well as the accompanying illegal harassment, arrest, imprisonment, and torture of Southern whites, was not new. It had been practiced by the North since early in the War, as Jefferson Davis attested in 1862:

Peaceful and aged citizens, unresisting captives and non-combatants, have been confined at hard labor, with hard chains attached to their limbs, and are still so held, in dungeons and fortresses.

Others have been submitted to a like degrading punishment for selling medicines to the sick soldiers of the Confederacy.

The soldiers of the United States have been invited and encouraged in general orders to insult and outrage the wives, the mothers, and the sisters of our citizens.

Helpless women have been torn from their homes, and subjected to solitary confinement, some in fortresses and prisons, and one especially on an island of barren sand, under a tropical sun; have been fed with loathsome rations that have been condemned as unfit for soldiers, and have been exposed to the vilest insults.

Prisoners of war, who surrendered to the naval forces of the United States, on agreement that they should be released on parole, have been seized and kept in close confinement.

Repeated pretexts have been sought or invented for plundering the inhabitants of a captured city, by fines levied and collected under threats of imprisoning recusants at hard labor with ball and chain. *The entire population of New Orleans have been forced to elect between starvation by the confiscation of all their property and taking an oath against conscience to bear allegiance to the invader of their country.*

Egress from the city has been refused to those whose fortitude withstood the test, and *even to lone and aged women, and to helpless children; and after being ejected from their homes and robbed of their property, they have been left to starve in the streets or subsist on charity.*

The slaves have been driven from the plantations in the neighborhood of New Orleans until their owners would consent to share their crops with the commanding general [Benjamin F. Butler], his brother, Andrew J. Butler, and other officers; and when such consent had been extorted, *the slaves have been restored to the plantations, and there compelled to work under the bayonets of the guards of United States soldiers. Where that partnership was refused, armed expeditions have been sent to the plantations to rob them of everything that was susceptible of removal.*

And even slaves, too aged or infirm for work, have, in spite of their entreaties, been forced from the homes provided by their owners, and driven to wander helpless on the highway. . . .

And, finally, *the African slaves have not only been incited to insurrection by every license and encouragement, but numbers of them have actually been armed for a servile war—a war in its nature far exceeding the horrors and most merciless atrocities of savages.*[284]

That these barbarous Yankee policies were continued *after* the War and well into the Reconstruction era, is attested to by numerous other witnesses. In 1906 former Confederate officer John William Headley made the following report of Union outrages against former slaves in the area around Nashville, Tennessee:

[During the postwar period] . . . the most aggravating conduct of the Federals, toward the miserable people of this and all

> other sections of the South, was *the employment of the slaves as soldiers and sending them around, under Northern officers, in their old neighborhoods to taunt, pillage, and burn out the families that had raised them. These licensed detachments would take possession of a house and drive the family out with pompous airs and then smash and pillage till satisfied, when the torch would be applied and everything reduced to ashes.* The jolly soldiers would then march away singing "John Brown's body lies moldering," etc., and other favorite songs.
>
> The darkies were organized in large numbers at Nashville, and after the retreat of [Confederate General John Bell] Hood in December *were sent all over the Murfreesboro country to take and destroy the remnants that might still be left among the people. Several of these crowds had been caught that had committed depredations and were loaded with plunder.*[285]

The Reconstruction KKK was formed, in great part, to combat these very types of atrocities against Southerners.

This 1925 photo of a KKK rally in Washington, D.C. (the Capitol Building can be seen in the center rear) reveals the truth about the organization and its official flag. It was not and never has been the Confederate Battle Flag. It was and always has been the U.S. Flag, the Stars and Stripes. Those who link the Confederacy and her military flag with the KKK and racism are victims of "The Great Yankee Coverup," which has purposefully buried the truth about the South under a mountain of false rhetoric, absurd propaganda, patent misinformation, and vindictive disinformation.

As part of their counter-Reconstruction efforts, white and black KKK members responded by carrying coffins through the streets with the names of prominent Bureau leaders on them. Underneath their names were the words: "Dead, Damned, and Delivered!" The Bureau, as it turned out, was not only unnecessary, as Southerners had long maintained, but it was an absolute hindrance to any kind of racial harmony in the South—one of the reasons Yankees created it to begin with. This is why former Confederates saw it as nothing less than the imposition of an alien government, reinforced by an occupying army.

One hundred years ago KKK rallies, like this one in Washington, D.C., featured only one flag: the U.S. Flag. Associating the Confederate Battle Flag with the Ku Klux Klan is a modern phenomenon, a wholesale perversion of history manufactured by the uninformed and perpetuated by the intolerant.

The Bureau's overt political efforts to create racial warfare in Dixie (by attempting to make former black servants hate their former white owners) were intended to further divide the Southern people by breaking down their morale. Ultimately, to the great remorse of Northern Radicals (Yankee abolitionists), it did not work. But various white elements in the Reconstruction KKK began to understandably turn their attention, some of it violent, toward African-Americans, particularly those who were committing hate crimes against white families under the directives of the U.S. government's Black Leagues.

Again, these particular white groups were acting out of self-preservation, not racism.

Proof of this is that when carpetbag rule ended that year, in 1869, this, the original or Reconstruction KKK, immediately came to an end as well all across the "Invisible Empire" (that is, the Southern states). For when Southerners were allowed to begin to take back political control of their own states, there was no longer any need for a self-protective social welfare organization like the KKK. This is why former Confederate officer and Southern hero General Nathan Bedford Forrest, the Klan's most famous and influential supporter, called in its members and shut the entire fraternity down in March of that year.[286] By the end of 1871 the Reconstruction KKK had disappeared from most areas of the South, and by 1877 Reconstruction itself ceased to exist—a disastrous, corrupt, and malevolent program by any standard.

Liberals have tried to tie the good name of Confederate General Nathan Bedford Forrest to the KKK and racism. But the facts tell a different story. He did not learn about the KKK until two years after it was formed, was never an official member, and was responsible for shutting down the organization in 1869. He then called for repopulating the South with new African immigrants, regarding them as superior workers to whites. Finally, an in-depth investigation by the U.S. government found Forrest innocent of all charges in connection with the KKK, facts that have been strenuously omitted from our history books.

Still, now inaccurately associated with bigotry, the damage had been done, and to this day the original Reconstruction KKK has been branded, unfairly and unhistorically, with the racist label.

Thus for the record, we must reemphasize here that the KKK of today, which emerged in the 1920s, is in no way similar or even connected to the original Reconstruction KKK of the Southern postbellum period, which lasted a mere three years and four months: December 1865 to March 1869. Indeed, there are indications that the modern KKK is far more popular in the North than in the South, with flourishing clans in Indiana, New York, California, Oregon, and Connecticut, just to name a few. Illinois, Lincoln's adopted home state, has also seen a recent resurgence of Klan activity.[287]

WHAT YOU WERE TAUGHT: The Confederate Battle Flag is a symbol of slavery, hatred, and racism. Therefore it should be banned from display.

THE FACTS: Enemies of the South have long promoted these ideas, all without a shred of hard evidence. Just opinion, emotion, and misinformation! And in fact they are nothing more than ludicrous and sinister inventions of the pro-North movement, which sustains itself by misrepresenting symbols, people, and organizations it dislikes.

"Hatred" by whom, and "racism" toward whom? As we have seen, this charge, like all the others fomented by South-loathers, is demonstrably false, for both the South and the Confederate military were multiracial, multicultural, and multinational.

Those who cannot accept the authentic history of the Confederate Battle Flag (which would include most Liberals and progressives) say that it must removed from the public arena because it causes them "pain." Since when do we remove something from public view because it causes someone "pain"? If we did, there would be no flags, signs, or symbols of any kind anywhere, because all of them cause distress to one group or another. It is part of the privilege and responsibility of being an American to learn to live with the cultural, social, racial, national, and religious differences that lawfully exist within our borders. If some of these differences inflict unbearable "pain" on someone, he or she should consider moving to a communist country where only one flag, one political idea, and one national symbol are permitted.

And what about the First Amendment and our constitutional right of freedom of speech and expression? This clause was created to prevent the very thing that is happening with the Confederate Battle Flag today: the censorship of a particular symbol by a single group. This idea was so important to the Founding Fathers that they inserted it in the opening of the Bill of Rights. But, of course, this is one of the many reasons Liberals have always disliked the Constitution: the First Amendment permits the free flow of historical facts that counter their personal views, beliefs, and ideologies, and which they can thus no longer deny, control, distort, revise, rewrite, or suppress.

The Confederate Battle Flag is also regularly attacked by the politically correct thought police as "a symbol of slavery." This too is erroneous, however, for as is clear from the foregoing history, it was a Confederate *military* flag, not a Confederate *national* flag; one that had nothing to do with social issues, civil institutions, or politics. It was used *only* by Rebel military officers and their soldiers, and never flew over the Confederate Capitol at Montgomery or later at Richmond.

True Southerners raise the next generation with an appreciation for the Confederate Battle Flag. This is a longstanding Southern tradition that began in the 1860s, and it is not going to cease, now or at any time in the future, no matter how loudly Liberals complain, how many facts they distort, or how many prohibitory laws they pass.

Even if the Confederate Battle Flag had been the national flag of the C.S.A., the Confederate government did not fight over slavery, so this accusation is equally fallacious. It is, in fact, just another worn out fairy tale created by the South-hating Left to stir up racial and regional strife, incite animosity toward Dixie, and divide the country, the same tactics used by Liberal Lincoln and his ilk prior to, during, and after the War.

What the anti-South movement does not understand, or understands but refuses to acknowledge, is that Southerners have lived under two national flags: the U.S. Flag and the C.S. Flag. Both are important to us here in the South (though for different reasons). *In a very real sense Southerners are dual citizens of the United States; citizens sharing a multiple history with the North, one that includes two countries and two flags—both American! Thus, Southerners are both Confederates (C.S.A.) and Unionists (U.S.A.), and so we have a double heritage and a double allegiance.*

In 1916 former Confederate officer Major T. H. Blacknall wrote a poem that perfectly expresses the sentiment of the South on this topic:

MY FLAGS
One I have sworn to defend and obey;
The other is the winding sheet of the gray.
Though the Stars and Stripes waves over land and sea,
I will forever love the banner I followed under Lee.
Should trouble come, under the Stars and Stripes I'd take my stand,
With the Stars and Bars embalmed in the heart of Dixie Land.[288]

The U.S. Flag and the C.S. Flag. The dual citizenship of every Southern man and woman is a fact of history, irrefutable and irrevocable. We do not deny it, and our heritage cannot be denied us. To enemies of the South we say, accept the obvious, embrace the inevitable, and move on.

This is reality; a reality that will never go away no matter how much hatred the Left directs toward our flag, and no matter how many laws they pass in an effort to suppress it. At one time even many Yankees understood this. In 1911 one of them, Colonel James Anderson of Holyoke, Massachusetts, for instance, wrote the following poem entitled:

LET THE "CONQUERED BANNER" WAVE
Why furl it and fold it and put it away,
The Banner that proudly waved over the Gray?
It has not a blemish, it shows not a stain,
Though it waved over fields where thousands were slain.
O, why should we furl it and put it away?

It's loved and respected by the Blue and the Gray.
They fought for a cause they thought was Just,
And this Banner they loved was trailed in the dust.
Their fight was lost and their hopes are dead,
And another flag waves proud o'er their head;
But still in their memory without boast or brag,
Wound around their hearts is this bonnie blue flag.

So unfurl that Banner; don't lay it away.
There is but one country—it's both Blue and Gray—
Just one united land for us all.
Each willing and ready to answer the call;
But no land on earth, no history can say
That braver men lived than those of the Gray.

Don't furl it and fold it and put it away.
Let our sons and daughters gaze on it and say:
"'Twill live on forever in story and song.
Brave men fought for it; they may have been wrong;
But they fought for it gladly, heroes and brave,
And the bonnie blue flag waves over their grave."

So unfurl the old Banner; let it float in the air;
Let all the old veterans salute it up there.
Though their cause it was lost, they were men tried and true.
And they loved their old Banner so bonnie and blue.
Now here's to old Dixie, the land of the brave:
"All hail to the bonnie blue flag; let it wave!"[289]

As Yankee Colonel Anderson readily recognizes, the dual citizenship of Southerners is part and parcel of American history, period: Southerners were once citizens of a foreign country, one that endured through America's bloodiest and most senseless conflict. An admirer of Jefferson Davis said the following after the president's passing in 1889:

> . . . those were eventful years through which he led us. Years of sunshine and of storm, in which, its flag flung to the battle and the breeze, there lived, ruled, and warred a nation, a Confederacy, with its president, its statesmen, its Congress, its leaders, its soldiers, and its people—men steadfast and true—and women (its flower and crown) who suffered and endured. *That is history*.[290]

The truth is that there have been far more racial crimes

The American slave trade was strictly a Yankee affair, one that the South never participated in. After a long voyage from the West Coast of Africa, these black slaves are being unloaded at a port in Boston, Massachusetts, after which they will be sold at auction to wealthy white and black families across New England.

committed under the U.S. Flag than the C.S. Flag, and if the Left truly practiced what it preaches, it would ban the former not the latter.

We could start with slavery, as just one example. As both American slavery and the American slave trade began in the North, we should not be surprised to learn that *every* American slave vessel to ever sail from the U.S. left from Northern ports aboard Northern slave vessels, that were designed by Northern engineers, constructed by Northern shipbuilders, fitted out by Northern riggers, piloted by Northern ship captains, manned by Northern crews, launched from Northern maritime ports, funded by Northern businessmen, all of this which was supported by the vast majority of the anti-abolitionist Northern population. The number of Africans who were abused and who died on these voyages is beyond counting.[291]

We never hear a word from Liberals about removing the U.S. Flag over this, however. Only the C.S. Flag, which had absolutely no connection to the slave trade, or even slavery for that matter!

WHAT YOU WERE TAUGHT: The last Confederate Flag was officially taken down on April 12, 1865, the day General Lee surrendered to General Grant.

THE FACTS: The last Confederate Battle Flag was officially furled nearly a half year later aboard the Confederate cruiser the *Shenandoah*. Here is the story as told by Confederate Captain W. C. Whittle, a participant in the event:

John Thompson Mason was a son of Major Isaac S. Rowland, a volunteer officer in the Mexican War, and Catherine Armstead Mason, of Loudon County, Va. He was born in 1844. His father died when he was only five years old, and his maternal grandfather John Thompson Mason, of Virginia, having no son of his own and wishing to perpetuate the distinguished name of Mason, requested that this child should take the name, which was done by act of Court. Young Thompson's friends secured for him an appointment to the United States Naval Academy, but the war came up before he entered, and he joined the Seventeenth Virginia regiment. Shortly after the battle of Manassas he was appointed midshipman in the Confederate Navy and sent to the naval school ship *Patrick Henry*. He served at Drury's Bluff, and was then sent abroad for service on one of the Confederate cruisers running the blockade at Charleston, S. C. Young Mason went to Abbeville, a quiet town in France, where he applied himself assiduously to the study of his profession and in gaining a thorough knowledge of the French language, succeeding admirably in both.

About this time Captain W. C. Whittle, a son of Commodore Whittle and nephew of Bishop Whittle, of Virginia, met Mason, who had passed his examination and secured his appointment as "passed midshipman." In October, 1864, he was assigned to a cruiser, gotten out from England for the Confederate Navy, and with Commander [James Iredell] Waddell and other officers of the prospective cruiser, except Lieutenant Whittle, sailed from Liverpool on the consort steamer *Laurel* to meet their ship elsewhere. Captain Whittle writes:

"I was assigned to the ship as her first lieutenant and executive officer, and sailed from London on board of her under her merchant name, *Sea King*. The two vessels, by preconcertion, met at the Madeira Islands and, leaving there in company, sailed to Desertas Island, where the *Sea King* was christened and commissioned the Confederate States Cruiser *Shenandoah*, and the guns, ammunition, and equipment were transferred from the consort *Laurel* to the cruiser *Shenandoah*, which promptly started on her memorable cruise. Her officers were Lieutenant-Commander James I. Waddell, of North Carolina; W. C. Whittle, of Virginia, First Lieutenant and Executive Officer; Lieutenants John Grimball, of South Carolina, S. S. Lee, Jr., Virginia; F. L. Chew, Missouri; Dabney M. Scales, Mississippi; Sailing Master Irvine S. Bullock, of Georgia; Passed Midshipmen Orris A. Brown, Virginia; and John T. Mason, Virginia. Surgeon C. E. Lining, South Carolina;

Assistant Surgeon F. J. McNulty, District of Columbia; Paymaster W. B. Smith, Louisiana; Chief Engineer M. O'Brien Law, Louisiana; Assistant Engineers Codd, Maryland; Hutchinson, Scotland; MacGreffery, Ireland; Master Mates John Minor, Virginia, Cotton, Maryland, Hunt, Virginia; Boatswain Harwood, England; Gunner Guy, England; Carpenter O'Shea, Ireland; Sailmaker Allcott, England.

The last Confederate cruiser, *Shenandoah*, which furled the last Confederate Flag on November 6, 1865. Note the C.S. Third National flying at the stern.

"Under these officers and subordinates this gallant ship made one of the most wonderful cruises on record. She was a merchant ship which had not about her construction a single equipment as a vessel of war. Her equipment—such as guns, ammunition, breechings, carriages, etc., were all in boxes on her deck, and these gallant officers and a few volunteer seamen from her crew and that of her consort were to transform and equip her on the high seas, and in all kinds of weather. None but the experienced can appreciate what a Herculean task that was. But it was enthusiastically undertaken and accomplished, and none were more conspicuous or untiring in their efforts to bring order out of chaos than young Mason.

"Our gallant little ship spread her broad canvas wings and sailed around the world, using her auxiliary steam power only in calm belts or in chase. We sailed around Cape of Good Hope, thence through the Indian Ocean to Melbourne, Australia, thence through the Islands of Polynesia, passing the Caroline, Gilbert, and other groups, on northward through Kurile Islands into the Okhotsk Sea, until stopped by the ice. We came out of the Okhotsk and went up the coast of Kamchatka into Bering Sea, and through Bering Strait into the Arctic Ocean, until the ice again prevented us from going farther, so we turned, passed again through the Aleutian Islands, into the Pacific Ocean. By this time we had absolutely destroyed or broken up the Federal [Yankee] whaling fleets.

"While sweeping down the Pacific coast, looking for more prey, we chased and overhauled a vessel flying the British flag. On boarding her we found it was the British bark *Barracoula*, bound from San Francisco to Liverpool. This was August 2nd, 1865. From her Captain we learned the war had been over since the previous April. The effects of this crushing intelligence on us can better be imagined than described. We found that much of our work of destruction to the whaling fleet of the United States had been done after the war closed, unwittingly of course, for from the nature of their work the whalers had been away from communication about as long as we had, and were equally ignorant of results. We promptly declared our mission of war over, disarmed our vessel, and shaped our course for England with well nigh broken hearts. We journeyed around Cape Horn, and on November 6th, 1865, arrived at Liverpool and surrendered to the British Government through their guard ship *Donegal* by *hauling down the last Confederate flag that ever floated in defiance to the United States, after having circumnavigated the globe, cruised in every ocean except the Antarctic, and made more captures than any other Confederate cruiser except the famous* Alabama.

James I. Waddell, commander of the *Shenandoah*.

"After a full investigation of our conduct by the law officer of the crown, it was decided that we had done nothing against the rules of war or the laws of nations to justify us in being held as prisoners, so we were unconditionally released by the

> nation to which we had surrendered. But the authorities of the United States considered us pirates and *in their heated hatred at that time* would have treated us as such if we had fallen into their hands, so we had to find homes elsewhere than our native land. Four of us (S. S. Lee, Orris A. Brown, John T. Mason, and myself) selected the Argentine Republic, in South America, and sometime in December 1865, sailed from Liverpool in a steamer for Buenos Ayres, via Bahia, Rio de Janeiro, and Montevidio. After prospecting a while, we went to Rosario, on Rio Parana, and near there bought a small place and began farming.
>
> "As the animosity of the Federal Government began to soften toward us, Brown and Mason returned home, Lee and myself coming sometime later.
>
> "On returning home Mason took a law course at the University of Virginia, graduated, and was brilliantly successful at his profession. He settled in Baltimore, and married Miss Helen Jackson, of New York, a daughter of the late Lieutenant Alonzo C. Jackson, of the U. S. Navy. His wife, two sons, and two daughters survive him."[292]

WHAT YOU WERE TAUGHT: We have always been one country, and still are. America has only *one* flag, the U.S. Flag, and it is this flag and only this flag that should be flown and honored by *all* Americans. This makes the South's love for the racist Confederate flag unnatural and irrational, which is why it should be banned.

THE FACTS: We have already debunked most of the mythical statements in this comment, so let us focus on the one we have not: the last one.

The South's attachment to its Confederate flags is right, proper, natural, and completely rational, for the existence—from 1861 to 1865—of the second Confederate States of America, the Southern Confederacy, was a *historical reality*. Some 12 million Southerners of all races were official citizens of this unique constitutionally created republic, and their modern descendants have every right, and every reason, to honor the flags that once represented their ancestors' country. "A Confederate Ditty" from the war period perfectly captures the feelings of "Johnny Reb," the everyday Confederate soldier:

Wrap me in a secesh flag,
Bury me by Jeff Davis,
Give my love to General Lee,
And kiss all the Southern ladies.[293]

This was not just a sentimentalized Southern romance. Thousands of Rebel soldiers asked to be literally enfolded and buried in the Confederate Flag. One of these, Colonel George Washington Rains (one half of the Confederacy's famous "Bomb Brothers"), placed a clause in his will to this effect, which was duly carried out at his death in March 1898.[294]

The enormous fondness we have for our Confederate flags began even before they were formally recognized by the Confederate government and hoisted up public flagpoles. Let us look at one example of this attachment between Southerner and flag from the time of Lincoln's War. It concerns the notorious Kentucky "bushwhacker" and Confederate guerilla Champ Ferguson, whose adherence to the Confederate Flag and the Southern Cause was so immense that it changed the course of the conflict. As the story goes,

> Champ was a citizen at his home when the tocsin was sounded, and stayed there until his own precincts were invaded. A rabid fire eater passed his house with a troop of Blues [Yankee soldiers]. You ask why he was so desperate. It was told in camp that Champ Ferguson's little three-year-old child came out into the porch waving a Confederate flag. One of the [Union] men in blue leveled his gun at Champ and killed the child. O, anguish! how that father's heart bled! His spirit welled up like the indomitable will of the primitive Norseman. In a moment of frenzy he said that the death of his baby would cost the "blue coats" a hundred lives. And it did. One hundred and twenty is believed to be the number he put to death. (Comrade S. H. Mitchell got this from Champ himself.)
>
> He took to the woods and for four years, his war upon them was unrelenting, and vengeance was never appeased. It increased like the raging torrent, as his family and friends were vilified and abused. In the Cumberland Mountains, clans formed and terrorized the section by petty warfare, until the cauldron of fear and apprehension invaded every home. The hunger for vengeance grew with the years, and Champ became the terror of the Northern side, while [Union guerilla Captain Elam] Huddleston

and Tinker Dave Beatty were the same to the Southern. The acts of the latter, because they belonged to the victorious side, are buried in the tomb, and the government perhaps honors their memory; but the acts of Champ Ferguson, because of the misfortunes of war, are bruited as the most terrible in history.

Champ Ferguson (right) and one of his guards.

If the sea could give up its dead, and the secrets of men be made known, Champ Ferguson's actions as bushwhacker, in comparison, would excite only a passive and not an active interest. Champ was a mountaineer; rude and untrained in the refinements of moral life, he had entertained that strict idea of right that belongs to the mountain character. Nature had instilled into him a consuming passion for vengeance for a wrong. *His method was indiscreet, his warfare contemptible; but, in palliation, how was it compared to the [Yankees'] open murder of starving out our women and children, burning our houses, and pillaging our homes?* Champ Ferguson was well to do in this world's goods when the war began. Had he been let alone, a career of good citizenship would have been his portion. Had he lived in the days of the Scottish Chiefs, the clans would no doubt have crowned his efforts; but now, since his flag has fallen, history marks his career as more awful than that of John A. Murrell [a famous antebellum Southern bandit], and caps it with

> a hangman's noose. The times in which he lived must be considered, the provocation, the surroundings, and then let history record Champ's actions.
>
> In his zeal for the South to win, he became hardened; and the more steeped in blood the more his recklessness increased until irritability occasioned by treatment of his home folk drove him to maniacal desperation.[295]

Captured by Union soldiers after the War, on October 20, 1865, the angry mountaineer swung on the gallows for his crimes. Some 120 Yankees had died at Ferguson's hand for killing his child and desecrating the Confederate Flag. While we cannot condone his murderous actions, we can certainly understand his passion for his family and the traditional Southern way of life. For it is this same passion which burns in the heart of every red-blooded Southerner today.

Southern heroine Rose O'Neal Greenhow and her daughter, who is visiting her in a prison in Washington, D.C. A fearless freedom fighter, Greenhow loved and cherished the Confederate Battle Flag and bemoaned its abuse by ignorant Yankees.

In 1863 renowned Washington socialite and Confederate spy Rose O'Neal Greenhow wrote of her feelings toward both the U.S. Flag of the Liberal North and the C.S. Flag of the Conservative South:

> To me . . . the days of my former abode in Washington seem to belong almost to another state of being. That time—when I, in common with all our people, looked up with pride and veneration to the banner of the stars and stripes—appears to be now with the years before the Flood. I look back to the scenes of that period through a haze of blood and horror. *Those [Northern] men whom I once called friends—who have broken bread at my table—have since then stirred up and hounded on host after host of greedy invaders, and precipitated them upon the beloved valleys where my [Southern] kindred had their peaceful homes. Many who were dear to me have been slain, or maimed for life, fighting in defence of all that makes life of value. Instead of friends, I see in those [Yankee] statesmen of Washington only mortal enemies. Instead of loving and worshipping the old [U.S.] flag of the stars and stripes, I see in it only the symbol of murder, plunder, oppression, and shame! and, like every other faithful Confederate, I dwell with delight on the many glorious fields where this dishonoured standard has gone down before the stainless battleflag of the Confederacy.*[296]

A hint of the importance the Confederate soldier attached to his flag can be seen in the following wartime description given by George M. Neese, a gunner in Jeb Stuart's Horse Artillery, Army of Northern Virginia:

> We had a grand review to-day. General Stuart's cavalry corps and horse artillery passed in general review before General R. E. Lee and John Letcher, Governor of Virginia. We arrived on the field early in the day. A great many of the cavalry were then already arriving on the review ground from two or three different directions, and the whole field was soon covered with bodies of horsemen in their cleanest attire and best appearance, all carefully prepared and trying to look pretty for review. Some of us men tried to blacken our shoes by rubbing them over a camp kettle.
>
> On the east side of the field on a small wave-like hill was a flagstaff with *a large, new, beautiful Confederate flag proudly floating in the crisp November breeze*. At twelve o'clock the troops were all formed and ready for the grand reviewing exhibition. General R. E. Lee and staff, General Stuart and staff, and Governor Letcher rode in a gentle gallop along the whole length of the line, then

quickly repaired to the review station and assembled in *the rippling shadow of the large Confederate flag that moved above their heads.*

When the resplendent and brilliant little cavalcade, with the grand old chieftain, R. E. Lee, in the center, had settled down for business, the column of horsemen began to move like some huge war machine. The horse artillery moved in front, then came the cavalry in solid ranks and moving in splendid order,—horsemen that have followed the feather of Stuart in a hundred fights. General Wade Hampton's mounted band was on the field and enlivened the magnificent display with inspiring strains of martial music.[297]

The cover of the sheet music of the national anthem of the Confederate States of America, 1862: "God Save the South." Music by C. T. De Coeniel, lyrics by Ernest Halpin. According to the text, the sheet music could be purchased at the composer's residence in Richmond, Virginia, or at "all principle book and music stores in the Confederacy."

Such sentiments continued long after Lincoln's War and, of course, they survive into the 21st Century. On April 26, 1898, at a Confederate Memorial Day service in Columbus, Georgia, former Confederate soldier Robert M. Howard made these remarks:

> Though there has been a lapse of thirty-three years since the flag of the Confederacy went down, *we turn to-day to the grand old emblem, and the hallowed cause it represented, with the same deathless love with which we hailed its glorious birth when we unfurled it to the breezes of high Heaven, and followed its spotless folds through its brief and brilliant life.* So long as the eagle shall wing its lofty flight to Alpine heights; so long as the babbling brooks shall mingle their crystal waters with the mighty rivers, in their clear winding to the sea; so long as the breeze shall beat the billows' foam; *so long as true manhood and noble womanhood shall inspire pure patriotism and exalted citizenship—so long will Dixie's brave sons and peerless daughters perpetuate and religiously observe this, our Memorial Day, in everlasting memory and love of our Confederate dead.* On each sad anniversary, with earth's sweetest, fairest flowers we will wreathe the graves of our immortal heroes, who went down to glorious death amid the shock and carnage of battle in the heroic discharge of righteous duty.[298]

WHAT YOU WERE TAUGHT: The Confederate Flag will never be used officially again.

THE FACTS: Convinced that it is time to disassociate from the decadent Union headquartered in Washington, D.C., millions of traditional Southerners are planning a second secession—and have been for quite some time. Why? Because the intolerant Left and the lukewarm Right are slowly but surely destroying the great Confederate Republic created by the Founding Fathers: the original Confederate States of America. The only way to preserve it is to separate from the North and recreate the C.S.A. in the South. This is exactly what our Southern ancestors attempted to do, and this is precisely why they fought the North.

As the C.S.A. was never officially closed down, when what I call "the Second Southern Secession" occurs, the Confederate Third National Flag will once again fly over every state capitol in the South, and the Confederate Battle Flag will once again billow from every flagpole.

This is not fanciful daydream. Do not underestimate the political, social, spiritual, and economic power of the Southern people. Southern secession happened once, and it can and *will* happen again. The South is not going to rise again in the future. It is *already* rising!

WHAT YOU WERE TAUGHT: Confederate soldiers claimed to be part of a "foreign country," the so-called "Confederate States of America." So, because their states tried to secede from the Union, they should all be regarded as traitors to the U.S., and, in turn, should not be honored or even recognized as U.S. veterans—because they weren't. In fact, their graves should be dug up and, along with their headstones, monuments, and statues, should be moved to private property or simply destroyed.

THE FACTS: These are statements of ignorance, hatred, bias, and intolerance, not facts of authentic history. Being personal beliefs based on emotion and disinformation, they are thus erroneous.

Part of the magnificent Confederate Memorial Monument at Montgomery, Alabama.

To begin with, neither Lincoln or most of the Northern populace considered the Confederate States of America to be a "foreign country." In fact the Yankee chief executive never once conceded what every Southerner knew to be true: that under the Ninth and Tenth Amendments, the C.S.A. (named after the original name for the U.S.A.) was a legal and constitutionally formed republic, with all the rights of a sovereign self-governing country.

Despite this bold fact of political history, naturally the U.S. government has sided with Lincoln on this matter into the present day, claiming that the C.S.A. was *not* a legitimate foreign commonwealth. What this means in plain English then is that *in the eyes of the U.S. government, Confederate soldiers were indeed U.S. military veterans*, recognition of which began early in the 20th Century when Congress approved "U.S. Public Law 810" on February 26, 1929. Now updated as "Title 38, Veterans' Benefits, Amendment 2306," it reads:

> Headstones, markers, and burial receptacles: (a) *The Secretary shall furnish*, when requested, *appropriate Government headstones or markers at the expense of the United States for* the unmarked graves of the following: . . . (3) *Soldiers of the* Union and *Confederate Armies of the Civil War.*[299]

On May 23, 1958, the idea of fully and legally Americanizing Confederate soldiers was made official when the U.S. Congress approved a regulation known as "Public Law 85-425." Though the last Confederate soldier died many decades ago, let us briefly review this act in order to further dispel the unhistorical statement above. The introduction reads:

> *To increase the monthly rates of pension payable to widows and former widows of deceased veterans of the* Spanish-American War, *Civil War*, Indian War, and Mexican War, and *provide pensions to widows of veterans who served in the military or naval forces of the Confederate States of America during the Civil War.*[300]

Further on the act states:

> Be it enacted by the Senate and House of Representatives of the *United States of America in Congress* assembled, That the Veterans' Benefits Act of 1957 (Public Law 85-56) is amended: [Clause] (e) For the purpose of this section, and section 433, *the term "veteran" includes a person who served in the military or naval forces of the Confederate States of America during the Civil War, and the term "active, military or naval service" includes active service in such forces.*[301]

According to the U.S. Congress, as U.S. veterans, all former Confederate soldiers, sailors, and marines were to be paid a monthly pension in accord with U.S. law, as stipulated in Section 410:

> Confederate Forces Veterans: The Administrator shall pay to each person who served in the military or naval forces of *the Confederate States of America during the Civil War* a monthly pension in the same amounts and subject to the same conditions *as would have been applicable to such person under the laws in effect on December 31, 1957, if his service in such forces had been service in the military or naval forces of the United States.*[302]

Thus, despite what Liberals, socialists, and the anti-South movement would like you to believe, according to no less than the U.S. Congress, *all* Confederate soldiers are indeed U.S. veterans (or more technically, are to be viewed as being the same as U.S. veterans), making it a crime to move, violate, or even disturb a Confederate gravestone, statue, or monument. This is so important that I will repeat it: *according to the U.S. government it is a crime to move, violate, or even disturb a Confederate gravestone, statue, or monument.*

The grave of Confederate Brigadier-General John C. Carter, Rose Hill Cemetery, Columbia, Tennessee, photographed by the author. Carter died on December 10, 1864, from wounds he received at the Battle of Franklin II (November 30, 1864). Though uneducated bigoted cultural cleansers would like Carter's remains completely removed from this location, under U.S. law he is considered the same as a U.S. military veteran, making it a crime to even tamper with his grave site.

On December 14, 1898, at Atlanta, Georgia, with the bitter sentiment of the "Civil War" still lingering in the air, our twenty-fifth president, William McKinley, *a former Union soldier*, spoke for many Americans when he made the following remarks before a Southern audience concerning both Union *and* Confederate soldiers—many who were still alive at the time:

> Sectional lines no longer mar the map of the United States; sectional feeling no longer holds back the love we bear one another. Fraternity is the national anthem, sung by a chorus of forty-five States and our Territories at home and beyond the seas. The Union is once more the common altar of our love and loyalty, our devotion and sacrifice. . . .
>
> The old [U.S.] flag again waves over us in peace with new glories, which *your [Southern] sons and ours* have this year added to its sacred folds. What cause we have for rejoicing, saddened only by the fact that *so many of our brave men fell on the field, or sickened and*

died from hardship and exposure, and others returned bringing wounds and disease from which they will long suffer!

The memory of the dead will be a precious legacy, and the disabled will be the nation's care. A nation which cares for its disabled soldiers as we have always done will never lack defenders. *The national cemeteries for those who fell in battle* are proof that the dead are cared for, and the living have our love. What an army of silent sentinels we have; and with what loving care their graves are kept. *Every soldier's grave made during our unfortunate civil war* is a tribute to *American* valor.

And while, when those graves were made, we differed widely about the future of this Government, these differences were long ago settled by the arbitrament of arms, and *the time has now come, in the evolution of sentiment and feeling, under the providence of God, when, in the spirit of fraternity, we should share with you in the care of the graves of the Confederate soldiers.*

The cordial feeling now happily existing between the North and South prompts this gracious act, and if it needed further justification it is found in the gallant loyalty to the Union and the Flag so conspicuously shown in the year just past by the sons and grandsons of those heroic dead.

What a glorious future awaits us if, unitedly, wisely, and bravely we face the new problems now pressing upon us, determined to solve them for right and humanity![303]

U.S. President William McKinley, a Northerner from Ohio who served in the Union army during Lincoln's War, understood why the Confederate Flag is important to Southerners, and encouraged his fellow Yankees to help care for the graves of Confederate soldiers. Sadly, many have ignored his sage advice.

Please note that President McKinley, a Yankee, asks his fellow Northerners to share with Southerners "in the care of the graves of the Confederate soldiers." Were he alive today, the chief executive from Ohio would not be happy to learn that other Northerners, and even many Southerners, are profaning, vandalizing, digging up, and requesting the removal, and sometimes the complete destruction, of the tombs of Dixie's "brave men in gray."

Just a few decades after Lincoln's War, many Union veterans themselves evinced tremendous respect and even awe for the fearless Rebels who they had once faced across the battlefield. After all, since the South withstood a fighting force three times its own size for four long years, the very term "Confederate soldier" became a synonym for courage in that day.[304] One of these Yankee vets was William M. Armstrong who, in 1898, penned the following:

> *I heartily endorse everything that will bring us [Northerners] into closer friendship with the people of the South. I have an intense admiration for them*, and it's odd that this was first awakened during a fierce engagement. It was in Tennessee. Our men were stationed on a slope of ground behind parapets with head-logs. . . . Well, the only danger to which we could possibly be exposed during an attack was from our own batteries, which were so placed that they could fire over our heads. In such cases shells often burst before they reach their intended destination, and thus play havoc in the ranks they are meant to serve. Everything was against any who should attempt to come up that line, *but a force of Confederates tried it*. Their front lines were mowed down by the batteries, but on they came, as though they meant to take everything before them, until one could but wonder what madness possessed them. Again and again they were repulsed by merciless firing, but *every time they would reform and come marching back as proudly as if on review*, until—would you believe it?—they charged us seven times, and every time they came nearer, until in the last desperate assault our defenses were reached, and, clambering upon them, *they fought like madmen* with the butts of their guns until our batteries swept them down in a heap. *I never saw anything that could equal it in my life, and I have seen some thrilling sights. While they were fighting so heroically I felt like cheering them myself. It was such a magnificent effort that, although victory was ours, it seemed trivial and mean because so easily won, especially when we watched the remnants of that gallant band fall slowly back, leaving the ground covered with gray-clad figures. Since then I have always thought that such foes would be worthy having as friends. I have made frequent visits in the South of late years, and have met many ex-Confederates, with whom delightful friendships were formed.*[305]

If only today's Liberals could be as benevolent and understanding toward the South as Yankee Armstrong, or President McKinley—a Union soldier who fought with the Twenty-Third Ohio Infantry!

Most cannot and never will be, however, because progressives, like Lincoln and his modern day political descendants, do not want peaceful coexistence between the South and the North, and never have. Conflict, whether military, political, racial, economic, social, or sectional, is what best serves the divisive agenda of the Left. As individuals like socialist Hitler have always known, *a divided country*—one filled with antagonistic intolerant opponents preaching contentious hate-filled ideologies—*is a weakened country*, one that is easier to lull or even force into dependence on the central government.

WHAT YOU WERE TAUGHT: The South lost the Civil War. Southerners need to accept this. Take down the Confederate Battle Flag and get over it.
THE FACTS: *The South did not lose the War. America lost the War.* For, contrary to what we have been taught, this was not a "rebellion" on the part of the South; it was not a"war between the states"; and it was not a "war of secession"; technically it was not even a "War for Southern Independence." And it was certainly not a "civil war," which Webster defines as "a battle between people or states belonging to the *same* country."

Thirteen inch mortars at a Union battery, the Battle of Yorktown, April through May 1862. The Civil War was neither a "civil war" or a "rebellion." It was a fight on the part of the South for the U.S. Constitution, on the part of the North to overturn the U.S. Constitution. Thus the North's victory was really America's loss, for every citizen gave up some of his or her freedom the day Lee stacked arms at Appomattox.

The four official flags of the Southern Confederacy, 1861-1865.
No. 1: The First National ("Stars and Bars")
No. 2: The Battle Flag ("Southern Cross")
No. 3: The Second National ("Stainless Banner")
No. 4: The Third National ("Blood-stained Banner")

An extremely obvious point that is continually ignored by the anti-South movement: *if these flags were actually symbols of "racism, slavery, and hatred," Southerners would not have loved them, displayed them, honored them, cherished them, or memorialized them for the past 150 years right into the present day!* Do not let the erroneous, delusive, irrational, silly, malicious, deceptive, fantastical, vengeful, unrealistic, error-filled, self-interested, and historically untrustworthy propaganda put out by the Left influence you against these beautiful American emblems. They are products of the Southern heart and mind. Thus, only a true Southerner, or at least one who has a thorough knowledge of authentic Southern history, has a right to define their true meaning.

The reason these terms are all incorrect is simple.

By the time the conflict began on April 12, 1861, the Southern states were *already* independent, for they had seceded and formed their own constitutional republic months before: the Confederate States of America, named after one of the names for the original U.S.A. And these states did not "rebel." They seceded, *peacefully* and *legally*, as was—according to the greatest legal scholars of that day—their constitutional right.

In reality then, *Lincoln's War was a battle between two confederacies*: the C.S.A. (the South) and the U.S.A. (the North) over the Constitution. The C.S.A. believed that, as guaranteed by the Ninth and Tenth Amendments, the states should retain their sovereign power as independent "nation-states," while the central government should remain strictly limited in its authority. The U.S.A. held the opposite view, namely, that the states should be stripped of all or most of their sovereign rights and the central government enlarged and empowered.

James Madison was a strong supporter of confederation and believed that states' rights were the foundation that held the Union together. He would not be pleased to see what Lincoln and his modern day fellow Liberals have done to the original confederate republic he and the other Conservative Founding Fathers worked so diligently to create.

Since the Founding Fathers intended the former, and indeed, created the Constitution to prevent the latter, the South's so-called "loss" was actually America's loss. For with Lee's surrender on April 9, 1865, every American citizen lost a number of important constitutional freedoms, rights, and privileges, whittled away and stolen by Liberal Lincoln and his progressive Northern followers.

What were these rights?

They were the "unalienable rights" laid out by the Founders in the Bill of Rights: freedom of religion and speech, the right to bear arms, the right of *habeas corpus*, the (tacit) state right of secession, the right against unreasonable searches, the right against excessive bail, etc. According to the Fathers, these "natural rights," as Locke called them, were meant to be ours *permanently*, because they were "endowed by the Creator" rather than given to us by the government. This means, in turn, that they cannot be taken from us by the government. They are spiritual gifts, freely inherited by you and me from God Himself, and thus are innate within us, built into our very DNA.

English philosopher John Locke held that each person is born with a set of "natural rights" (such as "life, happiness, liberty") that cannot be taken away by the government. This idea, of God-given inalienable rights, was embedded in the U.S. Constitution by the Founders. Ever since, American Liberals, from Lincoln to Obama, have been busy trying to erode it.

This belief, codified by the Constitution, is what makes America and our government special. It is a concept that is unique to us; and it has engendered a one-of-a-kind government, a "Confederate Republic," as Alexander Hamilton referred to it; one that has never existed at any other time in human history: a political system wherein *power flows from the people rather than from the government*.

But Liberals, many who are not religious or even spiritual, and most who have no love for the Constitution, do not appreciate the uniqueness of the U.S.A. and her confederate government. They would rather we imitate those European countries who have gone down the dark path of socialism, wherein power flows from the government rather than from the people. Though Lincoln was not technically a socialist, as a big government Liberal who was loved and supported by socialists and Marxists, he certainly possessed what can only be called socialistic tendencies, which is the real reason he went to war with the conservative South.

This certainly explains why Lincoln's modern political descendants, the Democrats (along with their cousins, radical progressives and the American Socialist Party), are still attacking our "unalienable rights," hell-bent on nationalizing every aspect of American life while reducing every American citizen to a slave of the Federal government. The Founding Generation would be horrified to see how Liberals have purposefully tried to foil their God-based plan for permanent personal independence and self-government.

The Gadsden Flag, designed in 1775 by Southerner and American Revolutionary War hero Christopher Gadsden, bears a rattlesnake on a yellow field. The Gadsden Flag has affinities with the Confederate Battle Flag: they represent, in great part, constitutional patriotism and freedom from governmental tyranny, which is why both have been adopted by the modern Tea Party and by libertarians. In an attempt to shut down debate and destroy their political opponents, history-ignorant Liberals have, of course, labeled the Gadsden Flag "racist." But Gadsden was not a bigot and the creation of his flag has never had anything to do with skin color. He was a military man and his banner was designed to be used by the U.S. Navy and the U.S. Marine Corps, both which still fly it to this day.

However, they would be elated to know that at least one group is carrying the torch of constitutional freedom forward: the proud descendants of Confederate soldiers, whose sacred banner of liberty is the Confederate Battle Flag. This makes the modern conservative, libertarian, and Tea Party movements merely extensions of the old Southern Confederacy, a fact that should gladden the hearts of all American traditionalists.

As a former Confederate said in 1889 concerning the South and our first president: "Mr. Davis and we fought for the Constitution framed by our fathers."[306] This is actually a reference to both of America's first two constitutions, the Articles of Confederation and the Constitution of the United States of America. In particular Confederates were interested in preserving the following three articles from the former:

> Article II. Each State retains its sovereignty, freedom, and independence, and every power, jurisdiction, and right, which is not by this confederation expressly delegated to the United States in Congress assembled;
>
> Article III. The said States hereby severally enter into a firm league of friendship with each other, for their common defense, the

> security of their liberties, and their mutual and general welfare, binding themselves to assist each other, against all force offered to. or attacks made upon them, or any of them, on account of religion, sovereignty, trade, or any other pretence whatever.
>
> Article IV. The free inhabitants of each State, paupers, vagabonds, and fugitives from justice excepted, shall be entitled to all privileges and immunities of free citizens in the several States.

The spirit, if not the exact meaning, of these three important clauses from the Articles of Confederation were brought forward into the U.S. Constitution (which replaced the former in 1789),[307] and it was this specific document—that is, the Constitution as it existed prior to Lincoln's election in 1861—which the freedom-loving, conservative Southern people fought to preserve starting that year. And this is precisely the same thing that today's Conservatives and Libertarians are fighting for: the preservation of the original liberties guaranteed to us by God, the Founding Fathers, and the U.S. Constitution.

In 1906 Captain John Levi Underwood, a chaplain in the Confederate military, wrote:

> *The Southern people* . . . and Democrats [the Conservatives of the day], *were devoted to the Union of the fathers as long as it was a reality. But as soon as they realized that it had become only a confederation of the Northern majority States, with the protecting features of the old Constitution directly discarded, the love for their own States led them heart and soul into the Confederate cause.* [Some] . . . might be satisfied with *a Union*, but nothing but *the Union* of the fathers could satisfy Southern men. *They loved the definite Union of 1789; they fought the indefinite Union of 1861*. The former was a union on a Constitution without a flag; the latter was a mere sentimental union under a flag without a Constitution. The Constitution had been thrown away.[308]

And the South wanted to retrieve and reinstate it!

Yes, in 1861 the Conservative South took up arms to defend the Constitution; the Liberal North took up arms to overturn it. In 1912, Confederate soldier Robert Milton Howard eloquently laid out this overt fact of history in what I consider the clearest and most precise essay ever written on this topic:

. . . I believe it to be the duty of every Southern man to do what he can to set forth these facts, and impress them on the minds of the new generation.

We [Southerners] stand charged at the bar of History with the crime of treasonably attempting to overthrow the best Government that the world ever saw in order to perpetuate human slavery; and if we refuse to make any defense the future will adjudge us guilty and consign us to infamy. The South can not refuse to plead her cause—*can not acquiesce in the misrepresentations of so-called history, written by men who have either misunderstood or wilfully defamed her*—without proving false to herself, false to the great statesmen and military leaders who guided her to glory in the past, and false to those indomitable heroes who, with no hope of reward save such as might be found in the consciousness of duty well and faithfully done, shouldered their muskets in answer to her call, and, on the field of battle, sealed their devotion to her cause with their blood.

Bear with me, then, while, in justification of the action of the men of the South, I endeavor to briefly indicate *the real issue in controversy which led to secession and war*.

However it may have been overshadowed and obscured by subordinate matters, *the real question in that controversy was: Shall this country be governed by the Constitution as construed by the men who framed it, by the States that ratified it, by the ablest jurists in the country, both North and South, and by the highest judicial tribunal in the land? The notion that the Southern States seceded and fought for the extension and perpetuation of slavery has no foundation in fact. "This whole subject of slavery, in any and every view of it," said Mr. [Alexander H.] Stephens, "was, to the seceding States, but a drop in the ocean compared with other considerations involved in the issue." Slavery was a matter of comparatively minor importance, the controversy about which brought to the front the far more important question of fidelity to the Constitution*. In the debate on the Nebraska Bill, [Illinois] Senator [Stephen A.] Douglas, speaking of the slavery agitation, said:

> "It has always arisen from one and the same cause. Whenever that cause has been removed, the agitation has ceased; and whenever that cause has been renewed, the agitation has sprung into existence. *That cause is, and ever has been, the attempt on the part of Congress to interfere with the question of slavery in the Territories and new States formed therefrom*. Is it not wise, then, to confine our action within the sphere of our legitimate duties, and leave

> this vexed question to take care of itself in each State and Territory in conformity to the forms and in subjection to *the provisions of the Constitution?*"

Mr. Douglas stated the case truly. *The sole cause of the controversy about slavery, in the councils of the nation, was the attempt of [the Northern influenced] Congress to go beyond the sphere of its legitimate duties and interfere with the question. The controversy was not about slavery itself—not whether it was right or wrong, not whether it ought or ought not to be abolished or restricted—but about whether Congress should exceed the powers which the Constitution granted to that body, and legislate against it.*

Like his leftist boss President Lincoln, Yankee Secretary of State William Henry Seward believed that the Constitution was not "the supreme law of the land"—despite the fact that the Constitution itself declares this in Article 6. The "higher law," as Victorian Liberals labeled it, was "justice," a subjective and arbitrary belief in the concept of fairness, something that means different things to different people; hence the need for an ultimate body of set laws. Here in the traditional South we respectfully refer to this document as the U.S. Constitution. Northern Liberals, however call it a "compact with the Devil and a league with Hell!"

As the Constitution did not give Congress the authority to legislate against slavery, the antislavery party [that is, the radical abolitionists in the then Liberal Republican Party], through its representative men, decried that instrument as an immoral and proslavery compact, and declared the purpose to be governed by a so-called "*higher law*."

"The [Liberal] anti-slavery faction in the North," says Mr. [George] Lunt, in his *Origin of the Late War*, "led by members of Congress from that quarter, by political and literary orators of every grade, and by the reverend clergy of most religious denominations, *were determined that there should be no more slavery territory,—law or no law*."

The chief exponent of that party's principles and purposes, [Yankee Liberal William H. Seward,] said: "*There is a law higher than the Constitution which regulates our authority over the domain*. Slavery must be abolished, and we must do it." *This was not merely a declaration of war against slavery; it was a declaration of war against Constitutional Government. It was a bold avowal of the purpose to set at naught the provisions of the Constitution*, and run the Government according to that party's judgment of what ought to be done, *which was presumptuously called "a law higher than the Constitution*."

This higher-law doctrine of Mr. Seward, as an eminent Northern jurist testifies,

> *"was adopted, avowed and acted upon by his party with almost entire unanimity, whenever and wherever they found their wishes opposed by a Constitutional interdict. By him and by them the old notion that the law of the land ought to be obeyed was scoffed at."*

The party's [Liberal] candidate for the Presidency [Lincoln] was committed to this doctrine. In a speech made in Boston in the summer of 1860, Mr. Seward declared that "*the people's standard-bearer, Abraham Lincoln, confessed the obligations of the higher law*;" and predicted the speedy and "*triumphant inauguration of this policy into the Government of the United States*."

In the [progressive] North the provision of the Constitution for the rendition of fugitive slaves [the Fugitive Slave Act] was indignantly repudiated, not only by public gatherings wrought up to a high pitch of excitement by the appeals of impassioned orators, but by deliberative bodies assembled to calmly legislate for the people. *The legislatures of a majority of the Northern States enacted laws to prevent the execution of measures adopted by Congress to make that clause of the Constitution more effective, and thus deliberately violated the compact of Union, and set their judgment above the fundamental law. "It is a singular political Nemesis," says Dr. [Jabez Lamar Monroe] Curry, "that Nullification and Rebellion, as terms of reproach, should attach to the South, while the North has escaped any odium attaching to the terms, although she openly and successfully nullified the Constitution, and the flag of rebellion against the Federal Compact and Federal laws floated over half her capitols."*

Lincoln's progressive belief that there is a "higher law" than the Constitution is what initiated the cascade of Southern secessions, and ultimately the War, not slavery.

While the [leftist] North thus flagrantly repudiated the Constitution, the men of the [traditional] South were unswervingly loyal to it. They opposed its violation even to serve their own interests. This was illustrated in the United States Senate when [Conservative] Jefferson Davis opposed a resolution looking to the establishment of an armed force along the line separating the free and the slave States, to prevent any invasion of the latter by men from the former, and to make more effective the execution of the Fugitive Slave Laws. Mr. Davis firmly opposed this measure, which was intended to protect Southern interests and secure Southern rights, on the ground that it tended to confer on the Federal Government the power to compel the Northern States to fulfill their Constitutional obligations.

He said: "It is providing to carry on war against States; and, whether it be against Massachusetts or Missouri, it is equally objectionable to me; and I will resist it alike in the one case and in the other as subversive of the great principle on which our Government rests." *The men of the South upheld the Constitution as the instrument in which the States had solemnly plighted their faith, each to the others, and the provisions of which could not be violated in any manner or degree without dishonor.* They were called "*Strict Constructionists*," because they protested against any loose interpretation of it to justify party policies and expedient measures. They faithfully fulfilled every obligation which it imposed on them, and urged its faithful observance by others as essential to the peace and prosperity of the country.

When the [Liberal] anti-slavery party had elected to the Presidency a man [Lincoln] avowedly hostile to her interests, all that the South asked was to be assured that the authority of the Constitution would continue to be recognized, and that the Government would continue to be administered according to its provisions. This assurance she could not get. On this point the testimony of Judge [Jeremiah Sullivan] Black, of Pennsylvania, in regard to an interview which he had with Mr. Seward, is conclusive. Mr. Seward was the recognized leader of his party, was slated for the head of the State Department under its rule, and was generally supposed to be the man who, "with law in his voice and honor in his hand," would shape its policy. To him Judge Black went, at the request of Southern men, to see if he would not give them some ground on which they could stand in the Union with safety. An account of their interview is given by Judge Black in an open letter to Mr. Charles Francis Adams, published in 1874. He says:

> "Many propositions were discussed, and rejected as being either impracticable or likely to prove useless, before I told him what I felt perfectly sure would stop all controversy at once and forever. I proposed that he should simply pledge himself and the incoming administration to govern according to the Constitution, and upon every disputed point of Constitutional law to accept that exposition of it which had been, or might be, given by the judicial authorities. *He started at this, became excited, and violently declared he would do no such thing.*"

This was the real issue, clearly and sharply defined—the issue to which slavery, and every other question, was subordinate. The South only asked to be assured that the country would be governed according to the Constitution as expounded by the judicial authorities; the chief exponent of the purposes of the party about to take the reins of government refused to pledge himself and the incoming administration to so govern, even when assured that such a pledge would settle all trouble at once and forever.

The [Conservative] South was dominated by the principle of law and order—the principle of conformity to the lawfully-established order, and the remedy of wrongs in a lawful way; the [Liberal] North was dominated by what Wendell Phillips called the "Puritan Principle"—the principle of which he saw a glorious exemplar in the "hero-saint" [John Brown] who, at Harper's Ferry, "flung himself against the law and order of his time," and attempted to carry insurrection, outrage and murder into the peaceful homes of Virginia—the principle of those whose motto, as Mr. Phillips declared, was not "Law and Order," but "God and Justice," and who, in all their history, never hesitated to trample law and order in the dust to compel others to conform to their notions of God and justice. The claim of the South was: The Constitution must be obeyed. Wherein it may be found wrong, amend it in the lawfully-prescribed way; but, until it is thus amended, its provisions, as they stand, must be faithfully carried out. The claim of the dominant party in the North, as voiced by Mr. Seward, was: "There is a law higher than the Constitution;" and, wherein the Constitution conflicts with that higher law, its provisions must be set at naught.

In an effort to prevent war from breaking out between the North and the South, Yankee Judge Jeremiah S. Black asked the Lincoln administration to promise the South that it would "govern according to the Constitution." This perfectly reasonable request was met with a violent "no."

> *The statesmen of the South reasoned that, if the provision of the Constitution in regard to slavery could be rightly violated on the ground of a so-called higher law, its other provisions could, with equal right, be violated on the same ground; that all Constitutional guaranties and safeguards would thus be rendered worthless; and that, instead of a Government acting as the agent of sovereign States, and having its powers clearly defined by the Constitution, we would thus come to have a Government defining its own powers, exercising sovereignty over the States, and doing whatever it might judge to be necessary, expedient or right.*
>
> *Hence, when it became clearly evident that the party elected to power [Lincoln's] intended to administer the Government on this higher-law theory, the Southern people felt that, in order to preserve the Constitutional Government inherited from their fathers, and hand it down unimpaired as a heritage to their children, they must, in their capacity as sovereign States, resume the powers delegated to the Federal Government, and form a new Union with the old Constitution as its organic law.*[309]

Not surprisingly, Liberals still cannot accept the fact that the South fought, not for slavery, but for the Constitution. As is clear from the history of the American Liberal Party (then the Republicans, today the Democrats), they have little attachment to the Constitution, and neither like it or understand it. They do not even care for the U.S., which they see as a fault-ridden, aggressive, egotistical country built on the European-American concept of "Manifest Destiny," along with "white privilege," "white racism," "white patriarchy," and "black slavery."

As for the Constitution, progressives view it as a conservative impediment to their socialist agenda to enlarge and strengthen the central government, convince American citizens that they are helpless without government, and nurture an infant-like dependence on unconstitutionally created government programs (the so-called "nanny state"). In 2001, one of America's leading socialists, Barack Hussein Obama, revealed to the public his own opinion of the Constitution:

> . . . I think it is an imperfect document, and I think it is a document that reflects some deep flaws in American culture . . .

This view is nothing new. Even before the start of Lincoln's War Northern Liberals, like meddlesome Yankee William Lloyd Garrison, were derogatorily referring to the U.S. Constitution—the world's most profound and unique political document—as a "compact with the Devil and a league with Hell."[310]

It is clear that without the efforts, intelligence, perseverance, and courage of Conservatives, Libertarians, Tea Partyists, and American traditionalists, Liberals would have deconstructed and altered, if not completely abolished, the U.S. Constitution long ago. And these patriotic individuals have Victorian Southern Confederates and their modern descendants to thank for keeping the flame of personal liberty, self-government, and constitutional rights alive into the present day.

Yankee busybody and radical abolitionist William Lloyd Garrison must be held responsible for helping inaugurate the Civil War. In 1830, with the South on the verge of fully committing to complete abolition, he began calling slavery a "sin" and Southern slaveholders "criminals." This false rhetoric provoked the Nat Turner Massacre in 1831, in which over sixty innocent whites were murdered in Virginia by a gang of black racists. This outrage caused the South to pull back from abolition and strengthen her slavery laws in an attempt to prevent further bloodshed. Garrison's ongoing demands for "immediate, complete, and uncompensated abolition" across Dixie sparked further resistance in the South to Northern interference in her affairs. By 1860, with newly elected Yankee President Lincoln promising to use the concept of "higher law" to overturn the Constitution, the die was cast. The beleaguered Southern states, for whom the Constitution was the heart and soul of American life, felt they had no choice but to secede. And "war came."

WHAT YOU WERE TAUGHT: The Confederate Battle Flag is nothing but the South's version of the Nazi Flag, and the Confederates were basically Nazis: cruel and barbaric racists.

THE FACTS: These are strong words coming from the North, the region where both the American slave trade and American slavery got their start! Let us set the record straight.

While foes of the South often associate the Confederate Flag with Nazism and the swastika, and those who fly it are routinely called "Nazis," such language only exposes the illiteracy of its users, not the alleged accuracy of their statements. In fact, the Confederate Battle Flag represents a political ideology that is the exact opposite of Nazism.

The word Nazi is actually an

acronym, one that therefore, technically, should be written in capital letters: NAZI. This acronym derives from the German term *Nationalsozialistische*, meaning "National Socialist," or more fully, the *Nationalsozialistische Deutsche Arbeiterpartei*, a phrase meaning the "National Socialist German Worker's Party." In the 1940s Nazi socialists espoused the same basic themes that the modern American Socialist Party does: big government, anti-capitalism, social welfare, dependence on government, and a rigid even violent intolerance of outsiders and opposing views and groups.

LITTLE SERMONS IN SOCIALISM

BY

Abraham Lincoln

Culled and Commented On

BY

BURKE McCARTY

Run in The Chicago Daily Socialist in 1910

This little pamphlet should be in the library of every Socialist speaker and agitator

Confederates were conservatives, the opposite of socialists, and therefore should not be equated with Nazis (German socialists). As the cover of this 1910 book shows, it was dictator Lincoln who was ideologically closest to socialist Adolf Hitler. Indeed, the Lincoln administration had much in common with Hitler's Third Reich.

There is some confusion about Nazism because in Europe it is associated with fascism, dictatorship, autocracy, and totalitarianism, all which are considered (radical far) *right-wing* there, while here in the U.S.A. socialism is seen as a *left-wing* ideology.

Whatever label we choose to give it, Nazism could not be more dissimilar to the Southern Confederacy, which was a conservative republic, founded on conservative-libertarian principles. Unlike the big government-loving Nazis, for instance, the Confederacy emphasized a small limited central government. Unlike the states' rights-hating Nazis, Confederates saw states' rights as one of the most important of the constitutional freedoms (see Amendments Nine and Ten). Unlike the bigoted and racist Nazis, 19th-Century Southern Confederates were well-known for their hospitality, racial tolerance, universal Christian love, and humanitarianism—all still true today.

Thus, on the *American* political spectrum, the Nazis and the Confederates were located on the extreme ends from one another, with the German socialists on the far left side and the American Southern conservatives on the far right.

To give this discussion the proper perspective, let us bring it back to Lincoln's War, the "Civil War" to Yanks.

Most American Liberals and Lincoln lovers are not aware that communists have always considered "Honest Abe" to be one of their own, which is why they displayed a picture of Lincoln alongside a picture of Russian dictator Joseph Stalin at the 1939 American Communist Party convention in Chicago, Illinois.

Since the South was mainly conservative, this can only mean that the North was mainly liberal, and in fact this is entirely correct—and the two regions remain so to this day. Confederate Vice President Alexander H. Stephens was only one of many Victorian statesmen who pointed out that the War was really nothing more than a conflict between Southern conservatives, or what he called "Constitutionalists" (because they believed correctly that the government derives its authority from the Constitution), and Northern Liberals, or what he referred to as "Consolidationists" (because they wrongly believed that the Constitution derives its authority from the government, and thus wanted to consolidate all political power in Washington, D.C.).

How can this be, some will ask, when Jefferson Davis was a Democrat and Abraham Lincoln was a Republican? It is because the party platforms were reversed in 1860, making the Democrats of that day conservatives and libertarians and the Republicans liberals and socialists.

This is why, after all, Lincoln surrounded himself with Marxists (Marxism is a form of socialism), was supported by a group of radical socialists called the "Forty-Eighters," and has been adored by nationalists, dictators, and communists from around the world ever since, including

Lincoln has long been compared to a host of dictators, communists, and socialists around the world, one of them being Russian revolutionary Vladimir Lenin.

famous American socialists like Francis Bellamy (author of America's *Pledge of Allegiance* and its notorious anti-constitutional reference to "one nation").

It is also why, in the 1930s, American communists formed a military organization called "The Abraham Lincoln Battalion," and it is why the 1939 Communist Party Convention in Chicago, Illinois, affectionately displayed an enormous image of Lincoln over the center of its stage, flanked by pictures of Russian communist dictators Vladimir Lenin on one side and Joseph Stalin on the other.[311]

One of Lincoln's greatest admirers was radical socialist Karl Marx, who once wrote the president a letter congratulating him on his reelection in 1864, adding that he hoped the American president would "lead his country through the matchless struggle for . . . the reconstruction of a social [that is, a *socialist*] world."[312]

It is plain then that calling those who love the Confederate Flag "Nazis" is both an oxymoron and a misnomer. For it is historically incorrect and wholly misrepresents the facts. It was the Union and its dictatorial leader Abraham Lincoln who were politically closely aligned with the German socialist party known as the Nazis. This is why, after all, arch socialist Adolf Hitler idolized Lincoln, even lovingly citing the Yankee chief executive's destruction of states' rights in his autobiography *Mein Kampf*.

Had socialist dictator Hitler been known to our Confederate ancestors, they would have automatically likened him to socialistic dictator Lincoln. In 1863, for instance, Rose O'Neal Greenhow commented on how "our Lord Abraham the First" swept from the South "every vestige of civil rights and freedom."[313] Some eighty years later Hitler would do precisely the same thing in Europe.

What follows is a list I have compiled of irrefutable similarities between Hitler and the German Nazis and Lincoln and the American Republicans (the U.S. Liberals of the 1860s):

- Hitler subverted Germany's government (a democratic republic) and replaced it with his own, an anti states' rights, centralist, Big Brother government, then abolished the office of president and set himself up as dictator; Lincoln subverted America's government (a confederate republic) and replaced it with his own, an anti states' rights, centralist, Big Brother government, then undermined the office of president and set himself up as pseudo-dictator.
- Hitler gave himself unlimited legislative, judicial, and executive power; Lincoln gave himself unlimited legislative, judicial, and executive power (under his self-created, unconstitutional fiction known as "military necessity").
- Hitler repeatedly ignored, violated, and finally overthrew the German Constitution; Lincoln repeatedly ignored, violated, and finally overthrew the U.S. Constitution.
- Hitler, a dictator, seized power from foreign countries; Lincoln, a Liberal with dictatorial ambitions, seized power from a foreign country.
- Hitler, head of the Third Reich, was an empire-builder (the German word *reich* means "empire") who sought to subdue and annex foreign countries; Lincoln, head of the Liberal Party, was an empire builder who sought to subdue and annex a foreign country.
- Socialist Hitler redistributed European land and wealth; socialistic Lincoln redistributed Southern land and wealth.
- Hitler altered the sense of non-German symbols (e.g., the swastika), giving them meanings they never had or were meant to have; Lincoln altered the sense of non-Northern symbols (e.g., the Confederate flags), giving them meanings they never had or were meant to have.
- Hitler engaged in total war (a war in which the aggressor acts without restrictions, limitations, or laws) on his enemies in order to achieve his aims; Lincoln engaged in total war on his enemies in order to achieve his aims.
- Regarding his enemies and minorities, Hitler was anti civil rights; regarding his enemies and minorities, Lincoln was anti civil rights.

- Hitler used white slaves to help build his empire; Lincoln used black slaves to help build his empire.
- Hitler used money from German white slavery to finance his political aspirations; Lincoln used money from Yankee black slavery to finance his political aspirations.
- Hitler was anti states' rights and purposefully set out to destroy them; Lincoln was anti states' rights and purposefully set out to destroy them.
- Hitler was pro big government; Lincoln was pro big government.
- Hitler used his power to further nationalize, strengthen, and centralize the German government; Lincoln used his power to further nationalize, strengthen, and centralize the U.S. government.
- Hitler purged Europe of cultural and political organizations and ideas he did not like; Lincoln purged the South of cultural and political organizations and ideas he did not like.
- Hitler was a war criminal who repeatedly violated the Geneva Conventions; Lincoln was a war criminal who repeatedly violated the Geneva Conventions. Both, for example, tortured and killed non-combatants and recklessly and purposefully destroyed civilian property (see below).
- One of Hitler's primary goals was to Germanize the countries of his enemies; one of Lincoln's primary goals was to Northernize the South.
- Hitler overthrew and militarily subjugated the local governments of various German cities; Lincoln overthrew and militarily subjugated the local governments of both Southern and Northern cities and even entire states.
- Hitler illegally arrested and imprisoned government officials; Lincoln illegally arrested and imprisoned government officials.
- Hitler tortured dissenters; Lincoln tortured dissenters.
- Hitler executed German soldiers for a variety of crimes, some of them petty; Lincoln executed Union soldiers for a variety crimes, some of them petty.
- Hitler produced millions of European refugees who tried to flee his death march across Europe; Lincoln produced millions of Southern refugees who tried to flee his death march across Dixie.

- Hitler had opposition leaders killed; Lincoln, or someone acting for him, had plans to assassinate Confederate President Jefferson Davis.
- Hitler burned books he did not like; Lincoln, a former newspaperman, shut down newspapers he did not like.

Who was more like German socialist Adolf Hitler: Abraham Lincoln, a Northern Liberal, or Jefferson Davis, a Southern Conservative? The answer comes from Hitler himself. In his 1925 autobiography *Mein Kampf* ("My Struggle") the Führer affectionately referenced Lincoln's subversion of states' rights in the American South. Hitler never admired or even mentioned Jefferson Davis, and for good reason. As a Conservative, Davis was a strong supporter of states' rights, a concept roundly detested by socialists and other progressives.

- Hitler confiscated and destroyed the printing equipment of anti-Nazi publishers and had them arrested and imprisoned; Lincoln confiscated and destroyed the printing equipment of anti-Union publishers (in the North) and had them arrested and imprisoned.
- Hitler used gangs and the military to intimidate the populace and sway public opinion; Lincoln used gangs and the military to intimidate the populace and sway public opinion.
- Hitler used threats of violence to prevent foreign nations from coming to the aid of Europe; Lincoln used threats of violence to prevent

foreign nations from coming to the aid of the South.

- Hitler used erroneous propaganda to brainwash the German masses; Lincoln used erroneous propaganda to brainwash the American masses.
- Hitler inadvertently and intentionally maimed non-combatants, including civilian men, women, and children, and bombed houses, stores, libraries, universities, and even hospitals; Lincoln inadvertently and intentionally maimed non-combatants, including civilian men, women, and children, and bombed Southern houses, stores, libraries, universities, and even hospitals.
- Hitler used bribery, deceit, fraud, coverups, and massive corruption to silence his critics and maintain power; Lincoln used bribery, deceit, fraud, coverups, and massive corruption to silence his critics and maintain power.
- Hitler harassed and deported protesters; Lincoln harassed and deported protesters.
- Hitler considered anyone who opposed him a traitor and punished them accordingly; Lincoln considered anyone who opposed him a traitor and punished them accordingly.
- Hitler detested minorities and subjected them to various humiliations, penalties, and strict rules and regulations; Lincoln detested minorities and subjected them to various humiliations, penalties, and strict rules and regulations.
- Hitler was the leader of a thugocracy; Lincoln was the leader of a thugocracy.
- While posing as a German patriot, Hitler committed some of the most heinous crimes and outrages in European history; while posing as an American patriot, Lincoln committed some of the most heinous crimes and outrages in U.S. history.
- Hitler knew his actions were illegal, but he took them anyway; Lincoln knew his actions were illegal, but he took them anyway.[314]

It is patently clear from this brief comparison that big government Lincoln and his Liberal Yankee constituents indeed resembled Hitler and the Nazis in many respects. But the same could not be said for the Old South. In fact, *not one of these crimes can be attributed to small government Conservative Jefferson Davis and the Southern Confederacy!*

A Confederate veteran presenting a Battle Flag wreath at a Confederate gathering in Arlington, Virginia, circa 1920s. Southerners have long allowed the descendants of Union soldiers to memorialize and even bury their dead in Dixie, but the North does not like to grant the same courtesy to descendants of Confederate soldiers.

The brutal Nazi-like treatment of the fine people of the American South continued long after the War, right up to the end and even through the Victorian period and into the 20th Century. At a United Confederate Veterans meeting in 1900, for example, when a resolution was proposed "calling for expressions of fraternal feeling between the North and the South," the old Rebel vets in attendance struck it down. Not because they were not ready to forgive the North, but because the haughty Yankee was not yet ready to repent of his crimes. *Northerners, for instance, would still not even grant a small parcel of soil in many Yankee cemeteries for a monument to honor the Confederate dead who had fought at the same battles.* Thirty-five years after the War, an aging Rebel soldier at the meeting that day spoke for many of his contemporaries:

> *The North wronged and robbed the South, and [we] will hate her as long as a Confederate lives to remind her of her crime. There is ten*

times more bitterness in that section toward the South than there is here [in the South] against the North. Why, look, the national cemetery at Germantown, Pa., is considered, in Grand [Yankee] Army circles, *ground too consecrated for a monument to Confederate dead to stand upon!* The injurer always hates the injured until the former repents and makes restitution. And *there will be no lasting good feeling restored to the sections until the North repents of the injuries she did us, and makes restitution for the millions of property of which the South was robbed by one stroke of Lincoln's pen*.

"If thy brother repent, forgive him." Forgiveness is based on repentance; and until the Yankees repent, the Confederates are under no obligation to forgive.

Instead of repenting, the Yankees are glorying in their crime against us. It is absurd, therefore, to hope to reconcile the sections by swallowing Yankee taffy and snobbishly appropriating honeyed phrases found floating in the air.

All the Camps belonging to the U. C. V. Association should by formal resolution respectfully but firmly repudiate this part of the proceedings . . . .[315]

These Confederate veterans at a Confederate reunion in 1917 understood that authentic American patriotism and history involve two countries, the C.S. and the U.S., and so displayed the flags of both—a custom still practiced in the South. Do the modern descendants of Union soldiers display both flags as well?

Late Victorian and early 20th-Century Yankees were not content to prohibit the erection of Confederate monuments in the North—even though Southerners have long allowed thousands of Yankee memorials to be constructed in Dixie! That "vile element," as Confederate veterans once called anti-South Yanks, also used the written word to "scatter poison" by inculcating Southerners against their own ancestors, history, and heritage,[316] self-interested demagogues only interested in currying favors, votes, money, and power.

The caption of this old illustration is: "The first flag of independence raised in the South, by the citizens of Savannah, Georgia, November 8, 1860." None of the Southern states had seceded yet, thus there was no Confederacy and no official Confederate flag. What they raised that night in Dixie's "Hostess City" was a rendition of what we now call the Gadsden Flag. On it were the words, "Our Motto: Southern Rights, Equality of the States," with a large rattlesnake in the center. At the bottom is the phrase, "Don't Tread On Me," borrowed from the American Revolutionary War period and the colonial secessionists. The trigger for this early Southern secession celebration? Lincoln's election two days earlier.

That revisionist, word-twisting, pro-North writers were busy from the very beginning trying to deconstruct the facts, blacken the reputation of the Confederacy, and replace authentic Southern history with a fake history of their own making, can be seen in the following article. It concerns a reunion of the Confederate Veterans Association at Bonham, Texas, in August 1900, where the growing problem of anti-South Yankee propaganda in Southern schools was discussed:

> There is now being sold and offered for sale in this

county a certain book, entitled the *Students' Cyclopedia*, which, as a historical work, is sectional, unfair, and untruthful in this: It refers to our Southern leaders in the great war between the States as "leaders of a rebellion." And while it thus stigmatizes Jefferson Davis, it refers to Abraham Lincoln as "one commissioned by the Most High." While it devotes four and one-half columns to Abraham Lincoln, it spares only one column to Jefferson Davis. While it devotes two columns to Gen. U. S. Grant, it spares only one-third of a column to Gen. Albert Sidney Johnston. While it devotes two and one-half columns to Gen. W. T. Sherman, it spares only one-half of a column to Gen. Joseph E. Johnston. While it devotes two columns to Gen. Phil Sheridan, it spares only one-fourth of a column to Gen. Bedford Forrest. While it devotes two and one-half columns to the infamous John Brown, of Harper's Ferry notoriety, it spares only one-half of a column to that mighty statesman, John C. Calhoun, of South Carolina. It defends the Hartford Convention [at which Yankees sought to secede from the Union and form the "New England Confederacy" in 1814-1815], and boldly acquits it of all "treasonable designs," and falsely states that such charges as to said Convention "are now regarded as baseless." In its accounts of the battles of the great War between the States it is vague, partial, and incorrect. Therefore be it

Resolved: I. That the aforesaid so-called *Students' Cyclopedia*, edited by one C. B. Beach and published by Howard and Dixon, of Chicago, is *altogether unworthy of the support or patronage of all fair-minded people*.

2. That we earnestly urge all persons—especially stationers, book agents, and school-teachers—to examine closely all literary and historic works which are or may be offered for sale, with a view of *banishing from our midst any and all books which teach false lessons, either of fact or sentiment, or which are in any way partisan or unpatriotic in tone [toward the South]*.

3. That we heartily indorse all the acts of the Historic Committee of the National United Confederate Veterans from its incipiency to the present time, and we heartily thank them for their arduous labors in this behalf.

4. That, as *the preservation and vindication of truthful history is and should ever be the prime object of all Confederate organizations*, a committee of three be appointed by this body, whose duty it shall be to watch closely the subject of history and to make a at each annual meeting of this Association, and to support and act in

concert with the State subcommittee of three as recommended by our National Historic Committee at the late Charleston reunion.

5. That we notice with pride and gratitude the zeal manifested by the sons and daughters of the Confederacy in behalf of *truthful history*, and the ability they have shown in repelling and throttling the epithets "traitor" and "rebel," which have been freely applied to their fathers, and which *are not sustained by the stubborn facts of history*.

6. That we especially *applaud the United Daughters of the Confederacy for their noble and untiring zeal displayed in the erection of Confederate monuments*, and we heartily indorse the report of their Historic Committee as read at their last annual meeting at Hot Springs.[317]

A rare photograph from the Spring of 1861 of Confederate forces at Fort Sumter, Charleston Harbor, South Carolina. Only seven Southern states had so far seceded at this early date: a large seven-star version of the First National Flag snaps in the wind atop a massive flagstaff overlooking the garrison. This was a sight that thrilled the heart of every true Southerner.

A month later, at Danville, Virginia, the Cabell-Graves Camp addressed the same problem in the Old Dominion. The discussion began with a recitation of the pronouncements of several intolerant Yankees regarding the education of Southern children, which they had uttered at a recent reunion of Confederate and Union veterans. At the time, Southern schools were, naturally, teaching Southern children Southern history, an idea that was rancorously opposed by the Northerners in attendance:

> Whereas at a reunion of the blue [former Yankee soldiers] and the gray [former Confederate soldiers] held at Atlanta, July 30, 1900, [Union] Gen. Albert D. Shaw, Commander of the G. A. R. [a Yankee organization, the "Grand Army of the Republic"], used the following words:
>
> > "The keeping alive of sectional teachings as to the justice and right of the course of the South in the hearts of the children *is all out of order, unwise, unjust*, and utterly opposed to the bond by which the great chieftain [Robert E.] Lee solemnly bound the cause of the South in his final surrender. I deeply deplore all agencies of this sort, because in honor and chivalric American manhood and womanhood *nothing of this nature should be taught or tolerated for an instant. There can now be but one bulwark of patriotic teachings for all and by all.*"
>
> And at a reunion of the [Yankee] G. A. R., held at Chicago August 30, 1900, *the school histories of the South were denounced by that organization.* The official declaration [of the North] was made that the Southern histories were written with the purpose of perpetuating in the minds of the children the sectional prejudices of the days of 1861. *Resolutions were adopted calling on the public in the name of the Grand Army to banish these books from the schools of the country [i.e., the South], and a committee was appointed to carry out the protest. And whereas the above words of Gen. Shaw and the resolutions of the G. A. R. show an intolerant and exceedingly narrow view of the case, and that the "sectional prejudice" which they are so eager to banish from the minds of Southerners flourishes like "the green bay tree" in their own; that if these words and resolutions mean anything they mean that the South should teach histories written by Northern sympathizers, the fairest of which have been repeatedly shown, even by Federal records, to be*

full of inaccuracies and glaring misstatements as to the facts of the war, besides teaching that the South was traitorous during that period. The knockdown argument seems to be infallible and conclusive with them. Therefore be it

Resolved: I. That *we yield to none in loyalty—faithfulness to law—to our Constitution*; that we have solemnly kept the only "bond" imposed upon us when surrendered by our great commander Lee, "to go home, abide by the laws, and not take up arms against the United States until properly exchanged;" and more, *we have worked earnestly for the good of the country at large.*

2. That *we have great respect for our brave [Yankee] opponents who are fair and honest, and we are always willing to meet them halfway in genuine fraternal reunions*, begot in the feeling of comradeship of soldiers who shared similar dangers and hardships, and to *forget for the time former and present differences and agree to disagree as to the issues of the past.*

3. That *in our histories we are earnestly striving for the truth, the whole truth, and nothing but the truth. We deny with indignation that we are striving to perpetuate the prejudices of 1861. If we can only get the facts before the grand tribunal, the public opinion of the world, we fear not the result of its decision. Truth can never be injurious; it is error which poisons.*

4. That *while earnestly desiring to teach our children the truth and to clear from the false imputation of treason those who took up arms in 1861-65 to repel armed invasion of their homes by the North, we gladly favor the cultivation of good will between the sections formerly at war, when done in a spirit of manliness, self-respect, and with an entire lack of servility on the part of the Southerner.*

5. *That if reunions of the blue and the gray are interpreted (as the above words and resolutions seem to indicate) to mean, a confession of error on the part of the Southern soldier—legal, moral, or in policy—in the stand he took in 1861-65, we deprecate any more such reunions. The one alluded to seems to have done much to turn backward the good feelings generating.*

6. *That we will continue to teach to our children the truth. We have studied the matter assiduously for thirty-five years to prove to the world that we had law and justice on our side in 1861-65. The more we study, the more overwhelming becomes the conviction of that truth. This conviction does not impair our fidelity to the Constitution.*[318]

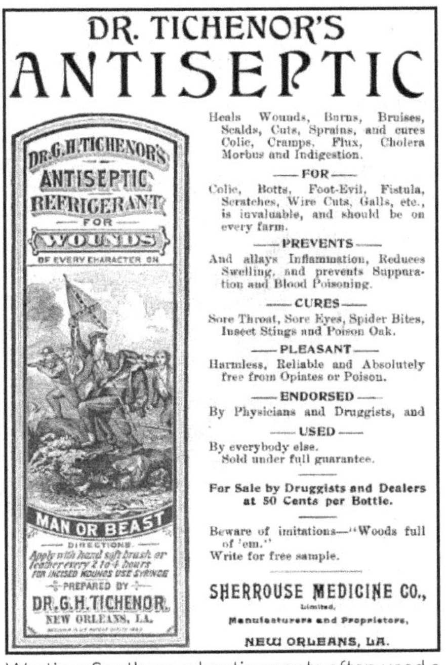

Wartime Southern advertisements often used a patriotic theme that included a picture of the Confederate Battle Flag. This magazine ad for "Dr. Tichenor's Antiseptic" featured a stalwart Confederate regiment with the color-bearer leading a charge on the enemy.

The 19th- and 20th-Century Liberal Yankees' insensitivity, arrogance, and intolerance, as well as their penchant for avoiding and stifling debate, denying authenticated facts, censoring and destroying opponents, meddling in the affairs of others, and rewriting history and aggressively promoting their own version, has carried on into the progressive movement of modern day America.

As I write these very words, bigoted Left-wingers are stigmatizing, criminalizing, ripping down, and burning the Confederate Battle Flag; banning and suppressing Southern history books; outlawing words such as "Confederate," "Confederacy," and "Dixie"; harassing, attacking and assaulting Confederate supporters and flaggers; defacing and destroying our Confederate monuments and grave sites; and belittling and prohibiting Confederate symbols, songs, and clothing—all in an effort to obliterate traditional Southern society and Northernize Dixie. Our modern day American Liberal Nazis are closely following the advice of fellow socialist Karl Marx, who said: "Take away a nation's heritage and they are more easily persuaded."

Unsurprisingly, some U.S. government-run Civil War sites, as well as a few of our country's largest retailers, have begun banning products with images of the Confederate Battle Flag on them. This would include, of course, my "Civil War" books, each one which is written from the South's perspective. My books depict the C.S. Flag on their covers because they are historical works about the Confederacy.

Does removing this symbol change how Southerners feel about their heritage, diminish Southern pride, or make four important years of American history disappear? Only a Liberal would think so!

The purging of the South, the virtual cultural genocide of an entire region of the U.S., continues unabated. In 1991, for example, one of America's most vocal hate groups, the race-baiting NAACP, ratified a resolution to prohibit and censor anything having to do with the Confederacy,[319] a sentiment that has spread like wildfire among uninformed Liberals and radical progressives ever since. In the wake of this virulent anti-South resurgence, the Confederate Battle Flag is currently being torn from flag poles, Confederate graves are being despoiled, and Confederate monuments are being toppled over.

The cross on this 1861 South Carolina Secession Flag is the Cross of Jesus, whose central message was love (Mt. 22:36-39). Declaring this flag a "symbol of hate" does not change this fact.

These actions are no different than the cultural cleansing now being perpetuated by terrorist groups in the Middle East—where wanton acts like the burning of books and the destruction of precious historic art and statuary are a daily occurrence. Yet it is the Confederate Battle Flag, emblazoned with the Cross of Christian Love, that is called a "symbol of hate" by ill-informed race-merchants and hate-mongers! Is there any question that many of today's American socialists and Liberals, had they lived during World War II, would have sided with big government socialist Hitler against the U.S.?

If any doubt remains as to the integral connection between American Liberalism and Nazism, terrorism, and authoritarianism, let us survey the following quotes:

> "Make the lie big, make it simple, keep saying it, and eventually they will believe it."
>
> "It is not truth that matters, but victory."
>
> "If you tell a big enough lie and tell it frequently enough, it will be believed."

"How fortunate for governments that the people they administer don't think."

"[We] use emotion for the many and reserve reason for the few."

"All great movements are popular movements. They are the volcanic eruptions of human passions and emotions, stirred into activity by the ruthless Goddess of Distress or by the torch of the spoken word cast into the midst of the people."

"It is always more difficult to fight against faith than against knowledge."

"All propaganda has to be popular and has to accommodate itself to the comprehension of the least intelligent of those whom it seeks to reach."

"By the skillful and sustained use of propaganda, one can make a people see even heaven as hell or an extremely wretched life as paradise."

Fact: In his campaign to subjugate the South, vanquish states' rights, annul the Constitution, and install big government in Washington, Liberal Lincoln used many of the same tactics as other tyrants, including Hitler, Stalin, and Mussolini.

These are well-known concepts used everyday by the modern liberal descendants of Lincoln and his Yankee minions, to spread their socialist ideology and persecute their conservative opponents—in particular *traditional Christian Southerners*. And indeed, these phrases sound as if they came straight from the Democratic Party's radical Left-wing playbook.

In actuality, they come straight from the mouth of socialist tyrant Adolf Hitler, the same man who, in his autobiography, praised big government liberal Abraham Lincoln for crushing states' rights in America.

WHAT YOU WERE TAUGHT: The Confederate Battle Flag is a symbol of white supremacy.

THE FACTS: Like all symbols the Confederate flag means something different to different people. Consequently it has picked up erroneous meanings over the years. The question is which is the right meaning and which is the wrong meaning?

The view that it is a symbol of racism or hate in any way, shape, or form is not just ridiculous, it is also false and historically inaccurate. It is, in fact, nothing but a product of the Liberal-run educational system, which makes it, by both definition and association, an automatic lie and a misrepresentation of authentic history—as I will now prove.

This group of Cherokee-Confederate veterans, meeting in New Orleans, Louisiana, in 1903, represents just a fraction of the thousands of Native-Americans who fought for the Confederacy against the imperialistic North from 1861 to 1865. An esteemed and battle-hardened wing of the Confederate military, they would be quite surprised to hear modern Liberals describe their beloved Confederate Battle Flag as an "emblem of bigotry" and their country, the C.S.A., as a "nation of white racists."

There were (and still are) three national Confederate flags: the First National, the Second National, and the Third National. These three flags are proudly displayed all over the U.S., and even in some foreign countries, without a whimper of protest. Why? Because they have never been used by hate groups.

It is the Confederate Battle Flag (a distinctive military flag designed, as we have seen, for specific use on the battlefield), with its striking blue cross, thirteen white stars, and bright red field, that has caused all the uproar. Why? Because it *has* been used by hate groups.

The very existence of Stand Watie destroys the Liberals' accusation of a racist Confederacy. A Native-American from Georgia, he was a celebrated Confederate general who led his command, the First Cherokee Mounted Rifles, to numerous victories throughout the War. Faithful to the Southern Cause to the end, on June 23, 1865, he laid down his arms, becoming the last Confederate general to surrender.

The reason such groups use this particular flag comes from a lack of knowledge of *authentic* Southern history. For as has been made plain throughout this book, the goals and dreams of the Confederacy were never about race, nor were they based on racism, or even slavery. The "Southern Cause," as it is called, was always about upholding the original Constitution of the Founding Fathers and this document's sacred Jeffersonian promise of states' rights, a small weak central government, self-determination, and personal freedom. If big government Liberal Abraham Lincoln had embraced these ideas as well, there would have been no "Civil War." It was his promise to override them, based on his leftist concept that there is a "higher law than the Constitution," that sparked the conflict.

Though thanks to "The Great Yankee Coverup" these facts are little known today,[320] they were well-known to both the average Confederate soldier and his superiors. In 1900 one of them, Confederate General Stephen Dill Lee, a cousin of mine and of General Robert E. Lee, said:

> We men of the South made as gallant a struggle as was ever made *for constitutional principles*. Upon the fields of battle the boys in gray fought with valor for *a great cause* . . .[321]

In 1919, Georgia's state historian emeritus, Lucian Lamar Knight, made a similar but even clearer statement on this topic:

> [When the South] drew her sword against the Union's flag, *it was in defence of the Union's Constitution!* . . . Nor was it African slavery for which the South contended, but Anglo-Saxon freedom—the old Teutonic birthright of *self-government and home rule!*[322]

In 1910, former Confederate First Lieutenant Randolph H. McKim of the Army of Northern Virginia wrote:

> . . . I am chiefly concerned to show that my comrades and brothers, of whom I write in these pages, did not draw their swords in defence of the institution of slavery. *They were not thinking of their slaves when they cast all in the balance—their lives, their fortunes, their sacred honor*—and went forth to endure the hardships of the camp and the march and the perils of the battle field. *They did not suffer, they did not fight, they did not die, for the privilege of holding their fellow men in bondage!*
>
> No, *it was for the sacred right of self-government that they fought. It was in defence of their homes and their firesides. It was to repel the invader, to resist a war of subjugation. It was in vindication of the principle enunciated in the Declaration of Independence that "governments derive their just powers from the consent of the governed."*
>
> Only a very small minority of the men who fought in the Southern armies—not one in ten—were financially interested in the institution of slavery. *We cared little or nothing about it. To establish our independence we would at any time have gladly surrendered it.*[323]

Most 19th-Century foreigners, like Charles Dickens, understood what is still unknown to many modern Americans: the Civil War was nothing but the North's attempt to dominate the South economically, masquerading as a fight over slavery.

Even most foreigners were aware of the truth about the War and the Yankees' intentions. One of them, English novelist Charles Dickens, declared:

> The Northern onslaught upon slavery was no more than a piece of specious humbug designed to conceal its desire for economic control of the Southern states.

Typical of the attitude of most Yankees at the time, in 1859 Massachusetts Senator Henry Wilson declared that, if need be, the North would not hesitate to use violence against the South in order to enforce its principles.

In 1863 Confederate icon Rose O'Neal Greenhow proved Dickens correct when she reported verbatim the words of several Yankee politicians. Honorable Henry Wilson of Massachusetts, for example, believed that "the country has been ruled long enough by Southern aristocrats, and our [Northern Liberal] party will enforce our principles at the point of a bayonet." Any state that resisted would be "crushed" beneath the North's "iron heel," he asserted. Likewise, a statesman from Rhode Island declared that the North's purpose in going to war with the Confederacy was to "reduce the South to a state of vassalage."[324] No mention of slavery, racism, or the Confederate Battle Flag here. Just the Liberal Yankee's obsession with power, control, and domination.

In essence then, the Southern Confederacy was fighting for *all* Americans; the Northern Union was fighting only for its own section, with anti-Constitution Lincoln, the first sectionally elected president in American history, leading the way.

In his "Gettysburg Address" Lincoln tried to pretend otherwise, claiming the North fought so that the "government of the people, by the people, for the people, should not perish from the earth." But even Northerners at the time saw through the hoax, noting that the president had reversed the facts to suit his own agenda. Maryland journalist, H. L. Mencken, for instance, had this to say about Lincoln's most infamous declamation:

> The Gettysburg speech was at once the shortest and the most famous oration in American history. . . the highest emotion reduced to a few poetical phrases. Lincoln himself never even remotely approached it. It is genuinely stupendous. But let us not forget that *it is poetry, not logic; beauty, not sense.* Think of the argument in it. Put it into the cold words of everyday. The doctrine is simply this: that the Union soldiers who died at Gettysburg sacrificed their lives to the cause of self-determination—that government of the people, by the people, for the people, should not perish from the earth. *It is difficult to imagine anything more untrue. The Union soldiers in the battle actually fought against self-determination; it was the Confederates who fought for the right of their people to govern themselves.*[325]

H. L. Mencken in 1935, one of many Yankees who saw through the great political charade known as "the Gettysburg Address."

Little wonder that, according to Lincoln himself, America's reaction to the Gettysburg Address was less than appreciative. "That speech fell on the audience like a wet blanket," he later complained to his friend Ward Hill Lamon. "I am distressed about it . . . It is a flat failure and the people are disappointed."[326]

Despite such bold facts of history, the misuse of the Confederate Battle Flag, as well as the ignorance surrounding it, surges onward. The situation is now so serious that some pro-South organizations are actually suing hate groups who use and display the flag in an attempt to make the practice prohibited.

The question we must ask ourselves is this: if a symbol is used by a racist hate group, does this automatically make that symbol one of racism and hate? We traditional Southerners rightly say, absolutely not.

Anti-South partisans say yes, which, of course, presents them with a dilemma: if they are correct, then the United States Flag must also be considered a symbol of hatred and bigotry, because not only is this the flag that flew on the masts of *all* American slave ships, it is the one most often seen at modern white racist rallies and on white racist Websites. In fact, the U.S. Flag is the actual official symbol of numerous hate groups, while *the Confederate Battle Flag is not the official symbol of any hate group*.

Rational people understand, however, that the U.S. Flag is not a symbol of intolerance, and that its use by bigoted groups does not make it a symbol of bigotry. They also understand that this same reasoning applies to the Confederate Battle Flag: as I have repeatedly shown, *it is not and never was a symbol of racism, and its use by racist groups does not make it one*.

A photo of the Confederate Battle Flag used by the Thirteenth Mississippi Regiment during Lincoln's War. The tattered banner survived the conflicts at Sharpsburg, Fredericksburg, Chancellorsville, Gettysburg, the Wilderness, and finally Appomattox. The men who fought under it treasured it until their final days, saying: "This flag is ever viewed with the fondest pride by a Confederate veteran and others who are interested in that cause for which so many died." That "cause" was freedom from governmental tyranny!

Still, this fact is habitually ignored, discounted, and suppressed by enemies of the South. Why? Because they need the Confederate Battle Flag to be a symbol of racism in order to divide and weaken the country and justify their attack on the conservatism, Christianity, and traditional family values of the South.

What then is the correct meaning of the "Starry Cross," as our fetching flag is proudly called?

Designed by South Carolinian William Porcher Miles around his state's secession flag, it is an emblem of Southern heritage, a heritage that includes *all* races. For not only did *all* races help settle and build the South, *all* races also fought against the Yankees under the Confederate Battle Flag. We will recall that the Confederate military was comprised of 1 million European-Americans, 300,000 to as many as 1 million African-Americans, 70,000 Native-Americans, 60,000 Latin-Americans,

50,000 foreigners, 12,000 Jewish-Americans, and 10,000 Asian-Americans.

These statistics prove to the world like nothing else can, that from the beginning the Confederacy was a multiracial, multicultural, multinational society, one that fought, not to oppress the black race or any other race, but for the constitutional rights and personal freedom of all her people. Those who say anything different are either lying or are ignorant of genuine Southern history, plain and simple.

The American South has been a multiracial and multicultural region since its inception. Here Georgia founder James E. Oglethorpe meets with Native-Americans in 1733, with whom he forged a strong bond. Like most Southerners, Oglethorpe was against slavery and had a complete ban on the institution placed in the colony's constitution, the first of the 13 colonies to do so.

Some from the anti-Confederate Flag movement, like the intolerant Northern-based NAACP, know full well the true meaning of what we in Dixie also call the "Southern Cross," for their Victorian forerunners, the *Independent Order of Pole Bearers*, were once proud to be friends with white Southerners like Confederate General Nathan Bedford Forrest.[327] But the NAACP (which even other blacks, like Reverend Jesse Lee Peterson, have labeled a "hate group") has a vested interest in fanning the flames of racism, for without racial divisiveness it would go out of business. Thus, the Confederate Battle Flag must be stamped and typecast as a "racist" banner.

Our most racist liberal president, Abraham Lincoln, thought along similar lines. He, along with the Radicals (that is, abolitionists) in his party, believed that by pitting whites and blacks against each other, the resulting tension, emotion, and fear would split and undermine the South, allowing him to manipulate and overcome her people easier. Happily, Lincoln's attempt to poison Southern race relations failed, for the majority of whites and blacks saw through the ruse and remained loyal to one another both during and after his War.

The South did not immediately become a multiracial, multicultural society in 1861 with the start of Lincoln's War, of course.

The South has always been a racially inclusive region. Native-Americans were inhabiting the South for thousands of years prior to European settlement, and blacks were in the area now known as Virginia as early as 1526, long before the European ancestors of most of today's white Southerners arrived. It is for this very reason that by 1860, 99 percent of all blacks were native born Americans, a larger percentage than for whites.

Hispanics too had a hand in the development of the Southern states. Spanish explorer Juan Once de León was in Florida in 1513, and in 1565 Spaniards founded St. Augustine, the oldest continually occupied city in the U.S. It is true, as has been said, that the American South once spoke Spanish.

Nelson W. Winbush, the grandson of black Confederate soldier Louis Napoleon Nelson, holding his grandfather's Confederate uniform and cap. Mr. Winbush is an award-winning African-American educator and a member of the Sons of Confederate Veterans.

Contrary to popular thought, the South is not a "white region," and never was. Indeed, Dixie is the unique and special place it is today because of the culinary, architectural, sartorial, political, social, artistic, musical, and literary contributions *made by all the races*. If one section of the U.S. had to be called a melting pot of multiracial influences, it would be the South, not the North.

The Confederate Battle Flag then turns out to be anything but a symbol of white racism or white supremacy. Those who created it never intended it to have this meaning, and those who fought under it never thought of it as having this meaning. The descendants of those soldiers today have also never perceived it in this way, as I myself, as well as living black Confederate-Americans, such as my friend, Nelson W. Winbush, can testify.[328]

If anything it would be more accurate to call our flag a symbol of racial inclusiveness and multiculturalism, one founded on the Christian principles extolled by Jesus, whose main tenants were love and universal brotherhood.[329] As we have discussed, the Confederate Battle

Flag itself was designed around the Christian crosses of Great Britain's flag (Saint George's Cross), Scotland's flag (Saint Andrew's Cross), and Ireland's flag (Saint Patrick's Cross).

Now you know why so many of our more educated 20th-Century U.S. presidents not only accepted and embraced both the Southern Confederacy and Confederate soldiers, but the Confederate Battle Flag as well. One of these was Theodore Roosevelt. When Captain John Levi Underwood, a former Rebel officer, wrote to him in the Fall of 1905, President Roosevelt responded with a letter that began:

> Dear sir: It is always a pleasure to hear from an old Confederate soldier, and I thank you for your letter . . .[330]

Another U.S. chief executive who had no issue with former Confederates was Calvin Coolidge, who met with a group of Confederate veterans in December 1927. The president even posed for photographs in front of the White House, with the Rebel veterans holding up several Battle Flags.

U.S. President Theodore Roosevelt, a New Yorker whose face is on Mount Rushmore, spoke respectfully of and to Confederate veterans, a civility no longer followed by many Americans.

In Washington D.C. this sentiment continued well into the latter half of the 20th Century. In 1992, for instance, the Democratic Party (by then America's Liberal Party) freely used the Confederate Battle Flag on its campaign posters and buttons, with the names "Clinton and Gore" prominently displayed over the Rebel banner. (This despite the fact that the Confederate Battle Flag had been the military symbol of a *conservative* country!)

In summary, our Battle

Flag, the beautiful Southern Cross—or as our Confederate ancestors sometimes referred to it, the "Red Cross Flag"[331]—is an emblem of American patriotism, strict constitutionalism, Christian love, and Southern heritage. And, after all, during his funeral service in 1889, it draped the coffin of our only president, Jefferson Davis, for years the leader of the conservative States' Rights Party.[332] As such, it is a flag that all Southerners, and all lovers of liberty, should display with pride and honor whenever and wherever possible. Conservative Southern Founder, Thomas Jefferson, the "Father of the Declaration of Independence," would heartily approve.[333]

In December 1927 U.S. President Calvin Coolidge, a Yankee from Vermont, took time from his busy schedule to meet with a group of Confederate veterans, then pose for this photograph in front of the White House. The Confederate Battle Flag is prominently displayed while the president looks on reverently. Unlike today's misguided anti-South bigots, Coolidge understood that Confederate soldiers were patriotic Americans and, as such, should be treated with the same dignity as Union soldiers. The U.S. Congress agreed, and in the first half of the 20th Century it passed numerous laws defining *all* C.S. service personnel as U.S. military veterans.

WHAT YOU WERE TAUGHT: Liberals rightly hate the Confederate Flag because of all its negative connotations.

THE FACTS: These "negative connotations" have been invented by people who know nothing about Lincoln's War, let alone the South's history and her symbols. Their hatred of our flag is based on an illusion which they themselves created. Since the "pain" and "anger" they feel toward it is being fueled by their own fabrications, it is not real. It is fake, just like the rest of their anti-South propaganda. Yet we are asked to take their feelings seriously. This is the epitome of "Liberal logic"!

At the time this Clinton-Gore campaign button was used in 1992, Democrats, and Liberals in general, had no issue with embracing the Confederate Battle Flag. That these same people now consider it a "symbol of hate and racism" just a few decades later, reveals the utter hypocrisy of the Left, which thinks nothing of twisting words, perverting the meaning of symbols, rewriting history, and misrepresenting an entire region of the country to achieve their nefarious agenda: divide and thus weaken American citizens in order to make them wholly dependent on an ever growing central government. It is little wonder that Hitler admired their Civil War president: big government Liberal Abraham Lincoln.

If we dig a little deeper into the psychology of the Liberal mind, we discover the real reasons progressives detest an emblem that has nothing to do with slavery, racism, or hatred.

1. Many white Liberals suffer from a psychological disorder known as *ethnomasochism*: gaining pleasure from the hatred of one's own race (in other words, extreme self-racism). At the same time, many black Liberals suffer from a psychological disorder known as *ethnosadism*: gaining pleasure from hating other races (in other words, extreme racism).[334]

Charleston, South Carolina, April 1865, shortly after the Confederate surrender. Lincoln turned many other Southern towns into rubble as well. Could all of this blood and mayhem have been over slavery, as Liberals maintain? Lincoln did not care about slavery enough to warrant this kind of destruction, few Southerners owned slaves (less than 5 percent), and both Union and Confederate soldiers said that they would not have enlisted had the cause been to either preserve or destroy slavery. Clearly, only one thing could have inspired millions of *Southern* men and women to risk their lives and bankrupt their federal treasury: the preservation of the God-given right of personal freedom, the same idea that motivated the fearless Greeks in their fight against the autocratic Persians at the Battle of Thermopylae in 480 B.C.

Why some individuals acquire or manifest these conditions while most do not, must be left to the psychologist, the anthropologist, and the sociobiologist. What we are interested in here is how these disorders relate to the South and her emblems.

In order to generate feelings of pleasure and garner public support for their racial hatreds, these two psychologically impaired groups often combine (as they often have since even before the "Civil War"), and seek out demographics, beliefs, ideas, writings, institutions, organizations, and symbols on which to focus their racist beliefs. One of the favorite emblems of the ethnomasochist and ethnosadist is the Confederate Battle Flag, the reasons for which follow.

2. The Confederate Battle Flag makes an ideal target for the Left, for it has the benefit of being one of the traditional South's most beloved symbols; guaranteed to cause the most intense emotional response, friction, and resistance from Dixie when attacked. Countless thousands of Confederate soldiers perished beneath this beautiful ensign, and it is often their descendants who fly the Confederate Battle Flag today in their ancestors' honor.

Confederate veterans on parade in front of the White House, Washington, D.C., 1917. As the Confederate First National Flag passes by, some individuals in the crowd applaud, others honor it by placing their right hand over their heart. What happened to the Confederate Flag between then and now is a travesty of history, justice, and honor; one that should concern every American.

A typical white Southern family at Cedar Mountain, Virginia, in 1862. The South has always been a peace-loving region, and did everything it could to avoid conflict with the North. But Lincoln was determined to go to war, and he did. Yet just as they felt in the 1860s, traditional Southerners still feel the same way today: they simply want the government to leave them alone.

The emotionally charged dynamics of Southern symbols, like the Confederate Battle Flag, is very important to Liberals and socialists, for their goal to continually consolidate more and more power in Washington, D.C. can only succeed if the lower and middle classes are convinced that our capitalist economic system works against them, and that their only chance for happiness is dependence on the central government.

To aid in this process, malevolent progressives polarize the populace in an effort to further weaken them, a "divide and conquer" strategy that has worked well for emperors, dictators, potentates, autocrats, tyrants, despots, and kings and queens since time immemorial. This Liberals accomplish through the use of false rhetoric and the invention of fake conflicts, such as the "race war," the "war on women," the "war on guns," the "gender war," and the "class war." Though these struggles exist only in the minds of their liberal inventors, using physical symbols like the Confederate Battle Flag makes them more visceral to the uninformed portion of the public, who readily rally around any Left-wing cause that is presented to them by their leaders.

Liberals need a dark force to fight against, and so they have created the myth that the Confederate Battle Flag is evil. But emblems in and of themselves are not evil. Those who imbue them with false meanings are.

3. One of the signs of intelligence is an urge to learn new things, thus intelligent people are naturally curious and open-minded. Intelligent individuals also base their knowledge of history on objective facts, researched by credible and authoritative writers, historians, and scholars.

A Confederate fort at Atlanta, Georgia. The South had no choice but to take up arms. Not to preserve slavery, as the Left continues to teach our children. But in order to defend its land, families, and honor from a "ruthless invader."

These characteristics are often wholly missing from Liberals and South-loathers, however, many who show absolutely no desire to grow intellectually. Along with this attribute, Liberals have a propensity for basing their historical knowledge on opinion, emotion, subjective feelings, principles, and ideology, usually culled from the works of highly biased pro-North, anti-South writers who, year after year, copy the same misinformation and disinformation from one another.

Of course, all of this is the exact opposite of how history should be approached. But *South-haters live in a fantasy world where propagandizing the public rather than educating the public is the focus.* For them truth is meaningless, fabricated lies are everything.

This utter abhorrence of the facts of true history infuses Liberals with an obsessive-compulsive need to rewrite and revise it, expunging everything that does not fit the view of history they want to promote, while appending to it completely unrelated items that do.

A Union battery with a 24 pound siege gun. We can be sure that few Yankees would have gone to war against the South had they not been lied to about the true motivation behind it. Lincoln claimed it was to "preserve the Union," and so his soldiers believed. But the Founding Fathers created the Union as a *voluntary* one, so this could not have been the real reason Lincoln sent 75,000 troops into Dixie in the Spring of 1861.

It is in this way that the Confederate Battle Flag has become an emblem of racism, slavery, and hatred. Not because it is, but because the fact-hating, idealistic Liberals who control the media in the U.S. want and need it to be. Note that these are the same individuals running most of our libraries, bookstores, schools, and universities, where they carefully screen out, reject, block, and suppress any and all literature they do not agree with, or which contains information they do not want the public to see. This would include, of course, *all* Civil War books written from the South's point of view.

With intellectually dead revisionists at the helm of our educational system, it is little wonder that our country is at a standstill when it comes to American history; or that today most high school students do not know who Jefferson Davis, Alexander H. Stephens, or Robert E. Lee are.

Southern black refugees crossing the Rappahannock River in Virginia in 1862. Lincoln's War turned millions of Southerners of all races into homeless vagrants. For what purpose? To "preserve the Union and abolish slavery"? No right-thinking person will ever believe this, and history itself does not support it.

4. Hate groups have adopted the Confederate Battle Flag as one of their many emblems. Why? Because they have read the same anti-South literature that Liberal South-haters read: historically inaccurate books, overflowing with slanderous lies and illogical propaganda, written by progressive historians with a distaste for truth and a bias toward the South. *If these individuals would read history books written by traditional Southerners instead of progressive Northerners, they would discover the facts, and would not associate white racism with the Confederate Battle Flag.*

Unfortunately, the illicit adoption of our ensign by hate groups has been used by the Left to further misrepresent the South while simultaneously supporting their spurious idea that the flag is indeed a symbol of "racism, hatred, and slavery"—despite the fact that it has no connection to these things, and is therefore patently untrue.

In the end, it is really not the flag they hate. It is what it represents: the conservative, Christian, traditional South. This is so childish, irrational, un-American, and just plain mean-spirited that they could never admit it publicly for fear of losing respect, supporters, and money. So they project their vitriol onto those Southern symbols which they have falsely suffused with immoral attributes, controversializing anything with the word Confederate attached to it.

As for traditional Southerners, the Confederate Battle Flag remains a powerful symbol of our history as a once proud, separate and sovereign country. And in honor of our heritage and the thousands of Southerners who gave their lives fighting to sustain the Constitution and escape Yankee tyranny, our flag will continue to fly across Dixie. It is, after all, as Southern journalist Don Hinkle calls it, "quintessentially Southern," a cloth standard that also symbolizes family, religion, tradition, farming, and patriotism.[335]

This Yankee anti-South propaganda painting from 1861, which depicts the Confederate First National Flag in flames, going down with a sinking Confederate ship, is called "The Fate of the Rebel Flag." Like most foes of the South, this artist did not understand that the Confederate Flag is not a piece of cloth that can be burned away or banned into oblivion. It is a Southern symbol of an idea; one of the most precious and miraculous concepts ever conceived by Man: we all possess the God-bestowed rights of "life, liberty, and the pursuit of happiness," untouchable by any government.

But it is far more than that; more than a physical flag.

It is a deeply spiritual emblem, a holy banner, that lives and breathes in the hearts of Southerners, echoing ancestral honor, regional pride, and a one-of-a-kind history. In 1912 Howard wrote of Confederate soldiers and their beloved emblem after Lee's surrender:

> The Confederate battle flag, which they loved so well, was furled with no stain or soil of dishonor thereon, but around it was wreathed the glory of hundreds of victorious battlefields, while its shell and shot torn rents and remnants were undying emblems of

> the heroic duty of the heroic men who fought beneath its folds and whose achievements shall deathless be upon the scroll of history and upon the lips of poetry.[336]

Likewise, in 1907 Confederate soldier John R. Deering, an infantryman in the Army of Northern Virginia, wrote of his time fighting beneath the "white-starred cross":

> I have been ashamed of many things in my life, but the recollection of my course as a Confederate soldier has been for forty years, my chief joy and pride! If ever I was fit to live or willing to die, if ever I was worthy of my father's name or my mother's blood, if ever I was pleased with my place, suited to my rank, or satisfied with my sinful self—it must have been whilst I was marching under that white-starred cross upon that blood-red banner against the invaders of my native Southland. For that I want no forgiveness in this world or the next. I can adopt the saying of my great Commander, General Lee: "*If all were to be done over again, I should act in precisely the same manner; I could have taken no other course without dishonor.*"[337]

With his hand on his hip, haughty Union General William T. Sherman (leaning on cannon, facing left) poses with a Yankee artillery piece and his staff. The North may have won the Civil War, but America lost our original Constitution, along with its promise of states' rights, limited government, and individual freedoms, established by God and the Founding Fathers. Was it worth the overwhelming sacrifice of American blood and treasure? We in the South say no.

Words like these represent a spiritual worship that is not going to change now or in the future, and the sooner this is accepted by enemies of the South the better for everyone. As Rose O'Neal Greenhow said to Lincoln's Secretary of State, William Henry Seward, in 1863: "You cannot defeat us, sir. A nation armed in the defence of her rights is under the protection of God."[338]

Few people could articulate the South's love for her military men like Lee's chaplain, Reverend John William Jones:

> In the summer of 1865 I was travelling one day along a country road in Virginia [with a companion], when I saw a young man plowing in the field, guiding the plow with one hand, while an empty sleeve hung at his side. I know not how others may feel about it, but for myself *I never see the empty sleeve or halting gait of the true Confederate soldier that I do not instinctively take off my hat in profound respect for the man*—I never pass his "vocal grave" without desiring to pause and cast at least one little violet upon it—and I hope never to see the day when I shall not count it a privilege to share with him, or with his widow or orphan, the last crust of bread that a good Providence shall give me. And so I said to the friend who was with me: "We must stop. I must speak to that young man."
>
> When he drew near, singing merrily at his work, I recognized him as a young man whom I had baptized in the army. I knew his history. Raised in the lap of luxury he had resisted its temptations, and when the war broke out he was about to bear off the highest honors of one of our colleges, and seemed destined to shine in his chosen profession, for which his tastes and talents fitted him. He was one of the first to step to the front when Virginia called on her sons to rally to her defence, and was one of the best of her noble soldiers.
>
> To see him thus, then, his hopes blighted, his fortune wrecked, and his body maimed for life, deeply touched my heart, and my words of greeting and sympathy were right warm. I shall never forget how the noble fellow, straightening himself up, replied, with a proud smile: "Oh, Brother Jones, that is all right. I thank God that I have one arm left and an opportunity to use it for the support of those I love." If my voice could reach all the young men of the South to-day, I would ring in their ears the words of that maimed hero, and would beg them to imitate the example of our returned Confederate soldiers, who, as a rule, went to work with an energy and patient industry which have made them a real power in the land to-day.

> I recollect that when, several months after, I met General Lee in Lexington, when he came to take charge of Washington [now Washington and Lee] College, and he asked me, as he frequently did: "How are our old soldiers getting on these hard times?" I related to him, among others, the above incident. The old chieftain's face flushed, his eyes filled with tears, and he said: "*It is just like them, sir! It is just like my poor boys! They were the noblest fellows that the sun ever shone upon.*" And so I believe they were.[339]

Understanding the sentiment so poignantly expressed by General Lee and Reverend Jones is important. Not just for Southerners, but for all Americans. For both the righteous cause (freedom) for which the Confederacy fought and the starry Christian cross that represents it are more relevant today than at any time since 1861. Those without a thorough knowledge of the true facts of Lincoln's War have no right to even question this statement. In 1898 an old Yankee veteran, Colonel W. A. Taylor, summed up his feelings about the South's love of its battle flag this way: "Thoughtful people do not malign the motives of the Southerners . . ."[340] How true!

The author's cousin Confederate General Jeb Stuart fought for the principles of personal liberty and freedom from governmental tyranny. This is why he, and every educated Southerner to this day, refer to the Confederate Battle Flag as "the banner of Southern independence."

The reason for this is that only those who have ancestors who fought under the Confederate Battle Flag can truly understand and appreciate it. Such men would include the illustrious Confederate General James Ewell Brown "Jeb" Stuart, who, in the midst of battle in March 1862, wrote the following to his wife from the field:

> What a mockery would liberty be, with submission. *I, for one, though I stood alone in the Confederacy, without countenance or aid, would uphold the banner of Southern independence as long as I had a hand to grasp the staff, and then die, before submitting.* I want my wife to feel the same enthusiasm . . . Tell my boy, when I am gone, how I felt; and *never to forget the principles for which his father struggled.*[341]

The truth, Southern Truth, marches on. It cannot be beaten down, ridiculed, harassed, censored, or outlawed out of existence. For the South and her Cause were no more defeated by the Civil War than Jesus and the Gospel were defeated by the Crucifixion.

Howell Cobb, a Southern Conservative, born in Georgia in 1815. An attorney who turned to politics, he eventually served as a U.S. congressman, speaker of the House of Representatives, governor of Georgia, and U.S. secretary of the treasury. He appears here, however, due to his most important position: president of the Provisional Confederate Congress (1861-1862), which officiated over the design of the Confederate First National Flag. After the Provisional Congress was dissolved, he became a major general in the Confederate army. In 1868, during a business trip to New York City, he passed away suddenly. His body was returned to the Peach State, where he was laid to rest in Oconee Hill Cemetery, Athens, Georgia.

THE OLD BRIGADES IN GRAY

They are passing in their glory,
Yet they'll live in deathless story—
Aye, until the years are hoary
And their past is far away.
By the world their deeds are spoken
And their fame is Glory's token,
For their ranks were never broken—
Those old brigades in gray.

I can see their camp fires quiver
By the fair and crystal river;
I can see them charging ever
Where the lights and shadows play.
Where their battle banner flaunted.
Brave, heroic, and undaunted,
In the wood by memory haunted
Stood the old brigades in gray.

I can see that banner streaming
In the sunset's glorious gleaming;
You may think that I am dreaming
Of a past that's far away.
Oft the storms of battle tore it
And the breezes bravely bore it,
Men of honor fell before it—
In the old brigades in gray.

O, how grand was their formation
When they fought to free a nation!
Fate was but their compensation,
Weak to-day is their array;
They are crossing to the others
Who have crossed, their hero brothers,
Sons of gentle-hearted mothers—
The old brigades in gray.

Like the enemy who met them,
They have trials and cares to fret them;
But the world will not forget them
Whilst among us yet they stay.
Weave for them a wreath of roses
Which the morning sun discloses,
See that it in love reposes
On the old brigades in gray.

Where their comrades now are sleeping
Angel-guarded vines are creeping,
And the rivers, onward leaping,
Seek the sea that's far away.
They were mustered in their glory
'Neath the pine and cypress hoary;
Now a remnant tells the story
Of the old brigades in gray.[342]

T. C. HARBAUGH, 1907

APPENDIX

Report of William Porcher Miles Concerning the Creation of the *Confederate First National Flag*

FROM THE "JOURNAL OF THE CONGRESS OF THE CONFEDERATE STATES OF AMERICA, 1861-1865," MARCH 4, 1861, VOL. 1

Mr. [William Porcher] Miles, from the Committee on the Flag and Seal of the Confederacy, made the following report:

The committee appointed to select a proper flag for the Confederate States of America, beg leave to report:

That they have given this subject due consideration, and carefully inspected all the designs and models submitted to them. The number of these has been immense, but they all may be divided into two great classes.

First. Those which copy and preserve the principal features of the United States flag, with slight and unimportant modifications.

Secondly. Those which are very elaborate, complicated, or fantastical. The objection to the first class is, that none of them at any considerable distance could readily be distinguished from the one which they imitate. Whatever attachment may be felt, from association, for "the Stars and Stripes" (an attachment which your committee may be permitted to say they do not all share), it is manifest that in inaugurating a new government we can not with any propriety, or without encountering very obvious practical difficulties, retain the flag of the Government from which we have withdrawn. There is no propriety in retaining the ensign of a government which, in the opinion of the States composing this Confederacy, had become so oppressive and injurious to their interests as to require their separation from it. It is idle to talk of "keeping" the flag of the United States when we have voluntarily seceded from them. It is superfluous to dwell upon the practical difficulties which would flow from the fact of two distinct and probably hostile governments, both employing the same or very similar flags. It would be a political and military solecism. It would produce endless confusion and mistakes. It would lead to perpetual disputes. As to "the glories of the old flag," we must bear in mind that the battles of the Revolution, about which our fondest and proudest memories cluster, were not fought beneath its folds. And although in more recent times—in the war of 1812 and in the war with Mexico—the South did win her fair share of glory, and shed her full measure of blood under its guidance and in its defense, we think the impartial page of history will preserve and commemorate the fact more imperishably than a mere piece of striped bunting. When the colonies achieved their independence of the "mother country" (which up to the last they fondly called her) they did not desire to retain the British flag or anything at all similar to it. Yet, under that flag they had been planted, and nurtured, and fostered. Under that flag they had fought in their infancy for their very existence against more than one determined foe; under it they had repelled and driven back the relentless savage, and carried it farther and farther into the decreasing wilderness as the standard of civilization and religion; under it the youthful [George] Washington won his spurs in the memorable and unfortunate expedition of [British officer Edward] Braddock, and [at the Battle of Quebec] Americans helped to plant it on the heights of [land owned by] Abraham [Martin], where the immortal

[British officer James] Wolfe fell, covered with glory, in the arms of victory. But our forefathers, when they separated themselves from Great Britain—a separation not on account of their hatred of the English constitution or of English institutions, but in consequence of the tyrannical and unconstitutional rule of Lord [Frederick] North's administration, and because their destiny beckoned them on to independent expansion and achievement—cast no lingering, regretful looks behind. They were proud of their race and lineage, proud of their heritage in the glories and genius and language of old England, but they were influenced by the spirit of the motto of the great [English politician John] Hampden, *Vestigia null retrorsum* ["No steps backward"]. They were determined to build up a new power among the nations of the world. They therefore did not attempt "to keep the old flag." We think it good to imitate them in this comparatively little matter as well as to emulate them in greater and more important ones.

The committee, in examining the representations of the flags of all countries, found that Liberia and the Sandwich Islands had flags so similar to that of the United States that it seemed to them an additional, if not in itself a conclusive, reason why we should not "keep," copy, or imitate it. They felt no inclination to borrow, at second hand, what had been pilfered and appropriated by a free negro community [i.e., the Liberians] and a race of savages [i.e., the Sandwich Islanders]. It must be admitted, however, that something was conceded by the committee to what seemed so strong and earnest a desire to retain at least a suggestion of the old "Stars and Stripes." So much for the mass of models and designs more or less copied from, or assimilated to, the United States flag.

With reference to the second class of designs—those of an elaborate and complicated character (but many of them showing considerable artistic skill and taste)—the committee will merely remark, that however pretty they may be, when made up by the cunning skill of a fair lady's fingers in silk, satin, and embroidery, they are not appropriate as flags. A flag should be simple, readily made, and, above all, capable of being made up in bunting. It should be different from the flag of any other country, place, or people. It should be significant. It should be readily distinguishable at a distance. The colors should be well contrasted and durable, and, lastly, and not the least important point, it should be effective and handsome.

The committee humbly think that the flag [the First National] which they submit combines these requisites. It is very easy to make. It is entirely different from any national flag. The three colors of which it is composed—red, white, and blue—are the true republican colors. In heraldry they are emblematic of the three great virtues—of valor, purity, and truth. Naval men assure us that it can be recognized and distinguished at a great distance. The colors contrast admirably and are lasting. In effect and appearance it must speak for itself.

Your committee, therefore, recommend that the flag of the Confederate States of America shall consist of a red field with a white space extending horizontally through the center, and equal in width to one-third the width of the flag. The red spaces above and below to be of the same width as the white. The union blue extending down through the white space and stopping at the lower red space. In the center of the union a circle of white stars corresponding in number with the States in the Confederacy. If adopted, long may it wave over a brave, a free, and a virtuous people. May the career of the Confederacy, whose duty it will then be to support and defend it, be such as to endear it to our children's children, as the flag of a loved, because a just and benign, government, and the cherished symbol of its valor, purity, and truth.

Respectfully submitted, William Porcher Miles, Chairman

NOTES

1. See Jones, TDMV, pp. 144, 200-201, 273.
2. See Seabrook, TAHSR, passim. See also, Pollard, LC, p. 178; Franklin, pp. 101, 111, 130, 149; Nicolay and Hay, ALCW, Vol. 1, p. 627.
3. See e.g., Seabrook, TQJD, pp. 30, 38, 76.
4. Seabrook, EYWTATCWIW, p. 13.
5. Anthropologists, in fact, no longer use the vague word race, which has been replaced with the more scientifically accurate term *ethnogroup*: "a population of people who share a common origin, background, nationality, culture, descent, religion, or language."
6. The word racism, which is now more correctly called ethnosadism, remains meaningful in one sense: those "race-baiters" who use this word to foment racial divisiveness are revealed as true "racists"; that is, these are individuals who judge others strictly by the color of their skin. For more on the topic of genetics and race, see my detailed discussion in Seabrook, EYWTAASIW, pp. 14-16.
7. Confederate Veteran, September 1896, Vol. 4, No. 9, p. 313.
8. See my book of the same name.
9. I am referring here to "global warming," one of the favored political weapons of the Left.
10. Richardson, pp. 5-6. Emphasis Richardson's.
11. Confederate Veteran, October 1916, Vol. 24, No. 10, p. 459.
12. Seabrook, AL, pp. 67-68. Emphasis added.
13. Underwood, pp. 247-248. Emphasis added throughout.
14. Underwood, p. 247.
15. Emphasis added. Emphasis added.
16. Boyd, Vol. 1, p. 44. Emphasis added.
17. Grady, p. 281.
18. Underwood, pp. 249-250. Emphasis added throughout. Note: In Madison's day the words confederal and federal were identical, and were used interchangeably by the Founding Fathers, the latter being merely an abbreviation of the former. Later, the two words came to have opposite meanings. A confederation (confederacy) was defined as a compact of friendly nation-states, each which retains its individual character and sovereignty. A federation (federacy) was defined as a compact between states that surrender their sovereignty to an all powerful central government.
19. The word democracy appears nowhere in the early official documents of the U.S.
20. Seabrook, TAOCE, p. 35. Emphasis added.
21. Debate continues as to whether these individuals were true U.S. presidents or merely heads of Congress. It is clear, in my opinion, however, that they were legitimate U.S. presidents, overseeing America's first Confederate States of America.
22. Seabrook, TAOCE, p. 41.
23. Jefferson, Vol. 8, p. 174.
24. Jefferson, for example, was in Paris, France, at the time.
25. Seabrook, C101, pp. 25-30.
26. Seabrook, C101, p. 37.
27. Seabrook, C101, pp. 39-40.
28. Seabrook, C101, p. 70.
29. Jefferson, Vol. 8, p. 4.
30. Davis, Vol. 2, p. 460.
31. Seabrook, C101, pp. 75-76.
32. Greenhow, p. 181.
33. Howard, p. 88. Emphasis added.
34. O'Ferrall, p. 151. Emphasis added.

35. Rutherford, p. 59. Emphasis added. Note: Rutherford missed a number of actual secessions, like the New England Secession of 1643, as well as several "threatened" ones, such as that which grew out of the Hartford Convention in 1814-1815, when the New England states gathered once again to discuss the formation of a "New England Confederacy," one that would have included New York, Pennsylvania, and even Nova Scotia. See Seabrook, C101, p 48.
36. Rawle, pp. 295, 296-297. Emphasis added.
37. Hodgson, pp. 470-471. Emphasis added.
38. Greeley, Vol. 1, p. 359. Emphasis added.
39. Seabrook, C101, p. 54. Emphasis added.
40. Seabrook, C101, p. 55.
41. Seabrook, C101, pp. 60-61.
42. Stephens, Vol. 2, p. 30.
43. Howard, p. 11.
44. Richardson, p. 430.
45. Howard, pp. 92-93.
46. McGehee, p. 103. Emphasis added.
47. McGehee, pp. 103-104. Emphasis added.
48. Stone and Myers, pp. 268-269.
49. Grant, p. 256.
50. Confederate Veteran, November 1894, Vol. 2, No. 11, p. 333. I have created my own title for this poem, as the original did not have one.
51. Cannon, pp. 7-9.
52. Confederate Veteran, May 1916, Vol. 24, No. 5, p. 197.
53. Seabrook, C101, pp. 75-76.
54. Confederate Veteran, May 1916, Vol. 24, No. 5, p. 196.
55. Journal, Vol. 1, p. 102.
56. Confederate Veteran, April 1894, Vol. 2, No. 4, p. 120.
57. Note: Though the secession of Texas had not yet been ratified, her seven delegates had been eagerly attending the Confederate proceedings at Montgomery, and so a star for the state was included on the original First National Flag.
58. Semmes, p. 97.
59. McHatton-Ripley, pp. 10-13.
60. Hopley, pp. 283-284, 324.
61. Confederate Veteran, May 1916, Vol. 24, No. 5, pp. 196, 199.
62. Confederate Veteran, May 1916, Vol. 24, No. 5, p. 199.
63. Confederate Veteran, May 1916, Vol. 24, No. 5, p. 199. Emphasis added.
64. Confederate Veteran, May 1907, Vol. 15, No. 5, pp. 227-228. Emphasis added.
65. Seabrook, EYWTATCWIW, pp. 35-39.
66. Grissom, p. 56.
67. Cannon, pp. 10-13.
68. Cumming, p. 25.
69. Grissom, p. 56.
70. Ellis, p. 856.
71. Sorrel, p. 34.
72. Journal, Vol. 6, p. 476.
73. Journal, Vol. 6, p. 477.
74. Confederate Veteran, May 1916, Vol. 24, No. 5, p. 198.
75. UCV, p. 3.
76. Confederate Veteran, May 1916, Vol. 24, No. 5, p. 198.
77. Confederate Veteran, May 1916, Vol. 24, No. 5, p. 198.
78. UCV, pp. 1-4.
79. Morgan, pp. 125-126. Emphasis added.
80. Semmes, p. 121.
81. Cannon, pp. 7-8.

82. Longstreet, p. 56.
83. Confederate Veteran, May 1916, Vol. 24, No. 5, p. 198. Note: There was no official uniform for either side in the Summer of 1861.
84. Confederate Veteran, May 1916, Vol. 24, No. 5, p. 197. Note: Hettie and Constance's surname is spelled "Cary" in some old records.
85. Confederate Veteran, May 1916, Vol. 24, No. 5, p. 198.
86. McCarthy, pp. 219-224. Emphasis added.
87. Cannon, p. 54.
88. Southwood, p. 107.
89. Confederate Veteran, September 1912, Vol. 20, No. 9, pp. 415-416.
90. Miller, Vol. 1, p. 351; Howard, p. 18; Mosby, p. 55; Brock, pp. 43-44.
91. Hopley, pp. 308-309.
92. Boyd, Vol. 1, pp. 56-61. Emphasis added.
93. Boyd, Vol. 1, pp. 67-69. Emphasis added.
94. Confederate Veteran, July 1894, Vol. 2, No. 7, p. 201.
95. Confederate Veteran, July 1916, Vol. 24, No. 7, pp. 298-299.
96. Jones, CITC, p. 459.
97. Hopley, p. 396.
98. Clark, Vol. 1, pp. 130-131.
99. Clark, Vol. 1, p. 284.
100. Clark, Vol. 1, pp. 151-152.
101. Wood, pp. 116-120. Emphasis added.
102. Worsham, p. 284. Emphasis added.
103. King, pp. 96-97. Emphasis added.
104. Murray, pp. 150-151. Emphasis added.
105. Cumming, p. 22. Emphasis added.
106. Gordon, pp. 445-446. Emphasis added.
107. Hinkle, p. 56.
108. Fortier, Vol. 3, pp. 61-78.
109. The Bonnie Blue Flag was the flag of the West Florida Republic from September 16 to December 10, 1810. It was the flag of the Republic of Texas from December 10, 1836, to January 25, 1839. It was the flag of the Republic of Mississippi from January 6 to January 26, 1861. Cannon, pp. 31-33.
110. Matthews, Brander, "The Song of the War," *The Century Illustrated Monthly Magazine*, May 1887 to October 1887, Vol. 34, New Series Vol.12, p. 625.
111. Confederate Veteran, May 1901, Vol. 9, No. 5, p. 213. "The Bonnie Blue Flag" is sung to the melody of the old Hibernian song "The Irish Jaunting Car."
112. The Bonnie Blue Flag was fashioned by Melissa Johnson, one of the freedom-loving English inhabitants of the province of West Florida that was then part of Spain, but which U.S. President James Madison considered part of France. The Bonnie Blue Flag, the official banner of "the little nation" of West Florida, flew over Baton Rouge for only four months. On December 10, 1810, it was replaced with the U.S. Flag. Cannon, p. 32; Encyc. Brit., s.v. "Florida."
113. Cannon, p. 33.
114. The Texas legislature convened on February 1, 1861, where its members voted 166 to eight for secession. On February 23, 1861, Texas citizens went to the polls and voted overwhelmingly for secession, which was made official on March 2, Texas Independence Day. Note: Other Southern states that have used the "Lone Star" in their flags: Florida, Louisiana, and Mississippi.
115. Confederate Veteran, July 1916, Vol. 24, No. 7, p. 289.
116. Seabrook, S101, p. 11.
117. Seabrook, S101, p. 15.
118. Seabrook, S101, p. 16.
119. Seabrook, S101, pp. 18-19.
120. Seabrook, S101, p. 20.
121. Seabrook, S101, p. 21.
122. Seabrook, S101, p. 22.

123. Seabrook, S101, p. 24.
124. Moore, p. 9.
125. Grady, p. 211.
126. Grady, pp. 212-214.
127. Seabrook, S101, pp. 38, 86.
128. Emphasis added.
129. Seabrook, S101, pp. 27-28.
130. The Weekly News and Courier, pp. 393-394.
131. Seabrook, S101, p. 29.
132. Emphasis added.
133. McKim, p. 19.
134. Seabrook, S101, pp. 30-31.
135. Seabrook, S101, p. 32.
136. Seabrook, S101, p. 38.
137. Seabrook, EYWTAASIW, pp. 431-432.
138. Emphasis added.
139. Howard, p. 184.
140. Emphasis added.
141. Emphasis added.
142. Emphasis added.
143. Emphasis added. Seabrook, EYWTAASIW, pp. 582-592, 666-669.
144. Cumming, p. 102. Emphasis added.
145. Seabrook, S101, p. 44.
146. Boyd, Vol. 1, p. 45.
147. Seabrook, TGYC, pp. 65, 67-68.
148. Cumming, pp. 179, 180. Emphasis added.
149. Cumming, p. 198. Emphasis added.
150. Cumming, pp. 113-114. Emphasis added.
151. See e.g., Boyd, Vol. 1, p. 45.
152. Lincoln called his "Emancipation Proclamation" exactly what it was: not a civil rights emancipation, but a "military emancipation." In other words, its true purpose was to "liberate" black servants, not so they could be free, but so the liberal Yankee president could use them in his armies. See e.g., Seabrook, L, p. 647.
153. Seabrook, S101, p. 45.
154. Seabrook, S101, p. 46.
155. Seabrook, S101, p. 47. Emphasis added.
156. Seabrook, S101, p. 50.
157. Seabrook, S101, p. 51.
158. Seabrook, S101, pp. 57-58. Emphasis added.
159. Cumming, p. 113. Emphasis added.
160. Seabrook, S101, pp. 61-62.
161. Seabrook, S101, pp. 63-64.
162. Seabrook, S101, p. 65.
163. Johnston, pp. 12-13.
164. Emphasis added.
165. Emphasis added.
166. Emphasis added.
167. For more on Stephens and his genuine attitude toward African-Americans, see Seabrook, TAHSR, passim; and Seabrook, TQAHS, passim.
168. Emphasis added.
169. Seabrook, S101, pp. 66-67.
170. Seabrook, S101, p. 68.
171. Only days after his inauguration Lincoln began working on his plan to deport American blacks by colonizing them in foreign countries. On April 10, 1861, for instance, he met with a representative from the Chiriqui Improvement Company, a coal mining operation in what is now Panama, to discuss the idea of

exiling African-Americans to the area. (See Long and Long, p. 55.) Lincoln apologists maintain that he eventually gave up on the idea of black colonization, but this is contradicted, not only by Lincoln's own words (see e.g., his Preliminary Emancipation Proclamation, issued September 22, 1862, wherein he urges black deportation), but by his friends and associates. One of these was Union General Benjamin F. Butler, who later wrote that the Yankee president met with him in the Spring of 1865, shortly before his assassination, to discuss black deportation. See Seabrook, EYWTAASIW, pp. 769-770.

172. Seabrook, EYWTAASIW, pp. 712-713.

173. Seabrook, S101, p. 71.

174. Seabrook, S101, p. 72.

175. Emphasis added.

176. Greeley, Vol. 2, p. 666. Emphasis added.

177. Davis, Vol. 2, p. 764.

178. Jones, TDMV, p. 625. Emphasis added.

179. Stiles, pp. 49-50. Emphasis added.

180. The Weekly News and Courier, p. 257.

181. Boyd, Vol. 1, p. 44. Emphasis added.

182. See Gilmor, passim.

183. See Taylor, passim.

184. Goodloe, pp. 5-6. Emphasis added. Note: Goodloe was a member of the John L. McEwen Bivouac No. 4, Franklin, Tennessee.

185. Watkins, pp. 13-14. Emphasis added.

186. Neese, p. 3. Emphasis added.

187. Alexander, pp. vii-viii. Emphasis added.

188. For more on this topic, see Seabrook, EYWTATCWIW, pp. 113-114.

189. Howard, pp. 191-192. Emphasis added.

190. Seabrook, EYWTATCWIW, p. 171.

191. For more on Lincoln's anti-black views and policies, see Seabrook, AL, passim; Seabrook, TGI, passim; Seabrook, L, passim; and Seabrook, TUAL, passim.

192. Marshall, pp. 587-590. Emphasis added.

193. The Weekly News and Courier, pp. 409-410. Emphasis added.

194. The Weekly News and Courier, p. 473. Emphasis added.

195. The Weekly News and Courier, p. 226. Emphasis added.

196. The Weekly News and Courier, pp. 473-474. Emphasis added.

197. The Weekly News and Courier, p. 116. Emphasis added.

198. Emphasis added.

199. The complete text of the Corwin Amendment reads: "No amendment shall be made to the Constitution which will authorize or give to Congress the power to abolish or interfere, within any State, with the domestic institutions thereof, including that of persons held to labor or service by the laws of said State."

200. Seabrook, EYWTATCWIW, p. 145.

201. Emphasis added.

202. Emphasis added.

203. Seabrook, EYWTATCWIW, pp. 38-40; Seabrook, TUAL, p. 40. Emphasis added.

204. Marshall, p. 184. Emphasis added.

205. Seabrook, AL, pp. 371-373.

206. Seabrook, EYWTAASIW, p. 706. Emphasis added.

207. Hagood, p. 370. Emphasis added.

208. For more on "The Great Yankee Coverup," see my book of the same name.

209. Seabrook, C101, p. 81.

210. Seabrook, S101, p. 79. Emphasis added.

211. Cumming, p. 25. Emphasis added.

212. Howard, p. 116.

213. Confederate Veteran, September 1900, Vol. 8, No. 9, pp. 395-396. In this one instance I have broken the original resolutions up into paragraphs for the modern reader. Emphasis added.

214. Seabrook, EYWTATCWIW, p. 204. Emphasis added.

215. Howard, p. 192. Emphasis added.
216. Howard, pp. 243-244. Emphasis added.
217. Seabrook, S101, p. 84.
218. Emphasis added.
219. Seabrook, S101, p. 85.
220. As I discuss, inexplicably, Union soldiers were also well-known to burn down schools, universities, laboratories, libraries, and even hospitals. In some cases they even dug up the graves of Southern men, women, and children in an effort to find valuable personal belongings that may have been hidden by Confederate families. See e.g., The Weekly News and Courier, pp. 116-127; Gragg, passim.
221. Let us note here that "uncle" was a common soldier's prefix, a term of endearment that was applied to both whites and blacks. See e.g., W. B. Smith, p. 77.
222. Confederate Veteran, September 1915, Vol. 23, No. 9, p. 425. Emphasis added.
223. Confederate Veteran, September 1900, Vol. 8, No. 9, p. 399. Emphasis added.
224. Confederate Veteran, September 1900, Vol. 8, No. 9, pp. 399-400. Emphasis added.
225. Confederate Veteran, June 1910, Vol. 18, No. 6, p. 294. Emphasis added.
226. Confederate Veteran, September 1903, Vol. 8, No. 9, p. 422. Emphasis added.
227. Confederate Veteran, September 1903, Vol. 8, No. 9, pp. 422-423. Emphasis added.
228. Confederate Veteran, September 1903, Vol. 8, No. 9, p. 423. Emphasis added.
229. Confederate Veteran, September 1903, Vol. 8, No. 9, p. 422. Emphasis added.
230. See Seabrook, EYWTATCWIW, passim.
231. Much of the information on black Confederates in this section came from the personal military collection of Ronny Mangrum—Adjutant for Roderick, Forrest's War Horse Camp 2072, Sons of Confederate Veterans—to whom I am indebted.
232. Johnston, p. 13. Emphasis added.
233. McKim, pp. 19-20. Emphasis added.
234. McKim, p. 19.
235. Emphasis added.
236. Seabrook, S101, pp. 90-91.
237. Seabrook, S101, p. 92.
238. Seabrook, S101, p. 93. Emphasis added.
239. Hague, p. 11.
240. Emphasis added.
241. Jones, CITC, p. 25.
242. Seabrook, S101, pp. 94-95.
243. Emphasis added.
244. Seabrook, S101, p. 102
245. Sorrel, p. 127.
246. Emphasis added.
247. Emphasis added.
248. Seabrook, EYWTAASIW, pp. 786-787.
249. Seabrook, S101, p. 103.
250. Nicolay and Hay, Vol. 2, p. 287. See also Confederate Veteran, November 1913, Vol. 21, No. 11, p. 545.
251. Seabrook, S101, pp. 109-110.
252. Wilson, Vol. 8, pp. 85-89. Emphasis added.
253. As I discuss, Lincoln's procrastination toward issuing the Emancipation Proclamation earned him numerous unflattering titles from fellow Republicans, such as "the tortoise president" and "the slow coach at Washington." Seabrook, EYWTAASIW, p. 696.
254. Seabrook, S101, p. 111.
255. Seabrook, S101, p. 112; Seabrook, EYWTAASIW, pp. 205-207, 696.
256. Confederate Veteran, September 1896, Vol. 4, No. 9, p. 296.
257. Evans, Vol. 7, "Mississippi," p. 9.
258. Seabrook, S101, pp. 113-114.
259. Seabrook, S101, p. 115. Emphasis added.

260. Seabrook, EYWTAASIW, p. 690.
261. Brock, pp. 351-352. Emphasis added.
262. Hagood, p. 98. Emphasis added.
263. Brock, pp. 177-180. Emphasis added.
264. DeLeon, p. 370.
265. Cumming, p. 195.
266. Stroyer, p. 47.
267. As one example of this, see Cumming, p. 194.
268. Johnston, p. 13.
269. Mosby, p. 5. Emphasis added.
270. Brock, p. 89.
271. Seabrook, EYWTAASIW, p. 329.
272. Hague, p. 120.
273. Seabrook, S101, p. 59.
274. Seabrook, EYWTAASIW, pp. 804-805. Emphasis added.
275. Confederate Veteran, February 1916, Vol. 24, No. 2, p. 64.
276. Davis, Vol. 2, p. 464.
277. Farrell and Presser, s.v. "Swastika."
278. Walker, TWDOSASO, pp. 52-61; Biedermann, s.v. "Swastika."
279. Metford, s.v. "Cross."
280. Walker, TWEOMAS, s.w. "Swastika."
281. Seabrook, JLOA, p. 33.
282. For example, see The Weekly News and Courier, pp. 38, 370, 473.
283. Jones, CITC, pp. 461-462. Emphasis added.
284. Butler, pp. 544-545. Emphasis added.
285. J. W. Headley, pp. 446-447. Emphasis added.
286. Note that Forrest was neither the founder or the leader of the Reconstruction KKK, as the anti-South movement continues to teach. For more on this topic, see my books on the general.
287. Seabrook, EYWTATCWIW, pp. 196-198.
288. Confederate Veteran, June 1916, Vol. 24, No. 6, p. 247.
289. Howard, pp. 54-55. While Union Colonel Anderson's poem expresses a Yankee view of the War and the Confederacy, his heart was in the right place. This is why, after reading his composition before a Confederate reunion at Petersburg, Virginia, he was made an honorary member of the town's A. P. Hill Camp. Confederate Veteran, March 1911, Vol. 19, No. 3, p. 103.
290. Jones, TDMV, p. 511. Emphasis added.
291. Seabrook, S101, p. 101.
292. Ridley, pp. 593-595. Emphasis added.
293. Howard, p. 320.
294. Wells, p. 96.
295. Ridley, pp. 522-523. Emphasis added.
296. Greenhow, pp. 3-4. Emphasis added.
297. Neese, pp. 233-234. Emphasis added.
298. Howard, pp. 137-138. Emphasis added.
299. United States Code, p. 386. Emphasis added.
300. Congressional Record, p. 8,327, Part 6. Emphasis added.
301. Congressional Record, p. 8,327, Part 6. Emphasis added.
302. Congressional Record, p. 18,121, Part 14. Emphasis added.
303. Gallison, p. 29. Emphasis added.
304. O'Ferrall, p. 149.
305. Confederate Veteran, June 1898, Vol. 6, No. 6, p. 253. Emphasis added.
306. Jones, TDMV, p. 514.
307. Grady, pp. 268-269.
308. Underwood, p. 250. Emphasis added.
309. Howard, pp. 78-86. Emphasis added.

310. Confederate Veteran, June 1914, Vol. 22, No. 6, p. 253.
311. Seabrook, TGYC, p. 60.
312. Seabrook, EYWTATCWIW, pp. 121-122.
313. Greenhow, pp. 106, 157.
314. For more on Lincoln's many crimes, see Seabrook, AL, pp. 293-318.
315. Confederate Veteran, September 1900, Vol. 8, No. 9, p. 397. Emphasis added.
316. Confederate Veteran, June 1898, Vol. 6, No. 6, p. 256.
317. Confederate Veteran, September 1900, Vol. 8, No. 9, pp. 397-398. Emphasis added.
318. Confederate Veteran, September 1900, Vol. 8, No. 9, p. 396. Emphasis added.
319. Hinkle, p. 19.
320. See my book of the same name.
321. Confederate Veteran, September 1900, Vol. 8, No. 9, p. 397. Emphasis added.
322. Knight, pp. 14, 138, 218. Emphasis added.
323. McKim, pp. 21-22. Emphasis added.
324. Greenhow, pp. 105, 106.
325. Emphasis added.
326. Seabrook, AL, p. 565.
327. For more on the 19th-Century forerunner of the NAACP, the "Independent Order of Pole Bearers," and Forrest, see Seabrook, ARB, pp. 459-461.
328. Mr. Winbush wrote the foreword for my book, *Everything You Were Taught About the Civil War is Wrong, Ask a Southerner!*
329. Matthew 22:36-40; John 13:34; 15:17; 1 John 4:8, 16.
330. Underwood, p. 216.
331. See e.g., Hagood, pp. 69, 173, 367.
332. Jones, TDMV, pp. 273, 536.
333. Seabrook, EYWTATCWIW, pp. 199-202.
334. Any race can suffer from either disorder, of course.
335. Hinkle, p. 19.
336. Howard, p. 344.
337. Deering, p. 166. Emphasis added.
338. Greenhow, p. 188.
339. Jones, CITC, pp. 463-464.
340. Confederate Veteran, June 1898, Vol. 6, No. 6, p. 254.
341. Southern Historical Papers, January to December 1880, Vol. 8, p. 455. Emphasis added.
342. Confederate Veteran, April 1907, Vol. 15, No. 4, p. 176.

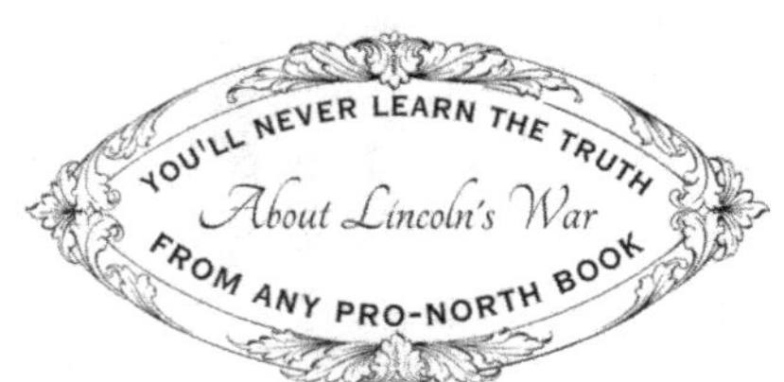

BIBLIOGRAPHY

LISTED BOOKS DO NOT NECESSARILY REFLECT AN ENDORSEMENT BY THE AUTHOR. SOME OF THESE TITLES ARE EXTREMELY ANTI-SOUTH, POORLY RESEARCHED, AND FILLED WITH ANTI-SOUTH PROPAGANDA AND DISINFORMATION (SEE E.G., CURRENT).

Adams, John Quincy. *The New England Confederacy of 1643.* (A discourse delivered before the Massachusetts Historical Society, at Boston, May 29, 1843.) Boston, MA: Charles C. Little and James Brown, 1843.

Alexander, Edward Porter. *Military Memoirs of a Confederate: A Critical Narrative.* New York, NY: Charles Scribner's Sons, 1907.

Alotta, Robert I. *Civil War Justice: Union Army Executions Under Lincoln.* Shippensburg, PA: White Mane, 1989.

Biedermann, Hans. *Dictionary of Symbolism: Cultural Icons and the Meanings Behind Them.* James Hulbert, trans. 1989. New York, NY: Facts on File, 1992 ed.

Blaisdell, Albert Franklin. *Stories of the Civil War.* Boston, MA: Lee and Shepard, 1890.

Boyd, Belle. *Belle Boyd, in Camp and Prison.* 2 vols. London, UK: Saunders, Otley, and Co., 1865.

Brock, Sarah "Sallie" Ann. *Richmond During the War; Four Years of Personal Observation.* New York, NY: G. W. Carleton and Co., 1867.

Butler, Benjamin Franklin. *Butler's Book: Autobiography and Personal Reminiscences of Major-General Benjamin F. Butler.* Boston, MA: A. M. Thayer and Co., 1892.

Cannon, Devereaux D., Jr. *The Flags of the Confederacy: An Illustrated History.* Memphis, TN: St. Lukes Press, 1988.

Clark, Walter (ed.). *Histories of the Several Regiments and Battalions From North Carolina in the Great War 1861-1865.* 5 vols. Raleigh, NC: "Published by the State," 1901.

Congressional Record: Proceedings and Debates of the 84th United States Congress, Volume 104, Part 6. Washington, D.C.: U.S. Government Printing Office, 1958.

Conyngham, David P. *Sherman's March Through the South, With Sketches and Incidents of the Campaign.* New York, NY: Sheldon and Co., 1865.

Cumming, Kate. *A Journal of Hospital Life in the Confederate Army of Tennessee.* Louisville, KY: John P. Morton, 1866.

Current, Richard N. (ed.). *The Confederacy.* New York, NY: Simon and Schuster, 1993.

Davis, Jefferson. *The Rise and Fall of the Confederate Government.* 2 vols. New York, NY: D. Appleton and Co., 1881.

Deering, John Richard. *Lee and His Cause, or the Why and How of the War Between the States.* New York, NY: The Neale Publishing Co., 1907.

DeLeon, Thomas Cooper. *Four Years in Rebel Capitals: An Inside View of Life in the Southern Confederacy, From Birth to Death; From Original Notes, Collated in the Years 1861 to 1865.* Mobile, AL: Gossip Printing Co., 1892.

Ellis, Edward Sylvester. *The History of Our Country: From the Discovery of America to the Present Time.* 1895. Los Angeles, CA: The Sanderson Whitten Co., 1900 ed.

Encyclopedia Britannica: A New Survey of Universal Knowledge. 1929. Chicago, IL: Encyclopedia Britannica, Inc., 1955 ed.

Evans, Clement Anselm (ed.). *Confederate Military History.* 12 vols. Atlanta, GA: Confederate Publishing Co., 1899.

Farrell, Deborah, and Carole Presser (eds.). *The Herder Symbol Dictionary*. 1986. Wilmette, IL: Chiron Publications, 1990 ed.

Fortier, Alcée. *A History of Louisiana*. 4 vols. New York, NY: Manzi, Joyant and Co., 1904.

Franklin, John Hope. *Reconstruction After the Civil War*. Chicago, IL: University of Chicago Press, 1961.

Gallison, Louis D. (ed.). *The American Hatter*. August 1898, Vol. 28, No. 5. New York: The Gallison and Hobron Co., 1898.

Gilmor, Harry. *Four Years in the Saddle*. New York, NY: Harper and Brothers, 1866.

Goodloe, Albert Theodore. *Some Rebel Relics From the Seat of War*. Nashville, TN: self-published, 1893.

Gordon, John Brown. *Reminiscences of the Civil War*. New York, NY: Charles Scribner's Sons, 1904.

Grady, Benjamin Franklin. *The Case of the South Against the North*. Raleigh, NC: Edwards and Broughton, 1899.

Grant, George. *The Life and Adventures of Sir William Wallace, the Liberator of Scotland*. Edinburgh, Scotland: J. Menzies, 1851.

Greeley, Horace. *The American Conflict: A History of the Great Rebellion in the United States of America, 1860-1865*. 2 vols. Hartford, CT: O. D. Case and Co., 1867.

Greenhow, Rose O'Neal. *My Imprisonment and the First Year of Abolition Rule at Washington*. London, UK: Richard Bentley, 1863.

Grissom, Michael Andrew. *Southern By the Grace of God*. 1988. Gretna, LA: Pelican Publishing, 1995 ed.

Hagood, Johnson. *Memoirs of the War of Secession*. Columbia, SC: The State Co., 1910.

Hague, Parthenia Antoinette. *A Blockaded Family: Life in Southern Alabama During the Civil War*. Boston, MA: Houghton, Mifflin and Co., 1888.

Headley, Joel Tyler. *The Great Riots of New York, 1712 to 1873, Including a Full and Complete Account of the Four Days' Draft Riot of 1863*. New York, NY: E. B. Treat, 1873.

Headley, John William. *Confederate Operations in Canada and New York*. New York, NY: Neale Publishing, 1906.

Hinkle, Don. *Embattled Banner: A Reasonable Defense of the Confederate Battle Flag*. Paducah, KY: Turner Publishing, 1997.

Hodgson, Joseph. *The Cradle of the Confederacy: A Sketch of Southwestern Political History From the Formation of the Federal Government to A.D. 1861*. Mobile AL: self-published, 1876.

Hopley, Catherine Cooper. *Life in the South: From the Commencement of the War*. 2 vols. London, UK: Chapman and Hall, 1863.

Howard, Robert Milton. *Reminiscences*. Columbus, GA: Gilbert Printing Co., 1912.

Jefferson, Thomas. *The Writings of Thomas Jefferson: Being His Autobiography, Correspondence, Reports, Messages, Addresses, and Other Writings, Official and Private*. 9 vols. Washington, D.C.: Taylor and Maury, 1854.

Johnson, Robert Underwood, and Clarence Clough Buel (eds.). *Battles and Leaders of the Civil War*. 4 vols. New York, NY: The Century Co., 1888.

Johnston, Mary. *The Long Roll*. Boston, MA: Houghton Mifflin Co., 1911.

Johnstone, Huger William. *Truth of War Conspiracy, 1861*. Idylwild, GA: H. W. Johnstone, 1921.

Jones, John William. *Christ in the Camp, or Religion in Lee's Army*. Richmond, VA: B. F. Johnson, 1887.

——. *The Davis Memorial Volume; Or Our Dead President, Jefferson Davis and the World's Tribute to His Memory*. Richmond, VA: B. F. Johnson, 1889.

Journal of the Congress of the Confederate States of America, 1861-1865. Vol. 1. Washington, D.C.: Government Printing Office, 1904.

——. Vol. 6. Washington, D.C.: Government Printing Office, 1905.

King, John Henry. *Three Hundred Days in a Yankee Prison: Reminiscences of War Life Captivity; Imprisonment at Camp Chase, Ohio.* Atlanta, GA: Jason P. Daves, 1904.

Knight, Lucian Lamar. *Memorials of Dixie-Land: Orations, Essays, Sketches and Poems on Topics Historical, Commemorative, Literary and Patriotic.* Atlanta, GA: self-published, 1919.

LaBree, Ben (ed.). *Camp Fires of the Confederacy.* Louisville, KY: Courier-Journal Job Printing Co., 1898.

Long, Everette Beach, and Barbara Long. *The Civil War Day By Day: An Almanac, 1861-1865.* 1971. New York, NY: Da Capo Press, 1985 ed.

Longstreet, James. *From Manassas to Appomattox: Memoirs of the Civil War in America.* 1895. Philadelphia, PA: J. B. Lipincott Co., 1908 ed.

Lunt, George. *Origin of the Late War: Traced From the Beginning of the Constitution to the Revolt of the Southern States.* New York, NY: D. Appleton and Co., 1866.

Madaus, Howard Michael. *The Battle Flags of the Confederate Army of Tennessee.* Milwaukee, WI: Milwaukee Public Museum, 1976.

Marshall, John A. *American Bastille: A History of the Illegal Arrests and Imprisonment of American Citizens in the Northern and Border States, On Account of Their Political Opinions, During the Late Civil War.* Philadelphia, PA: Thomas W. Hartley and Co., 1881.

McCarthy, Carlton. *Detailed Minutiae of Soldier Life in the Army of Northern Virginia 1861-1865.* 1882. Richmond, VA: B. F. Johnson, 1899 ed.

McGehee, Jacob Owen. *Causes That Led to the War Between the States.* Atlanta, GA: A. B. Caldwell, 1915.

McGuire, Hunter, and George L. Christian. *The Confederate Cause and Conduct in the War Between the States.* Richmond, VA: L. H. Jenkins, 1907.

McHatton-Ripley, Eliza. *From Flag to Flag: A Woman's Adventures and Experiences in the South During the War, in Mexico, and in Cuba.* New York, NY: D. Appleton and Co., 1889.

McKim, Randolph Harrison. *A Soldier's Recollections: Leaves From the Diary of a Young Confederate.* New York, NY: Longmans, Green, and Co., 1910.

Metford, J. C. J. *Dictionary of Christian Lore and Legend.* London, UK: Thames and Hudson, 1983.

Miller, Francis Trevelyan (ed.). *The Photographic History of the Civil War.* 10 vols. New York, NY: The Review of Reviews Co., 1911.

Moore, George Henry. *Notes on the History of Slavery in Massachusetts.* New York, NY: D. Appleton and Co., 1866.

Morgan, James Morris. *Recollections of a Rebel Reefer.* Boston, MA: Houghton Mifflin Co., 1917.

Mosby, John Singleton. *The Memoirs of John S. Mosby.* Boston, MA: Little, Brown, and Co., 1917.

Murray, John Ogden. *The Immortal Six Hundred: A Story of Cruelty Toward Confederate Prisoners of War.* Winchester, VA: The Eddy Press, 1905.

Neese, George Michael. *Three Years in the Confederate Horse Artillery.* New York, NY: The Neale Publishing Co., 1911.

Nicolay, John G., and John Hay (eds.). *Abraham Lincoln: Complete Works.* 12 vols. 1894. New York, NY: The Century Co., 1907 ed.

O'Ferrall, Charles Triplett. *Forty Years of Active Service.* New York, NY: Neale Publishing Co., 1904.

ORA (full title: *The War of the Rebellion: A Compilation of the Official Records of the Union and Confederate Armies.* (Multiple volumes.) Washington, D.C.: Government Printing Office, 1880.

ORN (full title: *Official Records of the Union and Confederate Navies in the War of the Rebellion*). (Multiple volumes.) Washington, D.C.: Government Printing Office, 1894.

Owsley, Frank Lawrence. *King Cotton Diplomacy: Foreign Relations of the Confederate States of America.* 1931. Chicago, IL: University of Chicago Press, 1959 ed.

Pollard, Edward A. *Southern History of the War.* 2 vols. in 1. New York, NY: Charles B.

Richardson, 1866.
——. *The Lost Cause*. 1867. Chicago, IL: E. B. Treat, 1890 ed.
——. *The Lost Cause Regained*. New York, NY: G. W. Carlton and Co., 1868.
——. *Life of Jefferson Davis, With a Secret History of the Southern Confederacy, Gathered "Behind the Scenes in Richmond."* Philadelphia, PA: National Publishing Co., 1869.
Rawle, William. *A View of the United States of America*. Philadelphia, PA: Philip H. Nicklin, 1829.
Richardson, John Anderson. *Richardson's Defense of the South*. Atlanta, GA: A. B. Caldwell, 1914.
Ridley, Bromfield Lewis. *Battles and Sketches of the Army of Tennessee*. Mexico, MO: Missouri Printing and Publishing Co., 1906.
Rutherford, Mildred Lewis. *Four Addresses*. Birmingham, AL: The Mildred Rutherford Historical Circle, 1912.
Rutland, Robert Allen. *The Birth of the Bill of Rights, 1776-1791*. 1955. Boston, MA: Northeastern University Press, 1991 ed.
Seabrook, Lochlainn. *Abraham Lincoln: The Southern View*. 2007. Franklin, TN: Sea Raven Press, 2013 ed.
——. *A Rebel Born: A Defense of Nathan Bedford Forrest*. 2010. Franklin, TN: Sea Raven Press, 2011 ed.
——. *Everything You Were Taught About the Civil War is Wrong, Ask a Southerner!* 2010. Franklin, TN: Sea Raven Press, revised 2014 ed.
——. *The Quotable Jefferson Davis: Selections From the Writings and Speeches of the Confederacy's First President*. Franklin, TN: Sea Raven Press, 2011.
——. *Lincolnology: The Real Abraham Lincoln Revealed In His Own Words*. Franklin, TN: Sea Raven Press, 2011.
——. *The Unquotable Abraham Lincoln: The President's Quotes They Don't Want You To Know!* Franklin, TN: Sea Raven Press, 2011.
——. *The Great Impersonator: 99 Reasons to Dislike Abraham Lincoln*. Franklin, TN: Sea Raven Press, 2012.
——. *The Alexander H. Stephens Reader: Excerpts From the Works of a Confederate Founding Father*. Franklin, TN: Sea Raven Press, 2013.
——. *Jesus and the Law of Attraction: The Bible-Based Guide to Creating Perfect Health, Wealth, and Happiness Following Christ's Simple Formula*. Franklin, TN: Sea Raven Press, 2013.
——. *The Quotable Alexander H. Stephens: Selections From the Writings and Speeches of the Confederacy's First Vice President*. Franklin, TN: Sea Raven Press, 2013.
——. *Give This Book to a Yankee! A Southern Guide to the Civil War For Northerners*. Franklin, TN: Sea Raven Press, 2014.
——. *Everything You Were Taught About American Slavery War is Wrong, Ask a Southerner!* Franklin, TN: Sea Raven Press, 2015.
——. *Confederacy 101: Amazing Facts You Never Knew About America's Oldest Political Tradition*. Franklin, TN: Sea Raven Press, 2015.
——. *Slavery 101: Amazing Facts You Never Knew About America's "Peculiar Institution."* Franklin, TN: Sea Raven Press, 2015.
——. *Confederate Blood and Treasure: An Interview With Lochlainn Seabrook*. Franklin, TN: Sea Raven Press, 2015.
——. *The Great Yankee Coverup: What the North Doesn't Want You to Know About Lincoln's War!* Franklin, TN: Sea Raven Press, 2015.
Semmes, Raphael. *Memoirs of Service Afloat, During the War Between the States*. Baltimore, MD: Kelly, Piet and Co., 1869.
Smith, Whitney. *The Flag Book of the United States*. New York, NY: William Morrow and Co., 1970.
Smith, William B. *On Wheels and How I Came There*. New York, NY: Hunt and Eaton, 1893.

Sorrel, Gilbert Moxley. *Recollections of a Confederate Staff Officer*. New York, NY: The Neale Publishing Co., 1905.

Southwood, Marion. *"Beauty and Booty": The Watchword of New Orleans*. New York, NY: M. Doolady, 1867.

Stephens, Alexander Hamilton. *A Constitutional View of the Late War Between the States; Its Causes, Character, Conduct and Results*. 2 vols. Philadelphia, PA: National Publishing Co., 1870.

Stiles, Robert. *Four Years Under Marse Robert*. 1903. New York, NY: The Neale Publishing Co., 1910 ed.

Stone, Ormond, and W. T. Myers (eds.). *Alumni Bulletin of the University of Virginia*, January 1912, Vol. 5, No. 1. Charlottesville, VA: The University of Virginia Press, 1912.

Stroyer, Jacob. *My Life in the South*. Salem, MA: Salem Observer Book and Job Print, 1885.

Taylor, Walter Herron. *Four Years With General Lee*. New York, NY: D. Appleton and Co., 1878.

The Weekly News and Courier. *Our Women in the War: The Lives They Lived; The Deaths They Died*. Charleston, SC: The Weekly News and Courier Book Presses, 1885.

Tocqueville, Alexis de. *Democracy in America*. 2 vols in 1. New York, NY: Pratt, Woodford, and Co., 1848.

Trezevant, Daniel Heyward. *The Burning of Columbia, S.C.: A Review of Northern Assertions and Southern Facts*. Columbia, SC: South Carolinian Power Press, 1866.

Trowbridge, John Townsend. *A Picture of the Desolated States; and the Work of Restoration 1865-1868*. Hartford, CT: L. Stebbins, 1868.

Underwood, John Levi. *The Women of the Confederacy*. New York, NY: The Neale Publishing Co., 1906.

United Confederate Veterans. *The Flags of the Confederate States of America*. New Orleans, LA: UCV Headquarters, 1907.

United States Code: Title 38, Veterans' Benefits (Supplement 4). Washington, D.C.: U.S. Government Printing Office, 2006 ed.

Walker, Barbara G. *The Woman's Encyclopedia of Myths and Secrets*. New York, NY: Harper and Row, 1983.

——. *The Woman's Dictionary of Symbols and Sacred Objects*. New York, NY: Harper and Row, 1988.

Warner, Ezra J. *Generals in Gray: Lives of the Confederate Commanders*. 1959. Baton Rouge, LA: Louisiana State University Press, 1989 ed.

——. *Generals in Blue: Lives of the Union Commanders*. 1964. Baton Rouge, LA: Louisiana State University Press, 2006 ed.

Watkins, Samuel Rush. *"Co. Aytch," Maury Grays, First Tennessee Regiment; or, A Side Show of the Big Show*. 1882. Chattanooga, TN: 1900 ed.

Weatherford, Willis Duke. *Negro Life in the South: Present Conditions and Needs*. New York, NY: Association Press, 1915.

Welch, Spencer Glasgow. *A Confederate Surgeon's Letters to His Wife*. New York, NY: The Neale Publishing Co., 1911.

Wells, Edward L. *Hampton and His Cavalry in '64*. Richmond, VA: B. F. Johnson Publishing Co., 1899.

Wilson, Woodrow. *A History of the American People*. 10 vols. 1901. New York, NY: Harper and Brothers, 1918 ed.

Wood, Robert Crooke. *Confederate Hand-book: A Compilation of Important Data and Other Interesting and Valuable Matter Relating to the War Between the States, 1861-1865*. New Orleans, LA: self-published, 1900.

Worsham, John H. *One of Jackson's Foot Cavalry: His Experience and What He Saw During the War 1861-1865*. New York, NY: The Neale Publishing Co., 1912.

Edmund Ruffin of Virginia, agriculturalist, author, state senator, and Southern nationalist. According to Southern legend, he fired the first shot of the War at Fort Sumter. A diehard Southern patriot who adored the Confederate Flag, tragically, after the War he committed suicide rather than live under a Yankee dictatorship.

INDEX

SEA RAVEN PRESS
FINE BOOKS
NASHVILLE TENNESSEE
SEARAVENPRESS.COM

TO THE STARS AND BARS

Battle-stained, time-worn, and tattered,
I saw you again to-day
Still floating, ragged and battered,
Above the thin ranks of the gray.

Fondly the old hands clasped you,
Their faded faces aglow
With something akin to the fire
Of fifty years ago.

But long have they left that struggle
And all that thereafter befell
With Him, the Lord of the battle,
Who doeth all things well.

And now their evening grows fainter;
The shadows around them fall;
Soon the old heroes will gather
To answer the great roll call.

But we, their children, will love you,
O flag, that our fathers unfurled,
When the last Confederate soldier
Has gone the way of the world.

And more, as with years you darken,
We honor your blackened scars,
For the South has not forgotten,
O gallant Stars and Bars.

EMMA EVE GARDNER, Georgia, 1914
(*Confederate Veteran*, June 1914, Vol. 22, No. 6, p. 248)

MEET THE AUTHOR

LOCHLAINN SEABROOK, winner of the prestigious Jefferson Davis Historical Gold Medal for his "masterpiece," *A Rebel Born: A Defense of Nathan Bedford Forrest*, is an unreconstructed Southern historian, award-winning author, Civil War scholar, and traditional Southern Agrarian of Scottish, English, Irish, Dutch, Welsh, German, and Italian extraction. An encyclopedist, lexicographer, musician, artist, graphic designer, genealogist, and photographer, as well as an award-winning poet, songwriter, and screenwriter, he has a 40 year background in historical nonfiction writing and is a member of the Sons of Confederate Veterans, the Civil War Trust, and the National Grange.

Due to similarities in their writing styles, ideas, and literary works, Seabrook is often referred to as the "new Shelby Foote," the "Southern Joseph Campbell," and the "American Robert Graves" (his English cousin).

The grandson of an Appalachian coal-mining family, Seabrook is a seventh-generation Kentuckian, co-chair of the Jent/Gent Family Committee (Kentucky), founder and director of the Blakeney Family Tree Project, and a board member of the Friends of Colonel Benjamin E. Caudill. Seabrook's literary works have been endorsed by leading authorities, museum curators, award-winning historians, bestselling authors, celebrities, noted scientists, well respected educators, TV show hosts and producers, renowned military artists, esteemed Southern organizations, and distinguished academicians from around the world.

Lochlainn Seabrook, award-winning Civil War scholar and unreconstructed Southern historian, is America's most popular and prolific pro-South author.

Seabrook has authored over 45 popular adult books on the American Civil War, American and international slavery, the U.S. Confederacy (1781), the Southern Confederacy (1861), religion, theology and thealogy, Jesus, the Bible, the Apocrypha, the Law of Attraction, alternative health, spirituality, ghost stories, the paranormal, ufology, social issues, and cross-cultural studies of the family and marriage. His Confederate biographies, pro-South studies, genealogical monographs, family histories, military encyclopedias, self-help guides, and etymological dictionaries have received wide acclaim.

Seabrook's eight children's books include a Southern guide to the Civil War, a biography of Nathan Bedford Forrest, a dictionary of religion and myth, a rewriting of the King Arthur legend (which reinstates the original pre-Christian motifs), two bedtime stories for preschoolers, a naturalist's guidebook to owls, a worldwide look at the family, and an examination of the Near-Death Experience.

Of blue-blooded Southern stock through his Kentucky, Tennessee, Virginia, West Virginia, and North Carolina ancestors, he is a direct descendant of European royalty via his 6th great-grandfather, the Earl of Oxford, after which London's famous Harley Street is named. Among his celebrated male Celtic ancestors is Robert the Bruce, King of Scotland, Seabrook's 22nd great-grandfather. The 21st great-grandson of Edward I "Longshanks" Plantagenet), King of England, Seabrook is a thirteenth-generation Southerner through his descent from the colonists of Jamestown, Virginia (1607).

The 2nd, 3rd, and 4th great-grandson of dozens of Confederate soldiers, one of his closest connections to Lincoln's War is through his 3rd great-grandfather, Elias Jent, Sr., who fought for the Confederacy in the Thirteenth Cavalry Kentucky under Seabrook's 2nd cousin, Colonel Benjamin E. Caudill. The Thirteenth, also known as "Caudill's Army," fought in numerous conflicts, including the Battles of Saltville, Gladsville, Mill Cliff, Poor Fork, Whitesburg, and Leatherwood.

Seabrook is a direct descendant of the families of Alexander H. Stephens, John Singleton Mosby, William Giles Harding, and Edmund Winchester Rucker, and is related to the following Confederates and other 18th- and 19th-Century luminaries: Robert E. Lee, Stephen Dill Lee, Stonewall Jackson, Nathan Bedford Forrest, James Longstreet, John Hunt Morgan, Jeb Stuart, P. G. T. Beauregard (approved the Confederate Battle Flag), George W. Gordon, John Bell Hood, Alexander Peter Stewart, Arthur M. Manigault, Joseph Manigault, Charles Scott Venable, Thornton A. Washington, John A. Washington, Abraham Buford, Edmund W. Pettus, Theodrick "Tod" Carter, John B. Womack, John H. Winder, Gideon J. Pillow, States Rights Gist, Henry R. Jackson, John Lawton Seabrook, John C. Breckinridge, Leonidas Polk, Zachary Taylor, Sarah Knox Taylor (first wife of Jefferson Davis), Richard Taylor, Davy Crockett, Daniel Boone, Meriwether Lewis (of the Lewis and Clark Expedition) Andrew Jackson, James K. Polk, Abram Poindexter Maury (founder of Franklin, TN), Zebulon Vance, Thomas Jefferson, Edmund Jennings Randolph, George Wythe Randolph (grandson of Jefferson), Felix K. Zollicoffer, Fitzhugh Lee, Nathaniel F. Cheairs, Jesse James, Frank James, Robert Brank Vance, Charles Sidney Winder, John W. McGavock, Caroline E. (Winder) McGavock, David Harding McGavock, Lysander McGavock, James Randal McGavock, Randal William McGavock, Francis McGavock, Emily McGavock, William Henry F. Lee, Lucius E. Polk, Minor Meriwether (husband of noted pro-South author Elizabeth Avery Meriwether), Ellen Bourne Tynes (wife of Forrest's chief of artillery, Captain John W. Morton), South Carolina Senators Preston Smith Brooks and Andrew Pickens Butler, and famed South Carolina diarist Mary Chesnut.

(Photo © Lochlainn Seabrook)

Seabrook's modern day cousins include: Patrick J. Buchanan (conservative author), Cindy Crawford (model), Shelby Lee Adams (Letcher County, Kentucky, portrait photographer), Bertram Thomas Combs (Kentucky's fiftieth governor), Edith Bolling (wife of President Woodrow Wilson), and actors Andy Griffith, George C. Scott, Robert Duvall, Reese Witherspoon, Lee Marvin, Rebecca Gayheart, and Tom Cruise.

Seabrook's screenplay, *A Rebel Born*, based on his book of the same name, has been signed with acclaimed filmmaker Christopher Forbes (of Forbes Film). It is now in pre-production, and is set for release in 2016 as a full-length feature film. This will be the first movie ever made of Nathan Bedford Forrest's life story, and as a historically accurate project written from the Southern perspective, is destined to be one of the most talked about Civil War films of all time.

Born with music in his blood, Seabrook is an award-winning, multi-genre, BMI-Nashville songwriter and lyricist who has composed some 3,000 songs (250 albums), and whose original music has been heard in film (*A Rebel Born, Cowgirls 'n Angels, Confederate Cavalry*, *Billy the Kid: Showdown in Lincoln County*, *Vengeance Without Mercy*, *Last Step*, *County Line*, *The Mark*) and on TV and radio worldwide. A musician, producer, multi-instrumentalist, and renown performer—whose keyboard work has been variously compared to pianists from Hargus Robbins and Vince Guaraldi to Elton John and Leonard Bernstein—Seabrook has opened for groups such as the Earl Scruggs Review, Ted Nugent, and Bob Seger, and has performed privately for such public figures as President Ronald Reagan, Burt Reynolds, Loni Anderson, and Senator Edward W. Brooke. Seabrook's cousins in the music business include: Johnny Cash, Elvis Presley, Billy Ray and Miley Cyrus, Patty Loveless, Tim McGraw, Lee Ann Womack, Dolly Parton, Pat Boone, Naomi, Wynonna, and Ashley Judd, Ricky Skaggs, the Sunshine Sisters, Martha Carson, and Chet Atkins.

Seabrook, a libertarian, lives with his wife and family in historic Middle Tennessee, the heart of Forrest country and the Confederacy, where his conservative Southern ancestors fought valiantly against Liberal Lincoln and the progressive North in defense of Jeffersonianism, constitutional government, and personal liberty.

LOCHLAINNSEABROOK.COM

MEET THE COVER ARTIST

For over 30 years American artist JOHN PAUL STRAIN has been amazing art collectors with his unique talent of capturing moments in time from the early days of the American Frontier, the glory and pageantry of the American Civil War, to contemporary scenic and romantic locations across the world. From the early age of twenty-one, Mr. Strain's paintings were represented by Trailside Galleries, America's most prestigious western art gallery. For fifteen years his beautiful landscapes, wild life paintings, and depictions of Indian life were represented by most every major western art gallery and top art auctions in the United States.

In 1991 Mr. Strain broadened his subjects to include historical art of the American Civil War. During the next seventeen years he focused his work on the world of daring horseback raids and epic battles with great armies and leaders, capturing and preserving a unique era in history. Over a period of years, Mr. Strain became known as America's leading historical artist, with over fifty magazine covers featuring his paintings.

John Paul Strain, America's premiere award-winning historical and military artist.

His work is featured in books, movies, and film. Mr. Strain's book, *A Witness to the Civil War*, released in November 2002, was a best seller for his publisher and quickly sold out of its first printing. The book is unusual among art books in that it is written by the artist. The Scholastic Resources Company purchased over 3,000 copies of the edition for school libraries across the US. His newest book was released in 2009.

Strain's paintings have helped to raise funds for many historical restoration projects and battlefield preservation organizations. The National Park Service uses his images in their publications and at battlefield sites. A number of historical private institutions have on site displays featuring his work such as General JEB Stuart's home and estate, and General Jubal Early's boyhood home.

Mr. Strain and his paintings were also featured on the television shows of C-Span's Washington Journal, The History Channel, and Extreme Makeover Home Edition. Throughout his career he has won many awards for his art. Reproductions of his work have won numerous first place awards and "Best of Show" honors, such as the PICA Awards, The Printing Industry of the Carolinas, and just recently at the PIAG 2008 Awards in Georgia, he won the Top Gold Award for his painting "New Year's Wish," and Best Of Category Giclée for "Fire In the Sky."

Strain is also a featured artist for internationally know collector art companies the Bradford Exchange and the Franklin Mint, where he has created a Civil War Chess Set, several limited edition plate series, sculptures, and many other collectable items featuring his paintings. Mr. Strain has also completed a number of commissioned works for the United States Army, which are on permanent display at Fort Leavenworth, Kansas, Fort McNair, Washington, D.C., and the battlefield visitor's center at Normandy, France.

Today, Mr. Strain's original paintings can be found in many noted museums such as the Museum of Fredericksburg, South Georgia Relics Museum, and at Thomas Jefferson's home, Monticello. His work is included in many private fine art collections, corporate collections, and is owned by dignitaries such as United States Senators, Congressmen and a number of State Governors.

JOHNPAULSTRAIN.COM

This Flag is Not Coming Down, Ever!

ENEMIES OF THE SOUTH HAVE AN AGENDA TO TURN THE PUBLIC AGAINST US. YET THEIR DIABOLICAL TECHNIQUES EXPOSE THEM FOR WHO THEY REALLY ARE.

☛ Those who say the Confederate Flag is "racist" are the real racists: they judge people by the color of their skin. Here in the traditional South we judge people by their character.

☛ Those who say the Confederate Flag is "divisive" are themselves divisive: they intentionally strive to pit groups of people against one another (a warring society is easier to manipulate). Here in the traditional South we seek to unify all Americans.

☛ Those who say the Confederate Flag "discourages diversity" are themselves discouraging diversity: they want an exclusive society made up only of people they agree with. We want an inclusive society that allows for differences between individuals.

☛ Those who say the Confederate Flag is a "symbol of intolerance" are themselves intolerant: they don't want those they disagree with to be able to express their First Amendment rights. As strict constitutionalists we support the First Amendment; not just for those who share our values, but for all law-abiding Americans.

☛ Those who say the Confederate Flag is a "symbol of ignorance" are themselves ignorant: they get their information about the South from biased, uninformed, malicious pro-North historians, then rewrite, ignore, marginalize, or try to suppress true Southern history—the very definition of ignorance.

☛ Those who say the Confederate Flag is a "symbol of hatred" are themselves hateful: their unrelenting efforts to ban our flag is a purposefully hurtful insult to the cultural heritage of millions of proud Southern-Americans. Here in Dixie we treat the symbols of the Union as part of American history and accept the right of the descendants of Yankee soldiers to honor and memorialize their dead however they see fit. In other words, we mind our own business.

In its effort to take over the U.S., the Left will stop at nothing in its war on the South, our flag, and our heritage. Use this book to combat the hate-filled lies, myths, slander, and propaganda invented by the so-called "party of compassion and tolerance." The South is not *going* to rise again. It's *already* rising again, and the information in this book will help lead the way!

CPSIA information can be obtained
at www.ICGtesting.com
Printed in the USA
LVHW031308180121
676757LV00001B/9